WARREN HASTINGS

WARREN HASTINGS:

A BIOGRAPHY.

CAPTAIN LIONEL JAMES TROTTER

GYAN

Published by

GYAN

Gyan Publishing House
5, Ansari Road
Daryaganj, New Delhi-110002
Phone: 011-47034999, 9811692060
E-mail: books@gyanbooks.com

Distribution Network
gyanbooks.com
India, USA, Canada, UK, Australia

ISBN: 978-81-212-4928-7 (HB)
First Published, 1878

2nd Impression 2024

Printed at: Gyan Press, Delhi.

WARREN HASTINGS
Author: CAPTAIN LIONEL JAMES TROTTER

WARREN HASTINGS: A BIOGRAPHY.

CHAPTER I.

"THE CHILD IS FATHER OF THE MAN."

ONE of the greatest names, if not the very greatest, in the annals of British India is that of Warren Hastings, who for thirteen years ruled over the provinces which British valour had lately won for the East India Company. The story of his troubled yet glorious career has been told at full length by Mr. Gleig, and summarised in glowing language by Lord Macaulay; to say nothing of the place he fills in every history of British India, from that of James Mill to the more succinct and impartial narrative of Mr. Marshman. But Mr. Gleig's biography, however rich in sterling value, has few attractions for the mass of readers in these days, while Macaulay's famous essay has charmed the world with a picture in which the lights and shadows are distributed with more regard for scenic effect than for historic justice. The wrong done to Hastings during his lifetime by Burke and other tools of his worst foe, Sir Philip Francis, has been heightened by the wrong which the most popular of English essayists, following in the steps of Mill, has inflicted upon his memory. For one reader of Mr. Gleig's volumes, Macaulay's essay counts scores. In aiming to correct the prevailing estimate of a statesman whose rule, according to Mill himself, was "popular both with his countrymen and the natives in Bengal," the present writer may seem to be attempting an Herculean task. In the interests of truth, however, and of fair play to one whose faults were few compared with his many virtues and his great public services, he is determined to dare the venture, let the result be what it may.

Warren Hastings was born at Churchill, a village in Oxfordshire, on the 6th of December, 1732. His mother, who died but a few days after his birth, was daughter of a Mr. Warren, who owned a small estate near Twining in

Gloucestershire. Her husband, Pynaston Hastings, was a boy of fifteen when he married Hester Warren; and a hard struggle for life the young couple seem to have had during the two years which elapsed before the birth of Warren, their second child. Pynaston himself was the younger of two sons born to their father, the Rector of Daylesford in Worcestershire, a poor clergyman who made himself still poorer by carrying on a ruinous lawsuit about tithes with the neighbouring squire.

Beyond the fact of his fatherhood to so great a son, Pynaston did nothing worthy of remembrance. Leaving his motherless babes to the care of their impoverished grandfather, who had now been driven to accept a curacy at Churchill, Pynaston went off to seek his fortune elsewhere. Lost to sight for a while, like a river flowing underground, he re-appears at Gloucester, married to a butcher's daughter. A little later he entered the Church and went out to one of the West Indian islands, where he died. Such is the meagre record which his own children cared to perpetuate of a parent to whom they owed so little.

Amidst circumstances so unpromising did poor

little Warren Hastings begin the world. Poverty and neglect seemed to mark for their own the descendant of an old English family whose origin may perhaps be traced to the Danish sea-king whom Alfred after long struggle overthrew. Be that as it may, it is certain that one of Warren's forefathers held in the days of Henry II. that manor of Daylesford in Worcestershire, which Pynaston's grandfather, Samuel Hastings, sold in 1715 to a London merchant. To one branch of the same family belonged Lord Hastings, the brave and faithful chamberlain of the fourth Edward, and the luckless victim of Richard III., who requited his loyalty to Edward's children by cutting off his head From another branch sprang the Earls of Pembroke of the fourteenth century, whose title was derived from the marriage of John Hastings with the heiress of Aymer de Valence, one of the great nobles who helped to put down Edward the Second's overweening favourite, Piers Gavaston. It was Earl John's son who fought in Spain under the Black Prince, and was taken prisoner with all his army by Henry of Castile, in the wars between Henry and his brother, Peter the Cruel. The family of the ill-starred Chamberlain received from a Tudor sovereign the Earldom of Huntingdon, which, says Macaulay, "after long dispossession was regained in our time by a series of events scarcely parallelled in romance." *

In the course of time the owners of Daylesford, who represented the oldest branch of the family, fixed their chief residence at Yelford, near Bampton, in Oxfordshire. Here, at the outbreak of the Civil War, lived John Hastings, a gallant gentlemen who proved his loyalty to Charles I. not only in the field, but by the help he gave him in other ways; raising money by the sale of his plate and the mortgage of his lands, until he was fain to rescue himself from utter ruin by making over his Yelford estates to Speaker Lenthal, who ruled the House of Commons in the days of the great Protector Cromwell. The decaying manor-house at Daylesford still gave shelter to its impoverished owners, until that too, as we have shown, passed as it seemed for ever into other hands.

Uuder his grandfather's care, little Warren

* The Barony of Hastings fell by marriage to the Earl of Moira in the latter part of the eighteenth century. But it was not till 1819 that the earldom of Huntingdon, after a suspension of more than 300 years, was recovered by Francis Hastings, as descendant of the second Earl.

spent the first years of his childhood, with the village children for his playmates, and the village school for his fount of learning. That he "took his learning kindly," his old schoolfellows loved to tell of him in after days; and his natural quickness may have been sharpened by the stories which he heard at home of the wealth, the greatness, the brave deeds, and splendid hospitalities of his own forefathers. Child as he was, he loved to lie beside the margin of a small stream which skirted the village of Churchill, and muse on the difference between things past and present. "There," as many year's afterwards he told a friend, "one bright summer's day, when I was scarcely seven year's old, I well remember that I first formed the determination to purchase back Daylesford." That dream, however wild it might seem then, or at any time thereafter, never faded from his resolute soul. In the darkest hours of a long life of storm and hard struggle, that beacon-fire never ceased to shine along his path.

When he was about eight years old, young Warren seems to have passed under the care of his uncle Howard, Pynaston's elder brother, a steady-going clerk in the Customs, who placed him at school at Newington Butts, near London. Here he remained for two years, half starved but not ill taught. From Newington he was removed to Westminster, then ruled by Dr. Nichols, who numbered among his masters the scholarly and well-beloved Vincent Bourne. Among Warren's new schoolfellows were Churchill, the elder Colman, Cowper, Lord Shelburne, and Elijah Impey, all of whom were destined in different ways to make some figure in the world. With some of these, especially the gentle bard of Olney and the future Chief Justice of Bengal, the new boy erelong formed a friendship which never afterwards died out. Both Impey and Cowper were older than himself, and both seem to have been apt scholars in the polite learning of their day. But Warren, whose eager spirit was clothed in a slight and somewhat delicate body, soon learned to handle an oar and to write Latin verse as deftly as any young fellow of his own standing. In swimming and "skiffing" he especially delighted, in preference to the more violent pastimes enjoyed by healthier and stronger boys. His gentle manners and sweet temper helped to make him popular with his schoolfellows, while his diligence and learning drew forth many a word of praise from Dr. Nichols himself.*

The purpose which the child of seven had conceived at Churchill, was not forgotten, we may be sure, at Westminster. In his fifteenth year, Warren's natural cleverness, backed by the perseverance in which clever boys are often wanting, won for him the first place on the list of King's Scholars admitted to the foundation in that year; Impey himself standing fourth. To a King's Scholar of fair abilities, the road to success at one of the great Universities lay invitingly open. But Warren was not destined to take that road. He was steadily working his way upwards at College, as the foundation at Westminster is called, when the death of his good uncle Howard gave a new turn to his worldly prospects. His new guardian, Mr. Chiswick, a distant relative, to whose care his uncle had bequeathed him, made

* Nothing could well have been wider of the mark than Macaulay's random guess that "whenever Hastings wished to play any trick more than usually naughty, he hired Impey with a ball or a tart to act as a fag in the worst part of the prank." The very contrary would be nearer the truth. In those days, it was Hastings who looked up to Impey, not Impey who fawned upon Hastings. See "Memoirs of Sir Elijah Impey, by his son," p. 6.

up his mind to send young Hastings out to India as a "writer" in the service of the East India Company.

In vain did the worthy Dr. Nichols plead hard against the proposed withdrawal of a scholar in whom he avowed a just pride. He even offered to educate at his own charge the favourite pupil whose success at College would redound, he frankly said, to his own credit. But the East India Director turned to all such pleadings a deaf ear. Towards the end of 1749, about two years after he had become a King's Scholar, Hastings parted from his many friends at Westminster to study book-keeping and accounts under a private tutor. In January, 1750, he set sail for Calcutta in company with several other youths destined for the same career. In those days, a voyage to India round the Cape took generally more months than it now takes weeks by the Suez Canal. The good ship *London* exceeded even the average limit of six months, for it was not till the first days of October that Hastings landed, lonely but high-hearted, on the scene of his future struggles and final renown. Of what he did or felt on that tedious voyage, Mr. Gleig can tell us nothing; but it may be assumed that these weary months were not passed in utter idleness by the youth whose dreams at Churchill had borne him company through years of profitable work at Westminster. That dreamy turn of mind, which so often unfits a man for the hard realities of his daily lot, seemed to act upon Warren Hastings, as it did upon Luther and Cromwell, like a powerful tonic, steeling his heart against all discouragements, and spurring him on to yet bolder efforts, with its never-failing visions of the success to come.

CHAPTER II.

1750—1753.

When Hastings landed in India he was not quite eighteen years old, and the famous Company whose service he had entered was still, to all seeming, little more than a chartered body of "merchants trading to the East Indies." For a century and a-half from its birth in 1600 down to the year 1750, that Company had played the part of a busy trader, on such conditions as the jealousy of rival merchants and the prudence or the greed of native rulers might allow. At Surat, Bombay, Madras, Calcutta, and a few other places on the coast or up the great rivers, the Company's servants carried on a trade which, spite of untoward checks and interruptions, brought much profit alike to their masters and themselves. The task of upholding their chartered monopoly against "interlopers" from England in the days of Charles I. and Cromwell had grown lighter with the return of the Stuart dynasty to power. With the cession of Bombay by Charles II. and the new rights lately secured to it by a new charter from the Crown, the Company continued to enlarge its trade, to found new settlements; to win by prayers, or gifts, or timely services, fresh powers and privileges from the officers of the Great Moghal. Its earliest forts at Madras and Surat had been built for the protection of its factories alone. The successful defence of Surat in 1664 taught Sivaji and his Maráthas a lasting lesson of respect for English valour, and earned from the politic Aurangzib a large remission of the duties hitherto levied on the Company's trade with that port.

In the twenty years that followed the Restoration the Company's Indian trade grew in value from £100,000 to a million sterling a year. Then came a time of wantonness and armed aggression, when the Company's servants in Bombay and Bengal, with the help of an English fleet and English soldiers, defied the might of Aurangzib, one of the ablest and most powerful princes of Bábar's Imperial line. In spite of some partial successes at sea, the Company's fortunes suffered for some years a perilous eclipse. But Aurangzib had no mind to press too hard on the turbulent traders who increased his revenue and brought wealth to his subjects ; nor did it suit him to wage a lingering war with foes who might still blockade his ports, and seize Indian vessels laden with merchandise, or worse still, with Mussulman pilgrims bound for Mecca. The East India Directors also, having learned with the loss of nearly all their factories to see the folly of their late doings, were now humbly suing for the peace which the Moghal Emperor was not slow to grant. In 1690 the forfeit factories were restored to their late owners, and Job Charnock once more hoisted his country's flag at Chatanatti, one of the three villages which afterwards grew into the capital of British India.

From that time for more than half a century the Company's servants in India kept clear of all perilous embroilments with the ruling powers. The old plague of interlopers, licensed and unlicensed, continued to vex them for a few years longer, and a new Company threatened for a moment to extinguish the old. But fortune still smiled upon the latter. In the first year of Queen Anne the rival Companies merged into one whose sole aim for many years afterwards was to increase its dividends and guard its own interests, amidst the clash of arms in either Continent, and the peaceful rivalry of Dutch, French, and other traders from the west.

Guarded by the guns of Fort William, the new settlement grew and prospered in the troublous days that followed the death of Aurangzib. Neither the exactions of an unfriendly Viceroy in Bengal,* nor the raids of plundering Marátha horsemen, availed to hinder the steady growth of a trade which the Viceroy's own officers found their profit in furthering, while the English entrenchments on the Hughli became an isle of shelter for thousands of natives flying, whether from Moghal oppression or Marátha greed. Nor did the wars that divided Europe ruffle the smooth course of our Indian trade. While Marlborough was beating the French in Flanders and on the Rhine, while "dapper little" George II. was adding at Dettingen to the laurels he had won at Oudenarde, the French and English merchants on the Hughli and the Coromandel coast still followed in peace the business which had brought them so many thousand miles away from their cool western homes.

But events were about to happen which would

* Murshid Kuli Khan, Subhadar or Viceroy of Bengal from 1702 to 1725, founded the city of Murshidabad.

give a new turn to the destinies of the rival nations in India. In 1744 France and England took opposite sides in the war of the Austrian Succession. While English soldiers under the Duke of Cumberland were bravely losing the battle of Fontenoy, an English fleet was worrying French commerce by sea; and Pondicherry itself, then governed by the bold and able Dupleix, was threatened with capture by Commodore Barnet. Anwar-ud-din, the Nawáb of the Carnatic, stepped between the French and impending disaster, under a show of friendliness for both his neighbours. But when the fiery Labourdonnais, fresh from his repulse of an English squadron, seized the moment for his long-planned attack upon Madras, the value of the Nawáb's professions was but too clearly seen. On the 18th September, 1746, the French batteries opened fire on a weak fort defended by three hundred Englishmen, of whom only two-thirds were soldiers. Three days later the garrison surrendered, and Madras for a time was wiped out of the list of English settlements in India. By the end of that year Fort St. David was the only possession left to the East India Company on the Coromandel coast.

From that time forth the English, at least in Southern India, are driven, rather by circumstances than of set design, to further the ends of their commercial being by other methods than trade alone. At the peace of Aix-la-Chapelle, in 1749, Madras was surrendered back into their hands. But Europe was a long way off, and the genius of Dupleix was already founding in Southern India a power which threatened the well-being, if not the very existence of his English rivals. With a few hundred Frenchmen and Sepoys* trained on the French pattern, his officers had beaten many times their own number of native troops led by native commanders. The English also began to drill their own Sepoys, to strengthen their defences, to seek allies among neighbouring princes, and to make their quarrels a means of gaining fresh advantages for themselves. In the wars which followed the death of Nizám-ul-Mulk, the long-lived founder of a kingdom in the Dakhan, still partly ruled by his descendants, the soldiers of the rival Companies were always to be found fighting on opposite sides; and the hero of Arkot gave rich promise of the greatness afterwards achieved by the victor of Plassy and the virtual conqueror of Bengal.

* More correctly *Sipáhis*, from *Sipah*, an army.

Thus far, however, the strife between the two nations had not extended to the settlements on the Hughli. When young Hastings landed at Calcutta in the cooler weather that followed the rainy season of 1750, he found his countrymen still employed in balancing accounts, in making bargains with "Gentoo" merchants, and in shipping off to England the muslins, silks, shawls, cotton, ivory, spices, gold and silver ornaments, which passed through their hands. In those days the rich and populous province of Bengal was ruled by Aliverdi Khan, a wise and able Viceroy, who encouraged trade with the foreigners, and did his best to guard his people from the raids of those ubiquitous Maráthas, who were already tearing to pieces the wide empire of the Moghals.

In Calcutta Hastings spent the first three years of his Indian service. The Company's servants were then divided into four classes. The writers, among whom he was now enrolled, had to conduct the smaller details of business, to keep the ledgers, and to look after the warehouses which held the goods collected by a staff of native agents, or *gomáshtas*, and their underlings of various grades. After five years, the writer became a factor, who discharged similar duties with somewhat higher powers. Three years of this service raised the factor into a "junior merchant," who after three more years passed into the grade of "senior merchants." From these last were chosen the members of council, the heads of factories, the chief officers of revenue and justice, the "political agents" at native courts, and even the governors of the three Presidencies, into which the Company's settlements had already been grouped.

Of the years which Hastings passed in the Secretary's Office at Calcutta, nothing seems to be known for certain. That he worked hard and lived uprightly, amidst many temptations to idleness and self-seeking, may be taken for granted. His taste for learning may have sharpened his desire to study the native languages as a means of rising in his new world; but the progress made by him in those studies can be measured only by our knowledge of the use to which he turned the fruits of such labours in after days. His pay at this time—five pounds a year—would barely have sufficed for the wants of an Indian Sepoy, or a very poor and thrifty husbandman in Bengal. His "commons," however, were found him by the Company, who further treated their ill-paid servants to a yearly grant of Madeira from their own stores. Five pounds a year could not go very far even towards the paying of a writer's house-rent, and the young men of that day were sometimes driven to seek their beds soon after the early sunset of Bengal, because they could ill afford the luxury of a candle or a supper. But the Company's servants were allowed, indeed expected to eke out their sorry *pittances with the profits of their private trade*; and so rich a field had thus been opened to some of them, that complaints were already heard in England of the extravagance of young fellows who sat down to dinner with a band of music, and rode about in a carriage and four.* As Warren Hasting was neither greedy nor corrupt, the amount of his earnings from private trade must have left him little room for such reckless spending, even if he had any great turn that way.

* The pay of the factors was £15 a year; that of the junior merchants, £30, and of the members of council £40, while even the President or Governor had no more than £300.

CHAPTER III.

1753—1757.

In October, 1753, Hastings was ordered up to the factory at Kásimbazár on the Bhágirathi, at that time the busy trading suburb of Murshidabad. Among the silk-weavers of that place, and the shrewd native middlemen who helped them to keep their shuttles going, and to bring the produce of their looms to an English market, he discharged his new duties with such steady skill, that within two years he found himself promoted to a seat in the council of the factory.

But the even tenour of his life was soon to be ruffled by a storm which altered the whole course of English affairs in India. In January, 1756, the aged Aliverdi Khán breathed his last, and his favourite grandson, the cruel, profligate, self-willed Suraj-ad-daula, filled his place. A new Viceroy, who cared nothing for the English reigned in Bengal. It was not long before Suraj-ad-daula had picked a quarrel with the Governor of Calcutta. Mr. Drake was ordered to surrender the refugee son of a wealthy Hindu officer, and to demolish the new defences he was said to have raised around Fort William. In vain he pleaded that the ramparts had merely been repaired against a possible attack from his French neighbours, and that honour forbade his yielding up a fugitive who claimed his protection. The imperious Subhadár at once began his march upon Calcutta, with the troops he had gathered for the chastisement of a rebellious vassal in Parniah.

What followed must be told in the fewest words. At the first sight of an army 50,000 strong a great panic seized upon our countrymen in Calcutta. On the 19th of June a general rush of men, women and children to seek shelter on board the English ships in the river was crowned by the flight of Mr. Drake and the Commandant himself of Fort William. For two days the small garrison, thus shamefully abandoned, held out under Mr. Holwell, with bootless courage and ever-waning strength, against the doom which the captains of the vessels in the river made no effort to avert. At last the soldiers, worn out with heat and watching, broke into the liquor stores. Amidst the ensuing drunkenness and disorder, while Holwell was parleying with the enemy, some of the Nawab's soldiers rushed into the fort and in a few minutes all its surviving defenders had fallen into the hands of their dreaded conqueror.

Then came the memorable tragedy of the Black Hole. In one of the hottest, sultriest nights of the Bengal year, with the air yet further heated by the blaze of burning warehouses, a hundred and forty-six wretches, including more than one woman, were shut up in an old guard-room barely eighteen feet square, pierced by two small windows strongly barred. What they suffered during that night of slow torture Holwell himself has told us in language powerfully simple as that of Defoe. Enough here to say that, next morning twenty-two men and one woman crawled out of that den of noisomeness into the air of a new day, looking hardly more alive than the dead they left behind them.

It is only fair to Suraj-ad-daula to add that this deed of hellish cruelty was neither ordered by himself, nor prompted by any instructions left with the officers into whose hands the prisoners were made over. The tragedy was enacted while he slept, and when the survivors were brought before him, Holwell alone and four others were sent off in irons to Murshidabad; the woman to adorn his harem, and the men as hostages for the extraction of more plunder. The rest were allowed to make their way to Falta, a barren island near the mouth of the Hughli, where Drake and his fellow-runaways were awaiting the issue of an appeal for help to their countrymen at Madras.

The ruthless conqueror of Calcutta lost no time in reaping the full fruits of his success. Every English factory in Bengal was seized and plundered, and Hastings among others found himself a prisoner at Murshidabad. It was not the Viceroy's policy to kill the victims of his greed, and Hastings for one remained a prisoner at large on bail offered by the head of a neighbouring Dutch factory. Amidst the dangers and discouragements of that dark hour he kept his head clear and his hands ready for such work as might still devolve upon him. His opportunity soon came. Famine threatened the fugitives at Falta, whose appeal to Madras had not yet been answered. In their despair they turned to Hastings as a means of softening the Viceroy's heart. He chose his own time and methods for carrying out their wishes; but erelong the opening of a bazár or native market rewarded his efforts to save the Falta party from dying of sheer hunger.

By that time the fainting hearts of Drake's followers were cheered with prospects of relief from another quarter. Kilpatrick's arrival at Falta with a small body of troops from Madras, if it had shortened their supplies of food, had prepared them to look for the coming of larger reinforcements in due time. It was not till August that the disasters at Calcutta were made known to the English at Madras. With mingled feelings of horror, wrath, and dismay was the news received; but the cry for action prompt and vigorous overbore all weaker counsels, and it only remained to get ready an armament strong enough to exact due vengeance for the past disgrace.

It took two months, however, not so much to prepare the armament as to choose for it the fittest leader and to define his proper powers. The Governor himself was quite ready to take the command if his colleagues could only have discovered his fitness for such a post. In default of the veteran Lawrence, disabled for the duty by failing health, the choice of the Madras Council at last fell upon his best subaltern, the brave young Colonel Clive,* whose brilliant defence of Arkot five years before had stamped him as a master of his art, and who had just gained fresh renown from his victories over the pirate chiefs in the Kánkan. Robert Clive had gone out as a writer to Madras in 1744, had manfully borne his part in the vain defence of that settlement two years afterwards, and had escaped in disguise from the captured stronghold to Fort St. David. Exchanging the desk for the drill-ground, young Clive proved his soldiership under Major Lawrence in the successful defence of Fort St. David, in Boscawen's bootless siege of Pondicherry, in the capture of Devikatta, and in the later campaigns provoked by the ambition and ended by the recal of Dupleix.

On every occasion Clive bore himself like a fighting Englishman; but the special qualities of a great captain were first displayed by him in 1751, when he persuaded the Governor of

* Orme, the eloquent historian of our early wars in India was then a member of the Madras Council, and voted warmly for Clive.

Madras to let him save Trichinopoly by a bold dash against Arkot, then held by the troops of Chanda Sahib, the new-made Nawáb of the Carnatic. With five hundred Englishmen and Sepoys, three guns and a few officers, mostly untried in war, he made his way through rain and storm to the gates of Arkot. Struck with panic at the sight of men whom even a heavy thunderstorm could not keep back, the garrison fled, and Clive marched into the fort. The event justified his forecast and clinched his fame as a bold yet trustworthy commander. For seven weeks his small garrison defied the attacks of ten thousand native troops aided by a powerful battering-train. On the fiftieth day of the siege one last tremendous effort was made to storm a weak stronghold defended now by only 320 fighting men. But Clive commanded them, and under his eye each man fought like twenty. Clive himself had to work one of his own field-pieces, while the men in front kept firing off their muskets as fast as those behind could load them. Thrice were the swarms of loud-shouting assailants flung back from the very arms of seeming victory, before any rest from that day-long struggle came at last to Clive and his wearied band.

Next morning Rájah Sáhib withdrew his shattered forces towards Vellór, and ere long the hero of Arkot was leading his reinforced columns to fresh victories over French and native foes. The relief of Trichinopoly by Major Lawrence and Captain Clive crowned the heroic defence of Arkot. Law himself, the French commander who was presently to fight against us in Bengal, surrendered at discretion, with all his troops, stores, and forty-one guns. The war in the Carnatic lingered on for two years; but Clive himself, after a few more feats of good soldiership, went home to England to recruit his health, to spend his prize-money like a prince, and to win his way, if he could, into the House of Commons.

Foiled in the last-named purpose, and only too successful in getting rid of his money, Colonel Clive was glad to return to India in 1755 as Governor of Fort, St David. He landed at Bombay in good time to join Admiral Watson in the siege and capture of Giriah, the main stronghold of the pirate chief Angria on the Western coast. The news of the Black Hole disaster found him at Fort St. David, free and ready to aid in repairing the ruined fortunes of his countrymen in Bengal. By the middle of

September, 1756, the refugees at Falta were gladdened by the arrival of the fleet, which Admiral Watson had led two months before out of the Madras Roads.

Among those who hailed the long-expected succours was Warren Hastings, who had fled to Falta from Murshidabad on finding his safety imperilled by the part he took in some secret correspondence between Drake and certain leaders of a plot against the Viceroy in his own capital. Whether from a sense of duty, or from a young man's eagerness for active work under a leader of Clive's renown, Hastings shouldered his musket, and shared as a volunteer in the capture of Bajbaj, and in Clive's victorious march upon Calcutta.* On the 2nd January, 1757, he saw the English colours once more flying over the ramparts of Fort William, and about a month later he bore his part in that daring attack on Suraj-ad-daula's camp, which first inspired the boastful despot of Bengal with a wholesome respect for English prowess.

It was not in arms, however, that Hastings was to win his special renown. Clive had

* He formed one of a separate volunteer company, consisting of Bengal Civil Servants and other English refugees.

already found him a trusty agent in his attempts to treat with Suraj-ad-daula. The negotiations begun in January, were resumed to better purpose after the Viceroy's hasty retreat from the neighbourhood of Calcutta. The demands he had once rejected were soon granted by the crestfallen Nawáb, and before the middle of February a treaty had been signed which not only compensated the English for most of their recent losses, but empowered them to fortify Calcutta and coin money in their own mint.

By this time Hastings was already a married man. During his brief sojourn at Falta, he had seen, wooed, and won to wife the widow of a Captain Campbell, who a few months before had arrived at Falta on his way out from England.* What sort of woman was this first wife of Hastings, how the two passed their few years of wedded life together, Mr. Gleig, after much searching, could not ascertain. All we know is that Mrs. Hastings died at Kásimbazár, not long after the birth of her second child, who was presently to follow his mother out of the world, which his elder sister had quitted after nineteen days.

* Such is the inference I gather from Broome's "History of the Bengal Army," Chap. I., p. 72.

Meanwhile things were happening which paved the way for Hastings' future greatness. It was known in Calcutta that France and England were again at war; and there was but too good reason to fear that Suraj-ad-daula, in spite of his new alliance with his English neighbours, was already seeking French aid for their destruction. His intrigues with Law and Bussy certainly looked that way, and his attempt to stop a hostile movement against the French settlement of Chandarnagar, was readily construed by the the Calcutta Council to the same effect. Be that as it may—and in those days the web of Indian politics was more hopelessly tangled than ever—the arrival of succours from Bombay and Madras emboldened the English in Bengal to grasp the nettle danger without more ado. The treaty with the French was cut short; Clive and Watson opened fire upon the defences of Chandarnagar; and in a few days, before the angry Viceroy had marched far to its relief, our troops had become masters of the foremost French possession in Bengal.

Erelong a plot for the dethronement of Suraj-ad-daula was quietly brewing at Calcutta and Murshidabad. The wretched Viceroy, conscious of impending evil, knew not whom to trust, nor whence to seek help against his many foes. At one moment he was imploring Bussy to hasten up to his rescue, at another he was sending the most civil messages to Clive, the man of all others he most dreaded. At the head of the Murshidabad plotters was Mír Jáfar, his own commander-in-Chief, a brother-in-law of Aliverdi Khán. His minister of finance, and Jaggat Sett, the foremost banker of Bengal, were in the plot. Clive's strong will and reckless daring overbore the scruples of his colleagues in the council, and with their help the plot grew and prospered. What part Hastings took in it does not plainly appear; but we may take it for granted that Watts's ablest subaltern at Kásimbazár was called into counsel over a matter which so nearly concerned himself.

At last, when all seemed ripe for action, Clive, in the burning month of June, led out his little army from Chandarnagar, on that famous enterprise which was to make the East India Company virtual masters of the largest, richest, and most populous province of the old Moghal Empire.

The victory of Plassy on the 23rd June, 1757, threw the future of India, as it were, into English hands. A few days later, Clive marched into Murshidabad, and installed the successful traitor,

Mír Jáfar, on the vacant *masnad* of Bengal. The seizure and death of the fugitive Suraj-ad-daula completed Mír Jáfar's good fortune. Mindful of Hastings' past services, the victor of Plassy sent him on special duty to Murshidabad, or, as the English then called it, Muxadavad. Some months later, when Clive became Governor of Fort William, Hastings succeded Scrafton as Resident at the court of the new Nawáb.

CHAPTER IV.

1758—1760.

HASTINGS' new office was no sinecure. As Resident at Murshidabad, he had to watch over the well-being of the English party at Kásimbazár; to see that Mír Jáfar fulfilled his engagements with the Calcutta Council; to keep the peace, if he could, between the new Nawáb and his chief officers; to discover and thwart the numerous intrigues which that time of general disorder, distrust, and ferment brought to an easy birth. It was not long before Mír Jáfar Khán began to plot against Rai Dulab Rám, and some other Hindu nobles, whose wealth might enable him to replenish a treasury exhausted by the payments due to his English friends as the price of his own elevation to the throne of Bengal.

For a time Hastings seems to have misread the real drift of the Nawáb's relations with Dulab Rám, the head of a powerful family of bankers and financiers named Sett. One evening in August, 1758, a number of Sepoys forced their way into the Nawáb's palace, clamouring loudly for their long withheld arrears of pay. To Hastings this was represented as a plot brewed by Dulab Rám against his master's life, and as such he repeated it to Clive himself. But his shrewd chief had not threaded the mazes of Indian roguery in vain. "You have not yet been long enough at the Durbar,"* he writes to Hastings, "to make yourself acquainted with the dark designs of the Mussulmans. The moment I perused your letter, I could perceive a design in the Nabob and those about him against Roy Doolub, and you may be assured what is alleged against him and his letters to Coja Huddee is a forgery from beginning to end. Roy Doolub is not such a fool as to give anything under his own hand." Besides, he would never dare to intrigue against a prince of our own selecting, with the knowledge that his own fate was in Clive's hands. "How easy is it," exclaims the writer, with possible reference to his own success in that line,†

* *Durbar*, or rather *Darbár*, answers to our "Court." For this letter of Clive's, see "Gleig's Life of Hastings," Vol. I., Chap. IV.

† The reader may remember that Clive had forged the signature of his colleague, Admiral Watson, to one copy of the treaty with Mír Jáfar, for the purpose of deceiving the traitor, Amín Chand.

"to counterfeit hands and seals in this country! and the Moors in general are villains enough to undertake anything which may benefit themselves at another's expense." Clive looks in short upon the whole matter as a plan to exasperate him against Dulab Rám, in order that the Nawáb "may have the plucking of him of all his money."

The letters which passed at this time between Clive and Hastings, bring out clearly enough the relation in which they stood to each other, and the spirit in which they worked together. Clive's imperious will, and keen, rough, ready understanding, flash out in short pithy sentences of advice, explanation, or command. His letters go straight to the point in the fewest possible words. Hastings writes rather more lengthily, with a more studied elegance of phrase, with the deference due to higher rank and older experience, and yet with a frankness equal to his chief's. Clive tells Hastings to be "a little severe in exacting the remainder of the last sixth. It is the nature of these people to do nothing through inclination. Ten sepoys or chokeys, now and then, will greatly expedite the payment of the money." Hastings promises to "use all possible means," for collecting the money, but Clive "must be sensible there is a wide difference between securing the payments due from a large amount, and that of collecting in several smal balances remaining on old accounts."

In another letter, Hastings complains of one Nand Kumár's seeming insolence in meddling with affairs, the whole management of which lay, he thought, in his own hands. This is the first time that a name, which was afterwards to be linked unpleasantly with that of Hastings, crops up in the story of Hastings' life. It was not, however, the first time that the zealous young Resident at Murshidábád had heard of the wily, well-born Hindu, the erewhile Governor of Hughli, whose deserts or intrigues had already won him from the Calcutta Council the important post of Revenue Collector for Bardwán, Nadiya, and Hughli, three large districts in the middle of Bengal.

Unaware of this arrangement, Hastings appeals to Clive for further instructions, so that he may not "appear to usurp an office for which he had no authority, or as abruptly dismissed from it for some misconduct or incapacity." Clive, in return, excuses himself for not having formally acquainted him with a fact of which his predecessors, Watts and Scrafton, ought to have made him aware; and he expresses "much concern" at the suggestion that Nand-Kumár's appointment was owing to any misconduct or incapacity on Hastings' part. "No one will be more ready to support your character and welfare than myself, when it can be done without prejudicing the concerns of the Company."*

Hastings' answer betrays the natural disappointment of one whose well-meant efforts have been thwarted by circumstances which he could not foresee. At the same time, he acts in prompt obedience to Clive's orders; merely asking for further enlightenment on certain points, and earnestly disclaiming the construction which Clive had put on a passage in his former letter. "I never," he says, "had the least suspicion that the transferring of the Burdwan and Nuddea affairs to Hughley proceeded in the least from any ill opinion of my conduct or capacity, but that it would be construed as such by everybody here, as it was universally believed that I was appointed at Moradbaug principally for the collection of those revenues." This disclaimer he

* Gleig's "Warren Hastings," Vol. 1, Chap. iv.

follows up by assuring his friend that the promises which Clive had made him, and the good things which Clive was reported to have said of him, were quite enough to preclude the notion of any wilful "slight or prejudice" on Clive's part.

One especial service which Hastings at this time rendered the Company must not be overlooked. The twenty-four Pargannas, a fertile district stretching from the Hughli to the Sundarbans, with Calcutta for its chief city, had been granted to the English by the new Nawáb of Bengal, in part payment of the victory which had raised him to power. But in the course of his researches at Murshidabad, Hastings discovered a serious flaw in the conditions under which the grant had been made. The ceded lands were held "only by virtue of the Nawáb's *parwána*," which might hold good, perhaps, during his lifetime, but was not unlikely to be set aside by his successor. Nor had they been entered in the accountants' books as lands directly belonging to the East India Oompany. In a letter to the Calcutta Council, Hastings pleaded that no time should be lost in clearing up all doubts on a matter which else might some day prove a bone of contention. With the ready consent of the

Governor in Council he set to work. Two months later he was able to inform the Council that his efforts to obtain the *Sanud*, or letters patent, which would secure the Company in their new possessions, would soon be crowned with full success. Of the value placed on those efforts, Clive himself at a later period made warm acknowledgement. "I am very sensible," he wrote to Hastings, "of the pains you have taken, and shall not fail acquainting the Company by the first opportunity, how much you have contributed to bring that important matter to so happy an issue."

The confirmation of the Company's title to these lands was not of course to be had for nothing. Two lakhs of rupees,*—or about £20,000—was the sum which Hastings agreed to pay for the promised *Sanad*; but to the Nawáb's request for the loan of an equal amount on the plea of temporary poverty, Clive turned an incredulous ear. In a letter to Hastings, who had backed this plea, he declared to his "certain knowledge" Mír Jafár possessed several lakhs of rupees in gold; and if, he added, "you were to hint to him, whenever he pleads poverty, that

* A lakh is a hundred thousand, and a rupee answers roughly to an English florin.

you are not ignorant of his hidden resources, I believe it might put an end to the disagreeable topic of borrowing money." So the Nawáb had to be content with his two lakhs down.

Amidst the stirring events and perplexing movements of the two following years, 1759-60, Hastings retained his post at Murshidabad, finding, doubtless, in his scholarly pursuits, and the zealous discharge of his appointed duties, a welcome relief from sorrowful memories of his lost wife. The steamy heat of Bengal, which seems to have killed Mrs. Hastings, wrought little harm upon her hard-working husband, who lived temperately, was seldom called upon to overstrain his bodily powers, and had no leisure, as it were, to fall ill. Those were busy and exciting years for our countrymen in India. The bold but ill fated Lally, beaten off from Madras by the soldiership of Lawrence, and the timely advent of an English fleet, was still revolving schemes full of danger to the Government of Madras. Bussy, recalled from the Dakhan, where, for seven years, he had virtually lorded it over the greatest Prince in Southern India,* led his seasoned troops to

* Salábat Jang, the Nizám or Subhadár of the Dakhan, was son of Chín Kilich Khán, one of Aurangzib's officers, who founded the dynasty that still rules at Haidarábad.

Pondicherry for the purpose of helping Lally to drive the English out of the Carnatic. In Bengal itself the shifty Nawáb, whom Clive's prompt march towards Patna had just saved from eminent disaster at the hands of Moghal invaders from Upper India, was intriguing with the Dutch at Chinsurah against allies already grown too powerful for his peace of mind. Not all Clive's personal influence, great as it was, could keep Mír Jafár from the crooked practices that seemed especially to flourish in the air of Bengal.

As for the Maráthas, whom our countrymen in those days called Morattoes, their swarms of wiry horsemen were raiding everywhere, from the Indus to the Kálarún, breaking to pieces the Moghal Empire in Hindustan, and winning for their Peshwa new provinces from the Nizám of the Dakhan. Delhi itself, the prize in turn of so many conquerors, from Muhammad Ghori to Nádir Shah and Ahmad the Abdáli, now for the first time fell into their hands; and it seemed for the moment as if all India was about to pass under the yoke of the wily Brahman who then reigned at Púna as Peshwa,* or virtual head of

* Bálají Vishwanáth, the first Peshwa or Prime Minister of Sivají's successor the Rajah of Satára, transmitted to his own family the title which in their case meant the real headship of the Marátha States.

that great Maráthа league against the Moghals, which Sivají had set in motion a century before.

The danger to the English in Bengal was met by Clive with his usual promptitude. A Dutch fleet from Java, laden with troops, had entered the Húghli. Although the two nations were then at peace, and Clive had lately invested the bulk of his wealth in Dutch securities, he took the only measures the need of the moment seemed to call for. The Dutch themselves, by their insolence and outrages, provoked the punishment that awaited them. On the 24th November, 1759, three of our men-of-war attacked and captured twice as many of the enemy's ships. On the same day, the bold Colonel Forde, fresh from his victories in Southern India, drove the Dutch troops, with much slaughter, back into Chinsura. On the following day a larger force of Dutchmen, Sepoys, and Malays, was utterly routed on the plain of Bidára by about half their number of Englishmen and Sepoys, whom Forde, encouraged by a hasty note from Clive, had led with equal skill and daring to the attack. Thoroughly humbled by these signal defeats, the Dutch at Chinsura were glad to accept peace on Clive's own terms, which, all things considered, were generous enough. Happily for our countrymen, the Nawáb's traitorous son, Míran, who was marching down with 6,000 horse to join the enemy if things went well with them, reached the scene of action three days too late. It was now his cue to side with the victors; and his threats against the vanquished made them bow the more readily to Clive's demands.

Early in the following year, two of Clive's best captains, Caillaud and Knox, were marching up the country from Murshidabad to drive back Shah Alam, the new, but homeless, Emperor of Delhi,* across the frontier of Bahár. One of the most brilliant feats of that fighting age was the hurried march of Captain Knox with about 1,200 men, mostly Sepoys, from Bardwán to Patna, a distance of 300 miles, in thirteen burning days of April; a movement rewarded by the timely relief of Patna, and the scattering of Shah Alam's troops, and followed up a few weeks later by the repulse and rout of an army twelve times stronger than his own, which the Nawáb of Parnia was leading to the Emperor's aid. Nor did the tireless Major Caillaud fail to teach the Moghal in-

* He had just succeeded his murdered father, Alamgir II., but Delhi was still in the hands of his father's foes.

vader a lesson of respect for the hardy warriors who, with small help from Mír Jafar or the cruel and cowardly Míran, hunted them back with heavy loss from Murshidabad to the borders of Bahár.

In the Carnatic, also, victory smiled upon our arms. Lally's dreams of French supremacy were cruelly shattered by the events of 1760. Coote's relief of Wandiwash, was followed by his crushing defeat of a French force which attempted to renew the siege. One strong place after another fell into the victor's hands. After the fall of Kárikál in April, Lally's prospects grew ever darker, until in September he himself was closely besieged in Pondicherry by the foe whom he had once hoped to drive into the sea. On the 15th of the following January, the capital of French India was surrendered by its starving garrison. and three months later the last French stronghold in Southern India succumbed to the prowess of the fiery Coote. So ended the fight for empire in India between the countrymen of Clive and Dupleix.

Meanwhile Clive himself had embarked for England to enjoy the wealth he had gotten together, and to reap the honours which an admiring nation, flushed with victories by land and sea, was ready, under the leading of its favourite minister, the elder Pitt, to bestow on "the heaven-born general" who had displayed a military genius worthy even of Frederick the Great. On the 25th February, 1760, he made over the keys of office to his senior colleague, Holwell, pending the arrival at Calcutta of his destined successor, Vansittart, a member of the Madras Council, whose after career did little to justify the preference which Clive had shown him over all his rivals in Bengal. It is pretty clear, however, that Clive selected the best man at that time eligible for so high a post. He knew that some of his own colleagues were about to follow his example; and he must have foreseen that none of those who signed the farewell letter of bold, but just, remonstrance addressed by him to the Court of Directors would have any chance of filling his place *

* In point of fact, Holwell, and the three others who signed the letter, were ordered to be dismissed from the Company's service.—Mill's India, Book 4, Chap. v.

CHAPTER V.

1760—1761.

When the new Governor of Fort William landed at Calcutta in July, 1760, the skies above him in that month of incessant rain lowered not more darkly than those which overhung the face of public business in Bengal. The Company's treasury in Calcutta, drained well-nigh of its last rupee, could be replenished only by drafts on England and loans from native bankers. The Court of Directors had themselves to borrow as they best could the means of defraying the costs of government in Bombay and Madras as well as Calcutta. The thriftless Nawáb of Bengal owed the Company large sums which he could not make good, and his troops were in open mutiny on account of their long-withheld arrears of pay. The crimes and vices of his infamous son Míran, who had just been killed by lightning at the age of twenty-one, had raised everywhere new enemies to his father's weak rule. Baffled and beaten by Knox and Caillaud, the young Shah

Alam still held his ground in a corner of Bahár, still asserted his claim to displace by a governor of his own choosing the puppet whom we had set up as the imperial viceroy in Bengal. Mir Jáfar's worthless favourites oppressed the people in his name. Amidst the prevailing strife, disorder, misrule and perplexity, the Maráthas renewed their old ravages unchecked, and, to crown all, some of Vansittart's worst foes were to be found in his own council.

It was hardly to be expected that Clive's successor would prove a second Clive. Vansittart was a man of comparative probity, judged by the standards of his day, but of middling talent and little strength of character. He was cursed with colleagues some abler, and nearly all far less upright than himself. Some of them hated him as an interloper from Madras, others feared in him a check upon their evil passions, especially their greed for ill-gotten gains.

His first movements were naturally guided by the advice of Holwell, whose impatient scorn of Mir Jáfar led him to take up any scheme that promised to rid Bengal of a worthless ruler and to recruit the Company's impoverished exchequer. Holwell, as acting Governor, had already proposed to win the favour of the Moghal Emperor by throwing over the poor old Nawáb; but his council were not prepared to break faith on such a pretext with their own nominee. It was agreed however to provide Mir Jáfar with a deputy who should wield the power of which he himself was to retain the outward symbols. With the hearty assent of Hastings, whose knowledge of the Nawáb's affairs lent due weight to his opinions, the council's choice fell upon Kásim Ali Khán, the old man's son-in-law, who, by dint of promises and money from his own purse, had just succeeded in pacifying the mutineers at Múrshidábád. In return for his promotion, Mír Kásim undertook to pay the balance of Mír Jáfar's debts to the Company, to make over to his patrons the revenues of Bardwán, Midnapúr and Chittagong, and to give five lakhs of rupees towards the war in the Carnatic.

All these preliminaries were settled before the end of September, 1760. On the 2nd of October Colonel Caillaud escorted Vansittart towards the capital where Mir Jáfar was drowning care in amusements and amidst companions suited to his easy, pleasure-loving nature. In his first interviews with the English Governor, he readily promised to mend his administrative ways in accordance with the views of his English friends and advisers. But, when he was finally bidden to get rid of his worthless favourites and instal Mir Kásim as his deputy and future successor, the old man's rage, which had not wholly concealed itself in the presence of his son-in-law, burst for a moment beyond all bounds. He would hear nothing that Caillaud, the bearer of the summons, had to say in explanation. Rather than accept the terms thus offered, he would hold out to the last, come what might.

This mood, however, was too hot to last. Caillaud's troops were at hand to compel submission; but there was no need to use force. As the Nawáb cooled down, Hastings and Lushington brought to bear upon him an array of reasons which served to quicken his change of purpose His wounded dignity, or his fears for his own safety, still forbade him to play the part of puppet to his hated son-in-law; but the Company were welcome to make Mir Kásim Viceroy in his place, if they would only let him retire under their protection into private life.

To this proposal there could only be one answer. It was equally impossible to throw Mir

Kásim over and to let things go on as they had done under Mir Jáfar. At that time no one dreamed of what was to happen a few years later, of the actual displacement of native by English rule throughout Bengal. To leave Mir Jáfar a sovereign in name while Kásim ruled in fact, would probably have been tantamount to signing the former's death-warrant, in a country whose chief men were always ready to kill off an inconvenient rival or a suspected foe. So Mir Kásim Ali was formally installed in the room of his helpless father-in-law, who, placing his life and fortunes in Caillaud's hands, took boat forthwith for Calcutta. A strong guard of Englishmen and Sepoys saw him safe to his journey's end. Lodged with his family and followers in the shady suburb of Chitpúr, we may leave the fallen prince to reflect with the calmness of a good Mussulman on the vanity of human greatness, and to amuse himself in his own fashion with the liberal income settled upon him by his fortunate successor.

Among those who waited on the new Nawáb, and took part in the ceremonies marking his preferment, Warren Hastings was of course included. But he seems to have made no personal profit out of an event which placed large sums of money, ranging from 13 to 50 lakhs of rupees, in the pockets of Vansittart, Holwell and five other gentlemen of the Company's Service. Such was the price at which Mir Kásim bought his way to power; and such were the means by which our countrymen in India were ready enough in those days to amass the fortunes which enabled them to win place, power, or social prominence after their return home.* It was no easy matter for the new Nawáb to fulfil his share of this unseemly bargain; and some of those who were left out of that bargain or got less than their fancied deserts had the face to condemn Vansittart's policy as a needless breach of faith.

For some months longer Hastings continued to discharge his former duties at the new Viceroy's capital. His knowledge of business, his conversance with native languages and ways, and his known character for steadiness and official honesty combined to make him a useful and trustworthy channel of intercourse between

* Vansittart obtained 500,000, Holwell 270,000, Sumner and M'Guire 255,000 and Cailland 200,000 rupees. Cailland at first refused to accept his proffered share, but it was transmitted to him after his arrival in England. *See* Broome's "History," chap. 4.

the Governments of Calcutta and Bengal. For a time, too, all went well in the provinces ruled by Mír Kásim. His predecessor's favourites were dismissed from office and compelled to disgorge the bulk of their ill-gotten wealth. Heavy arrears of pay were disbursed to the English troops at Patna, while the clamours of his own soldiery were appeased for a time by the same process. With the money which he scraped together for the Company's use, our countrymen at Madras were enabled to bring the siege of Pondicherry to a prosperous issue, and thus seal the doom of French dominion in the South. Able and active, the new Nawáb inspired and overlooked the reforms which his servants carried out in every branch of government. Never since the days of Aliverdi Khán had justice been administered with so firm a hand, or the revenues been employed to such useful purpose, as in the first two years of Kásim's rule.

In the field of arms, also, much was accomplished with small means. In the first days of 1761, Carnac, who had replaced Caillaud in the command of our troops, marched out from Patna to fight the Moghal Emperor posted at Suan, near the town of Bahár. Our bold infantry, aided by a few well-served guns, made short work of Shah Alam's native warriors, who speedily left M. Law, and his small French brigade, to bear the shock of battle by themselves. Law made up his mind to bear it at all hazards; but his guns were taken with a rush. Scared at the victors' unbroken advance with swift steps and levelled bayonets, his infantry also broke and fled. A few officers and men still stood firm beside their brave commander, whose noble madness saved him from the death he seemed to court. Followed by a few of his own officers, Carnac went forward, took off his his hat to Law, and in words of befitting courtesy and just compliment invited him to yield. "We are willing to surrender ourselves, but not our swords," was the Frenchman's* answer. To this condition Carnac at once agreed; the officers on both sides shook hands, and Carnac's prisoners entered the English camp as friends and honoured guests.

Meanwhile, in the Birbhúm highlands and on the rich plains of Bardwán, a few hundred Englishmen and Sepoys, under Yorke and White,

* Law was in fact a son of John Law, the clever Scotch financier, who founded a French Bank, became for a time Comptroller-General of the Finances, and sent France wild over the Mississippi scheme.

had broken the neck of a powerful revolt against the new Nawáb. Higher up the Ganges, in the neighbourhood of Monghír, the dashing Ensign Stables followed up and routed ten times his own number of rebel troops, led by the Rajah of Karakpúr. The records of that century teem with such instances of Sepoy courage, aided by a few English leaders and a mere sprinkling of European soldiers, against the heaviest odds. Nor did some, at least, of the native commanders who fought by our side fail to bear themselves like men of mettle. In the memorable fight near Patna, of which I have already spoken, the brave Hindu Rajah, Shitáb Rai, won the unstinted praises of so competent a critic as Captain Knox himself; and his name was ever afterwards held in deserved honour by our countrymen in Bengal.

Carnac's successes in Bahár were speedily crowned by the peace which Shah Alam, overborne by reverses and want of funds, was glad to accept from his untiring pursuers. Before the end of February, the homeless descendant of Bábar entered Patna under the protection of British bayonets. In the following month he agreed, in return for a fixed yearly tribute, to recognise Mir Kásim as Subhadár of Bengal, Bahár, and Orissa; and tempting offers were made to his new friends, if they would only help to replace him on the throne of his murdered father.* For various reasons these offers were unwillingly refused; but when, soon afterwards, the Emperor set out from Patna to try and recover his capital with the aid of his own feudatories in Oudh and Rohilkhand, Carnac escorted him with all honour to the banks of the Karamnása, beyond which the Nawáb of Oudh lay waiting to receive and shelter his ill-starred suzerain.

The same events which opened to Shah Alam the road to Delhi, had freed Bengal itself from one source of constant trouble. In the great battle fought on the plains of Pánipat in January, 1761, between the famished Marátha hosts and the allied Afghan and Moghal armies, led by the victorious Ahmad Shah, the far-reaching power of the still young Marátha League received in the hour of its greatest triumphs a blow from which it could never quite recover. Pánipat was the Flodden Field which broke the heart of the great Peshwa, Bálaji Ráo, and left all Mahá-

* Alamgir II. was murdered in 1759 by his Vizier, the infamous Ghází-ud-dín.

ráshtra wailing for the loss of her foremost leaders and stoutest sons. For some years to come the imperial cities of Delhi and Agra saw no more of their late despoilers; and the villagers of Bengal could reap their harvests without fear of a visit from the active freebooters, who made plundering a fine art, and coveted nothing which they did not carry away.

All this time Warren Hastings seems to have been watching the course of events from his "bungalow" in the suburbs of Murshidábád.* Hitherto he had played an useful, but still subordinate part in the Company's affairs; but the time was now come when his abilities and experience were to be tested in a higher sphere. The dismissal of three members of the Calcutta Council, for their bold remonstrance to the Court of Directors against the jobbery and injustice which these had prompted or connived at, took place in August, 1761; and one of the vacant seats in the Council was bestowed on Hastings, who entered on his new duties at a moment specially unfavourable to "the making of splendid names."

* ("Suburbs of Murshidâbâd)." The suburb in which Hastings lived was Moràdbàgh, on the opposite side of the river to Murshidâbâd.

CHAPTER VI.

1761—1764.

"There is no page in our Indian history so revolting as the four years of the weak and inefficient rule of Mr. Vansittart." So speaks Sir John Malcolm in his "Life of Clive," and the evidence of known facts seems to bear out that dismal verdict. Macaulay himself did not overstate the truth in declaring that the interval between Clive's first and second administration "has left on the fame of the East India Company a stain not wholly effaced by many years of just and humane government." Had all Vansittart's colleagues been like Warren Hastings, that page of our Indian history might have brought no blush of shame to the reader's cheek. But before Hastings entered the Calcutta Council, the first step had already been taken in that course of blundering, extortion, and high-handed violence, which ended only with Clive's return to power.

In the spring of 1761 Mir Kásim began to find himself in want of money. Rajah Rámnarain, the Hindu Governor of Patna, was reported to have amassed such heaps of treasure as a needy Nawáb, following the practice of his time and country, might easily be tempted to claim for his own use. It was easy also to find a pretext for an act of spoliation which Mir Kásim, for all we know, may have honestly regarded as fair payment of monies due to the State by one of its chief officers. Rámnarain, of course, like every native of rank, had his enemies who charged him with plotting against the Nawáb. He had however, or should have had, a powerful friend in the East India Company, if treaties with the English and repeated promises of protection were worth more than blank paper and wasted breath. Mir Kásim ordered him to account for the revenues of his province during the past three years. The Governor of Patna shirked compliance with this demand, pleading that the cost of defending a province overrun with hostile armies had swallowed up all his receipts, and asking for time to complete the balancing of accounts which, in their present state, could not well be laid before his master.

Both parties appealed to Calcutta. On Rámnaráin's side were Carnac and Coote, who succeeded Carnac in command of the Company's troops at Patna. Both of them had been tempted by large bribes to betray the Governor, but both to their honour stood firm against all temptation. Vansittart also shrank at first from gratifying the Nawáb's thirst for revenge or plunder at the cost of a subject whose guilt, if any, was yet to prove. But his opponents in the Council sided with the Rajah's friends, and Vansittart's sense of justice was clouded by distrust of the colleagues who for once seemed ready to back him against his usual supporters. There must, he argued, be something wrong in a cause thus strangely defended. His mind thus biassed, he soon lent an easy ear to the tales which Mir Kásim's agents kept pouring into it; and Ramnarain's doom was hastened by the Nawáb's assurance that the balance of his own debt to the Company should be cleared off out of the Hindu's forfeit wealth. Before the end of June Coote and Carnac were both recalled from Patna. Rámnarain and all his treasures, real or imaginary, fell into the hands of a prince whose anger was not allayed by his failure to find the booty of which he had dreamed.

The friends of the luckless captive were tortured in vain. The treasure actually found barely sufficed for the daily expenses of the government; and Ramnarain presently paid with a cruel death the penalty due in Eastern countries to disappointed greed.*

By his conduct in this matter Vansittart went far to destroy the confidence which the native nobles and gentry of Bengal had been wont to place in English promises of protection. Rámnarain's fate discouraged the friends as much as it emboldened the enemies of English influence in Bengal. Among these latter Mir Kásim Ali himself, the Nawáb of our own making, was ere long to be enrolled.

Gratitude for past favours was already burning low in the breast of a ruler who aspired to free his kingdom from all foreign control, and who knew that among Vansittart's present colleagues and agents the successful supplanter of Mír Jáfar could count upon few friends, besides the Governor and Warren Hastings. Disputes concerning the rights and privileges of English traders and their native friends were already claiming his attention. For the ends which he

* The weight of evidence, as quoted by Mill (Book IV., Ch. 5) bears out this view of the supposed treasure.

had in view Murshidabad was too near Calcutta, and so Mir Kásim ere long transferred his capital to Monghír, where the Ganges almost washes the foot of the Rájmahál Hills. New works of defence sprang up around that city. Within its walls he proceeded to found a large arsenal, to cast guns, and to manufacture muskets of the newest pattern for an army that might blunt the edge even of English daring. It was not long before he found himself master of 15,000 horse and 25,000 foot, trained for the most part by deserters from our own ranks or adventurers in quest of service under whatever flag.

Meanwhile his smouldering quarrel with the English was being daily fanned into fresh life by provocations which Hastings and Vansittart were powerless either to prevent or punish. Outvoted in council, they might deplore but could not restrain the high-handed violence with which Ellis, the new chief of the Patna factory, gratified at once his zeal for the Company's interests and his rancorous dislike of the Nawáb. Mír Kásim's dignity, affronted by an attempt to seize and imprison one of his officers for questioning the right of a Company's servant to pass his private wares free of duty, was yet further outraged by the insults heaped on another of the Nawáb's servants, whom Ellis seized and shipped off in irons to Calcutta, for having dared without his leave to buy some saltpetre for his master's use, in alleged defiance of the Company's monopoly. In the former case the attempt was frustrated by the good sense of an English officer, who, disobeying the order received from Patna, referred the grievance to the Nawáb himself. In the other case it needed all Vansittart's address and influence to save the offender from the brutal vengeance demanded by Ellis's partisans, in order that he might be punished by his own master.

Early in 1762 Ellis ordered a body of troops to search Monghír, Mir Kásim's new capital, for some deserters from the Patna garrison. The governor of that stronghold refused to admit the troops; but allowed two of their officers to accompany him round the fort. Ellis's wrath blazed up at what he called the governor's insolence, and the troops were ordered to keep their place outside the walls pending the issue of his demands for redress. Mir Kásim appealed to Calcutta, and Vansittart answered the appeal by deputing his best adviser, Hastings, to inquire into the whole affair and to allay as he best could a quarrel which was daily growing more embittered.

Hastings went up the country in April—saw some of the Nawáb's chief officers—looked in at Monghír, where any search for deserters seemed to him as hopeless as the attempt to "find a stray pebble on the mountains around it," and in due time got speech at Sarsarám, near Patna, with the Nawáb himself. Ellis, for his part, seems to have shirked a meeting with Vansittart's peacemaker; a fact which Hastings noted with regret. But the Nawáb had already agreed to compromise the matter, by allowing the officer of Hastings' escort to search the fort of Monghír. None of the missing deserters could be found, but one cause of quarrel disappeared with the return of the Sepoy force to Patna.

Other causes of quarrel, however, were not far to seek. The Nawáb's friendly dealings with Shujá-ad-daula, the Moghal Viceroy of Oudh, for their mutual benefit, were construed by Mír Kásim's ill-wishers into an alliance against the English. Even his sternness in suppressing plots against his own life gave his enemies a fresh handle for complaint and misrepresentation. Hastings inquired into these matters also; but his inquiries taught him only to laugh at rumours "so opposite to the Nawáb's character, his interest, and to common sense," that, but for "the uncommon pains which had been taken to make them plausible," he would have scorned to demonstrate their falsity to so shrewd an observer as Colonel Coote.*

Guilty or innocent of all the crimes and purposes laid to his charge, Mír Kásim could not avoid his fate. In his letter of April 25, Hastings had already besought the Governor's attention to the "oppressions" daily committed in Bengal under the sanction of the English name. To his surprise not a boat that passed him on the river but bore the English flag, which was also flying from many places along the bank. At almost every village on his way up, he found the shops shut and the people fled, for fear of exactions like those from which they had already suffered at the hands of his countrymen and their followers, real or pretended. He saw enough to convince him of the evils wrought and threatened by the lawless doings of the Company's servants, and the powerlessness of their victims to obtain redress. It was the old tale of strong men lord-

* Gleig's "Life of Warren Hastings," Vol. I., Ch. 5.

ing it without a scruple over neighbours too weak, timid, or indolent to withstand them. On the one side towered "the strength of civilisation without its mercy;" on the other crouched a multitude of feeble, down-trodden folk, whom centuries of foreign rule, of caste tyranny, and of life under a steamy tropical sun had long since debased from the type of their warlike, Sanskrit-speaking forefathers. What resistance could these herds of Bengáli deer offer to those ravening English wolves—

> "quos opimus
> Fallere et effugere est triumphus?"

The abuse of the Company's rights of trade had indeed grown to an unbearable pitch. Under the *phirmán* granted by a Moghal emperor the Company's merchandise had been allowed to pass up and down the country free of all duty, by virtue of a *dastak*, or pass, signed by the President of the Council. As the power of the Company waxed greater, their servants proceeded to turn this public privilege to their own account. The high duties and the frequent toll-houses, which hampered the private trade of Bengal, offered no hindrance to the bold factor who could display a dastak duly signed, or trust at need to the guarding influence of the Company's flag. Every *gomashta* or agent of a factory, every native merchant who had any interest with his English customers, adopted the same device; and it was said that the youngest "writer" in the Company's service could make his two or three thousand rupees a month by selling passes to native purchasers.

The Nawáb himself, in a letter to Vansittart, had already complained of the harm done to his own government and people by these acts of lawlessness and fraud. "From the factory of Calcutta to Kásimbazár, Patna, and Dacca, all the English chiefs with their gomashtas, officers, and agents in every district of the government, act as collectors, renters, and magistrates, and, setting up the Company's colours, allow no power to my officers. And besides this, the gomashtas and other servants in every district, in every market and village, carry on a trade in oil, fish, straw, bamboo, rice, paddy, betel-nut, and other things; and every man with a Company's *dastak* in his hand regards himself as not less than the Company."* Loud also grew the complaints of the Nawáb's officers at the way in which their

* Mill's "India," Book 4, Chap. v.

mildest efforts to carry out their master's orders were hindered and set at nought by the insolence and the threats of those strong-handed "Sahibs," whose agents forced the people, under pain of a flogging, to buy and sell goods at the Sahib's own price, and played the part of judges in their own causes without the least regard for the decrees of the Nawáb's regular courts.

Hastings felt that outrages so gross and frequent could "bode no good to the Nawáb's revenues, the quiet of the country, or the honour of our nation." Nor was Vansittart less blind to the dangers involved in abuses which, if not swiftly remedied, must end by plunging the Company into war with the Nawáb. To avert that issue he tried such arts as a well-meaning but weak-handed governor might fairly use against offenders conscious of his weakness and their own strength. His first efforts to abate the growing nuisance tended only to inflame an open sore. "Nothing," wrote Hastings, "will ever reach the root of those evils, till some certain boundary be fixed between the Nabob's authority and our privileges." Vansittart accordingly sketched out a number of proposals which Hastings, after careful revision, laid before the Nawáb. They were accepted with hardly a murmur, Mir Kásim asking only for their embodiment in a treaty guarded by the Company's seal.

But the plan which looked so promising was scornfully rejected by Vansittart's colleagues, as an insult to the English name and a grievous inroad on the rights of the Company's servants. The reign of violence and fraud went on with redoubled vigour; and Hastings, after three months of bootless labour in Bahár, returned to Calcutta to take fresh counsel with his bewildered chief. With sore hearts these two, the only honest members of the Calcutta Council, strove hard to win from their greedy and unscrupulous colleagues the desired permission to treat once more in a friendly spirit with the now indignant Nawáb. At last they seemed to have so far succeeded, that, early in the cold season of 1762, Vansittart set out with Hastings to talk over matters quietly with Kásim Ali at Monghir.

The Nawáb received them with a cordiality none the less marked for the bitterness of his language against the invaders of his lawful rights, and the despoilers of his helpless people. After some discussion it was agreed that the inland trade should remain open to the Company's servants, chargeable only with an *ad valorem* duty of nine per cent. on the prime cost of their goods at the place of purchase.

The manner in which a concession that still placed the English at a great advantage over the native traders was received at Calcutta, showed Vansittart that he had reckoned without his host. His opponents in the Council were furious at this surrender of any part of their pretended privileges. Their wrath was heightened by the ill-judged haste with which Mir Kásim carried out the new arrangement notified in Vansittart's letter to himself, before that arrangement had been confirmed by the Governor's Council. Against men thus furnished with an excuse for wrong doing, it was hopeless to argue. Vansittart's work was undone with every circumstance of needless insult to all concerned in it. The Nawáb's temper, never of the long-suffering sort, gave way beneath this new trial, coming as it did close upon the failure of his attempt to conquer Nipál. If the English would not trade with him on fair terms, he could at least extend to his own subjects the immunities which the Company's servants claimed so arrogantly for themselves alone. Accordingly, in the middle of March, 1763, the Nawáb abolished all transit duties throughout Bengal, and thus opened the trade of that country to merchants of all nations alike.

Then arose a fresh clamour against the prince who thus dared to rescue his own subjects from the shackles devised for them by English greed. In vain did two honest Englishmen point out the injustice of barring a whole nation from the right of trading in their own country on equal terms with a few foreigners from unknown seas. By a vote of the majority in the Council, it was resolved to let the Nawáb know how grievously he had wronged the authors and guardians of his political being. While two of their body were hastening up the country to demand from Mir Kásim the swift annulment of his obnoxious decree, the chiefs of the various factories and the commanders of the troops were ordered to prepare for that collision which our countrymen seemed so eager to provoke.

The Nawáb saw what was coming, but refused to purchase a brief respite from his growing troubles by accepting the demands of the English envoys. Despairing of help from his friends in the Calcutta Council, who still tried their best to avert the inevitable, he turned for deliverance to the Nawáb of Oudh and his nominal master but virtual dependant, the exiled Emperor of Dehli. In spite of fresh outrages and provocations from his old enemy, Ellis, he still wavered on the brink of armed resistance. On the 19th of June, 1763, he agreed to surrender the boatloads of arms which his officers had stopped on their way up to Patna. About the same time he wrote to Vansittart a letter plaintively reviewing his past conduct, and warmly protesting his innocence of the treachery laid to his charge. "In what way" —he asked—"have I deceived or betrayed you? I never devoured two or three crores of rupees of the treasure of Mír Jafar Khán. I never seized a biga* of the land belonging to Calcutta, nor have I imprisoned your gomashtas. Have I not discharged the debts contracted by the Khán aforenamed? Did I procure from you, gentlemen, the payment of the arrears of his army, or put you to the expense of maintaining the Company's forces? . . . . I gave you a country which produced a crore of rupees. Was it for this only, that after two or three months

* A "biga" is about two-thirds of an acre.

you should place another on the *masnad* of the Nizámat?" And he ended by retorting the charge of treachery on those who made it.

It shows how far the Nawáb's anger misled him, that he could tax one of his best friends with having brought him into his present plight. "All this distraction and ruin brought upon my affairs are owing," he wrote, "to Mr. Hastings," who had persuaded him to accept the fatal gift of government from Calcutta, and had counselled him to "engage the English in his interests." Only a few days before this letter was written, the alleged "author of all these evils" had been roundly abused by one of his colleagues for defending the Nawáb's cause with the unscrupulous zeal of a "hired solicitor;" and the abuse was followed up by a blow, for which Batson found himself severely censured by the Council, and obliged to offer a full apology, in terms dictated by his censurers.*

Do what he would, however, to keep the peace with his troublesome neighbours, Kásim Ali failed, as the best of rulers at such a moment might well have failed, to walk clear of all the snares and stumbling-blocks that beset his path.

* Gleig's "Life of Hastings," Vol. I., Ch. v.

In spite of Hastings' earnest remonstrances, the Council had entrusted Ellis at Patna with full power to act as he and his colleagues might think fit in their own and the Company's interests, if these should be imperilled by the Nawáb's conduct. This discretion that hot-headed Englishman was already using as indiscreetly as all who knew him must have foreseen. Once more the Nawáb lost his temper, and the arms which he had just surrendered were again seized on their way up the river. An English gentleman was also detained as hostage for some of the Nawáb's imprisoned officers. One angry movement provoked another. On the night of June 24 the city of Patna was suddenly attacked and taken by troops acting under Ellis's orders. The Nawáb retorted by commanding the arrest of every Englishman in Bengal. Amyatt, a leading member of the Council, paid with his life the penalty of armed resistance to the Nawáb's officers. Patna was recovered as easily as it had been lost, and erelong Ellis himself with many English fugitives from Patna and Kásimbazár fell into the hands of a conqueror on whose forbearance they had little reason to count.

In spite of the heavy July rains a force of

English and Sepoys under the daring Major Adams at once took the field. Never was a hard campaign more splendidly fought in India against heavier odds. In five months Adams had led his little army from Calcutta to the Káramnása, defeating in two pitched battles many times his own number of disciplined troops, winning four strong places by siege or assault, and capturing more than 400 pieces of cannon. Smarting with rage under the memorable rout of Giriah, the Nawáb gave the reins to his cruel nature. Rámnarain and other prisoners of mark were put to death. After his next reverse the two great Hindu bankers of the Sett clan were thrown into the Ganges. The capture of Monghír sealed the doom of his English prisoners. Walter Reinhardt, an Alsatian soldier of fortune, who had transferred his services from one flag to another until he rose to high command under Kásim, undertook the deed of butchery which was to make him for ever infamous in the annals of British India. This ruffian, better known by his nickname of Sombre which the natives turned into Sumru, carried out his bloody work with a thoroughness only to be equalled, a century later, by the massacre of Cawnpore. A hundred and fifty helpless soldiers and civilians, with several women, were shot down or cut to pieces within the walls of their prison-house at Patna. Ellis himself was among the fifty gentlemen who perished on that woful 5th of October, 1763.*

On the 6th of November Patna was stormed by Adams's heroes. But Kásim and the butcher Sumru had escaped the vengeanee of their pursuers by timely flight. Adams renewed the chase as far as the Karamnása; but before the year's end his prey had found shelter with Kásim's new ally, the Nawáb-Vazír of Oudh. Shuja-ad-daula refused to give up to certain death the fugitives who had become his guests. Worn out with toil and illness Adams resigned into the weaker hands of Carnac the task which he had brought so near completion. His own days, indeed, were numbered, for he reached Calcutta only to die.

Meanwhile a vote of the Calcutta Council had replaced Mír Jáfar, now old, leprous, and half doting, on the forfeit *masnad* of Bengal. In his readiness to resume even the show of power, the

* Broome's "Bengal Army," Chap. iv. Some of the bodies were thrown yet living into the well which served for their common tomb.

poor old man agreed to a number of conditions which left him the mere slave and tool of his greedy taskmasters. He pledged himself to reimpose the duties which Mir Kásim had repealed, to exempt from those duties the trade of the Company's servants, and to pay large sums into the Company's treasury as compensation for public and private losses. In these arrangements Hastings seems to have taken no active part, nor did he soil his fingers with any of the money which his colleagues pocketed in return for losses incurred in the prosecution of an illegal trade.

The famous victory of Bakhsar, won on the 23rd October, 1764, by Major Munro, with barely 7,000 Sepoys and Europeans over 50,000 of Shujá's troops, including Sumru's highly drilled brigades, and numbers of those Afghan horsemen who had fought so well at Pánipat, brought Shujá's schemes of conquest and Kásim's hopes of vengeance to a disastrous end. In effect it placed all Oudh at the feet of the victorious English, brought Shah Alam a suppliant into the English camp, sent Mir Kásim a friendless fugitive into Rohilkhand, and drove the infamous Sumru to sell his sword to the Játs of Bhartpúr. When the welcome news reached Calcutta, Hastings was already preparing for his voyage home. Before the close of November he had resigned his seat in the Council; and soon afterwards he embarked in the same ship with his friend Vansittart for the dear home-land where his little son lay dying, and his dream of retrieving the family fortunes had first been conceived.

BOOK II.

CHAPTER I.

1765—1769.

After a residence of more than fourteen years in India, Hastings returned to England, a poor man by comparison with other "Nabobs" of his day. Of the moderate fortune which he had scraped together, not a rupee appears to have been obtained by methods alien from the moral standards of our own time. While men like Drake, Clive, and Vansittart, were making thousands of pounds at one stroke out of the needs or the gratitude of native princes, while other of the Company's servants grew rich on perquisites drawn or wrung from native merchants, landholders, and placemen, Hastings seems to have kept his hands clean of all unworthy or even questionable gains. As Resident at a Native Court, and again as Member of the Calcutta Council, he had many opportunities of securing some of the wealth which flowed so steadily into the pockets of less scrupulous colleagues. To any one living in such an atmosphere of greed and corruption, the temptation to enrich himself by whatever means must have been very great; and Hastings, as we know, had a special reason for seeking after wealth. But his proud self-respect or his native honesty rose above temptations by which Macaulay, in his case, has set too little store; and he came home with money enough to keep him in comfort, but with little to spare for the indulgence of his generous instincts.

Before leaving India, Hastings sent his sister, Mrs. Woodman, a present of £1,000. This, no doubt, was the lady to whose charge, in 1761, he had entrusted his little son George, for what proved to be the brief remainder of his young life. On his aunt Elizabeth, widow of his kind uncle, Howard Hastings, he settled an annuity of £200; a large and timely addition to her very slender means.

The first news that greeted him on his return to England in 1765, was the death of his only son from an ulcerated throat. For months and years afterwards, the bereaved father mourned in silence over a loss which even his second marriage was destined never to repair. He might live to become the Lord of Daylesford, but no heir of his own loins ever succeeded to his name and estate.

The few years which he now spent in England remain to us almost a blank. At the age of thirty-two he must still have possessed a fund of youthful energy, which the circumstances of his past career had done little to exhaust. The shadow which his boy's death seems to have cast upon his life, may have disabled him from enjoying thoroughly the new world in which, after fifteen years of industrious exile, he found himself master of his own time, and of a fortune not too small for his reasonable wants. A restlessness born of sorrow drove him, it seems, in the winter of 1765, to ask the Court of Directors for early reëmployment in India. Their refusal turned his thoughts into other channels. Learning and literature erelong gave their votary a sweet distraction from melancholy musings. He studied the classics of two continents; he wrote and sometimes published verses and essays which never repaid the cost of publication. Among the men of genius or talent with whom at this time he became acquainted, was Dr. Johnson, whose name had already risen high in the world of literature, and whose personal knowledge of Hastings, if small, was enough, he afterwards wrote, to make him "wish for more."*

The acquaintance seems to have sprung out of Hastings' efforts to plan a scheme for encouraging in England the study of Persian, in those days the classical language of most Indian Courts. To establish somewhere a chair for Persian, filled by professors obtained from India, was an object worthy of the support which it failed to win. It has been said that Hastings selected Oxford for this purpose, and himself for the first Persian Professor. Mr. Gleig, however, on the best authority, declares that Hastings never thought of himself or Oxford in connection with such a scheme. He proposed, in fact, that the East India Company should found a seminary for its own servants, in which Persian should be taught

* Boswell's "Life of Johnson," Vol. 4, Chap. iii. (Routledge's Edition.)

by a competent native of India. "I formed a plan," wrote Hastings himself, "for such an institution, but I never offered, nor intended to superintend it. I was not qualified for it; indeed my intention was to obtain professors from India."* It was left for a later age, and a more enlightened Court of Directors, to embody in the College at Haileybury the cherished dream of Hastings, and the slowly rewarded efforts of Lord Wellesley.†

It was not long, however, before Hastings' services were again to be required in the field for which he still yearned. In 1766, the House of Commons had begun a careful inquiry into the affairs of the East India Company. Among the witnesses summoned before the Committee, not the least conspicuous was Hastings himself. So strong was the impression which his quiet bearing, his clear straightforward answers, and his manifest mastery of the subjects brought before him, left upon the minds of all who heard or read

* Gleig's "Warren Hastings," Vol. 1, Chap. vi.

† Lord Wellesley, in 1802, founded in Calcutta a college for the training of Indian civil servants, but an order from the Court of Directors led to its speedy abolition, in the form, at least, which he had hoped to give it. Four years afterwards, a college was opened at Haileybury, which was finally closed in 1858.

his evidence, that his second request for employment in India was not made in vain. His means were already becoming straitened, partly through the loss of savings left to fructify in Bengal, and partly through the help he gave so liberally to friends or relations in need. The Court of Directors had learned to see in him one of their ablest and most upright servants, one of the very few in whom they could put their trust at any pinch. An opening for him was at length found at Madras, for which place he set sail in the early spring of 1769. About a year earlier, his old friend Clive had returned home in broken health, but with his heart as high as ever, from his short but glorious second term of government in Bengal. In two years the victor of Plassy had done much to retrieve the fortunes and fair fame of the East India Company. He had won from the humbled Emperor of Delhi the charter that placed his masters upon the throne of Bengal;* he had put down a serious mutiny among his own officers; had reduced the ruler of Oudh into an obedient

* On the 12th August, 1765, in Clive's own tent, from a throne made up of two tables surmounted by a chair, Shah Alam bestowed on the Company the Dewáni, or Government, of Bengal, Bahar, and Orissa; provinces now peopled by sixty million souls.

ally of the new English power; had swept away many of the abuses which disgraced the Company's rule, and done all, in short, that one man, armed with uncertain powers, and thwarted or ill-succoured by his masters at home, could well do to atone for the misrule, corruption, and financial blundering of the past few years.

That Clive and Hastings met in England after the former's return home, is a likelihood which, for want of evidence, must not be taken for a solid fact. It may fairly be assumed, however, that such a meeting happened more than once, and that Hastings learned from the lips of his old friend how things were going on in Bengal and Madras.

The destined head of the Madras Council at this time was Du Pré, its senior member, a gentleman whose abilities were equalled by his great industry, and whose gentle manners covered a kind heart, while they lent a sweetness to his frankest utterances. To him and his colleagues the Directors announced their selection of "Mr. Warren Hastings, a gentleman who has served us many years upon the Bengal establishment, with great ability and unblemished character," for a seat in the Madras Council. "We have," they added, "from a consideration of his just merits, and general knowledge of the Company's affairs, been induced to appoint him one of the Members of our Council at your Presidency, and to station him next below Mr. Du Pré."

After making due provision for those whom he had hitherto helped to live, Hastings found himself driven to borow money for his own outfit. With a few words of loving farewell, written off Dover, to his "dear brother and sister," Mr. and Mrs. Woodman, he closed the first evening of his life on board the *Duke of Grafton*. An event which brought out the mingled strength and weakness of a nature essentially noble, happened during the long voyage round the Cape of Good Hope.

Among Hastings' fellow-passengers was a certain lady, whose husband, Baron Imhoff, a native of Franconia, was going out to Madras to mend his fortune by painting portraits. Between him and his wife, a lady, says Mr. Gleig, who came to know her in after years, "of singularly attractive manners, of a very engaging figure, and a mind highly cultivated," the love that should hallow wedlock seems to have burned but feebly, if it ever burned at all. Macaulay, without any warrant, assumes that the wife heartily despised her husband; but Mr. Gleig's narrative merely implies that the two were little suited to each other. With Hastings the lady was soon brought into social contact, under conditions which neither could have prevented if they would. Shut up with their companions for six or seven months in their floating prison, these two were naturally drawn together by those fine threads of mental and sexual sympathy, whose power for good and evil the great master-mind of Germany has set so movingly before us in his "Wahlverwandschaften." An acquaintance fed by daily, almost hourly intercourse, ripened into friendship, and friendship gradually passed into love.

At length a new temptation opened their eyes to the secret which their hearts had cherished unawares. Hastings fell dangerously ill. For days he lay hovering between life and death; his sick-bed watched by the Baroness with all the patient tenderness of her sex. It was she who gave him his medicines, and sat beside him while he slept. With returning health, he awoke to his new relations with another man's wife. Even then, the voice of honour or prudence held him back from the path of lawless self-indulgence. It appears that Imhoff was duly made aware of the passion which his wife and Hastings could no longer hide from each other. The marriage laws of his own country held out to him a way of escape from his awkward position; and his poverty, no doubt, inclined him to accept the salve which his wife's lover was prepared to place upon his wounded pride. It was soon arranged between them that the Baron and his wife should continue to live together as before, pending the issue of a divorce suit which Imhoff was to carry on at Hastings' expense in the courts of Franconia.

The bargain was honourably fulfilled on both sides. Some years had to elapse before the desired decree laid low the barrier which still parted Hastings from his future wife. Meanwhile Mr. and Mrs. Imhoff lived together "with good repute," according to Mr. Gleig, first at Madras, and afterwards, when Hastings rose to a higher sphere of duty, at Calcutta. In due time the spouseless Baron returned home, "a richer man than he ever could have hoped to become by the mere exercise of his skill as a painter" The lady's children by her first marriage, were adopted by her second husband, who never found cause to repent of the union thus quietly brought about.

CHAPTER II.

—1769.

When Hastings landed at Madras in the late summer of 1769, he found Du Pré installed as President in the room of Mr. Palk, the last days of whose government had been marked by an abrupt and rather inglorious ending to an undesirable and costly war. A foolish clause in an ill-advised treaty, had brought the Company into collision with the most formidable of its native foes in Southern India. The Northern Sarkárs, a tract of low seaboard, varying from eighteen to a hundred miles in breadth, and stretching some 450 miles north-eastward from the Kistna delta to Ganjam and the Orissa border, had been wrested, in 1759, from Bussy's countrymen by Colonel Forde. They were afterwards restored to their nominal master, Nizám Ali, the ruler of Haidarábád, who presently offered them as a Jaigír, or military fief, to the Madras Government. The offer was declined; but troops were sent from Madras to aid Hussain Ali, the Nizám's deputy, in collecting the revenues, and keeping the peace in his new domain.

Of the five Sarkárs, or provinces, the new Governor engaged to place three at any moment in the hands of his English allies, who saw their French rivals once more peacefully established in Pondicherry. To Lord Clive, as he went up the country in 1765 to receive the title-deeds of Bengal, Bahár and Orissa, from the nominal Emperor of Hindustan, came a letter from Palk, suggesting that the five coast provinces should also be added to the dominions of the East India Company. On this suggestion Clive acted, and in October of the same year a despatch from Madras informed the Directors that a "Sanad," or decree of the Great Moghal had formally invested them with the lordship of the Northern Sarkárs.*

Early in the following year fresh troops were marched into the new territory. But Nizám Ali, displeased at an arrangement which ignored

* Auber's "Rise and Progress of the British Power in India" (chap. 5) shows that this step was taken "at the instance of Mr. Palk."

his own rights over the ceded provinces, prepared to enter them with a large force. Thinking mainly of their exhausted exchequer, the Madras Council compromised the quarrel by agreeing to hold the Sarkárs in fief of the Nizam, under a treaty which bound them to pay him tribute and to aid him with their arms in time of need.

It was not long before that need arose. By this time the old Hindu kingdom of Maisúr, seated among the woody highlands of Southern India, had passed under the yoke of Haidar Ali Khan, a Mohammadan soldier of fortune, whose great-grandfather had left the Panjáb to gain a livelihood in the Dakhan as a Fakír, or mendicant devotee.* When Haidar was born, in 1702, his father, Fath Mohammad, was serving as a Naik or petty officer of armed police under the Nawáb of Séra. A few years later Haidar Ali's widowed mother was glad to place herself and her two sons under the charge of her kind-hearted brother, a Naik in the service of the Commandant of Bangalór. The elder youth soon rose to distinction, while Haidar idled away his time in hunting and pleasure-seeking. It was not till 1749 that he

* The Mussulman "Fakir" corresponds to the Hindu "Yogi' or "Bairági."

first made his mark as a volunteer soldier in the service of Nanjiráj, who then ruled Maisúr in the name of its titular Rajah.

Under the shelter of his new patron he soon gave full play to the talents and energies which had hitherto lain dormant, or been turned to little account. It is needless to follow him through each step of his remarkable career. Unlettered, but able, daring, crafty, and unscrupulous, he let slip no occasion which his greed or his ambition pointed out to him for bettering his own fortunes, at whatever cost to his friends or rivals. At one moment fighting the Maráthas or the English, at another harrying insurgent Pálikárs, he gathered round him a body of troops who lived by plundering friends and foes alike, and shared with their leader the profits of their frequent raids from his strong castle of Dindigal. Cattle, sheep, grain, clothes, earrings, turbans, all were fish for Haidar's wide-sweeping net. Of the booty which his followers won by force of arms or sleight of hand, one-half always went into Haidar's own coffers, enabling him to swell the ranks of his little army, and to draw pay from the Government for troops nearly half of whom existed only on paper.*

* Wilks's "History of Mysoor," vol. I.

In a few years the Constable of Dindigal became a power in Maisúr. His patron, Nanjiráj, looked to him not in vain for help, now against his own unpaid and therefore turbulent soldiery, anon against the ever-raiding Maráthas, and presently against a swarm of state creditors whose claims, real or pretended, the harassed Minister had no heart to examine for himself. His successful services on each occasion won for Haidar the gratitude or the respect of all ranks and classes in Maisúr. The Rajah greeted him with the title of "Bahádur;" Nanjiráj publicly embraced the saviour of his country; his former rivals kept a becoming silence, or openly paid their court to the successful soldier and diplomatist. His boldest opponent, Harri Singh, he had already through his faithful soldiers done to a violent death. The foremost man at the capital, the Governor by this time of Bangalór, the Minister's blindly-trusted friend, the General of established worth, Haidar saw in 1759 but one more step between him and the highest place in the government of Maisúr.

That step was soon taken. With the art of which he was a finished master, he so contrived that the disgrace of his old patron should seem to be the handiwork of the helpless Rajah, who little dreamed of the pit he was thus digging for his own downfall. Haidar rose at once into the banished Minister's place; but ere long he too had to taste of the cup which Nanjiráj drank to the dregs. His trusted agent and well-rewarded accomplice, Kandi Rao, plotted against him with the Rajah and the Rajah's mother, and ruin for a moment stared him in the face. But his matchless cunning, cool effrontery, and quick-witted strength of will bore him safe through a hurricane of black disaster into the light of a new and fairer day. So deep at one time grew the darkness, that he himself for a moment knew not which way to turn. One card only remained to play. Stealing away by night from his beleaguered stronghold, Haidar rode in wild haste to Kunúr, where his old patron Nanjiráj still hugged the memory of his former state. At the feet of one whom he had so grievously wronged, the daring hypocrite poured out such a tale of sorrow for the past, of promised reparation in the future, that the heart of the fallen minister became at once touched with pity for an old friend, and fired with new hopes of a good time coming for himself.

It was the gambler's last throw for safety, and Haidar had won it. Aided by the name, the influence, and the resources of his new ally, he succeeded after a few more shifts and failures in turning the tables upon his worst foes. At the head of a victorious army he entered Seringapatam in May, 1761, and the helpless Rajah received a message which told him in other words that henceforth Haidar Ali Khán Bahádur regarded himself as the actual ruler of Maisúr. As for Nanjiráj, it was not long before he learned the folly of trusting the honied words of a man who had once before outwitted and betrayed him.

Happily for our countrymen in Madras, Haidar's return to power came several months too late to arrest the overthrow of French rule in Southern India. The troops which Haidar had despatched to Lally's aid in the middle of 1760 had soon to be recalled for their master's own defence; and the fall of Pondicherry in the following January sounded the knell of those schemes of conquest which Dupleix and Labourdonnais had first sought to realise.

The self-made ruler of Maisúr now proceeded to carry out against neighbouring countries the policy which had proved so successful at home.

In the course of the next few years one province after another fell by force, or fraud, or purchase, into his greedy hands. The vast wealth of Bednór filled his treasury—the brave Nairs of Malabar paid for their resistance with the loss of Calicut—the internal troubles in the Dakhan and the weakness of the Maráthas after the rout of Panipat gave him a motive and a pretext for fresh raids. The bold Marátha horsemen sometimes found their match in the well-trained cavalry of Maisúr. At other times Haidar had to succumb to the force of superior numbers, and prudently surrendered a part of his new conquests in order to save the rest.

At last in 1766 a new lion stood before him in the shape of a league between the Nizam and Mádhu Rao, the new Marátha Peshwa,* whose famous father, Bálaji Rao, had died heart-broken after Pánipat. Into this league our countrymen at Madras were dragged by the treaty of which

* The office of Peshwa, or Lieutenant to the Marátha sovereigns of the house of Sivaji had for many years past been held by lineal successors of the Brahman, Bálaji Vishwanáth. Under Báji Rao and his successor Bálaji, the power of the Peshwas gradually supplanted that of their nominal masters who reigned in Satára, until at Balaji's death the Peshwa of Puna had become the acknowledged head of the whole Marátha League.

mention has already been made. Haidar's cleverness or his good fortune still befriended him. He bought off the Maráthas with a heavy ransom and then set himself to break up the alliance between the English and Nizám Ali. So cunningly did he play his cards, that the Nizam agreed to join him in attacking the very force which had been sent from Madras to the Nizam's aid.

Happily our troops, if few, were commanded by one of the ablest soldiers whom the needs of Indian warfare ever brought to the front. With an army of only 7,000 men and sixteen guns, Colonel Smith in 1767 twice defeated 70,000 of the enemy, and in the second fight took sixty-four of their guns. Disheartened by these reverses and by the swift advance of a Bengal column towards his capital, the faithless Nizam was soon ready to throw over his new ally. This was the moment chosen by the Madras Council, not to annul their former treaty, but to renew it with even worse additions. Palk and his colleagues promised to help the Nizam with troops and guns against "Haidar Naik," as they scornfully described him, and to hold in fief* of

* So in effect says Mill (book IV., ch. 8), while Auber (ch. 5) states that "care was taken so to word the treaty," that the

that prince not only the Sarkárs, but even those districts which they designed to wrest from the kingdom of Maisúr.

To the folly of such proceedings the Court of Directors were keenly alive. They had already condemned the policy which aimed at turning the Company into the "umpires of Indostan." They were for letting the Indian princes "remain as a check upon one another." It was not for their interest that either the Nizam or Haidar Ali should be altogether crushed. They wanted to hold aloof from the quarrels of the "country powers;" they dreaded the Maráthas more than Haidar Ali; and very strong was the language in which they denounced the bargain made in 1768 with the Nizam for the possession of a province still held by the ruler of Maisúr. In the large fortunes suddenly amassed by their servants in India, they saw only fresh grounds for the popular belief that "the rage for negotiations, treaties and alliances" aimed rather at private advantage than the public good.

But long before these censures reached Madras,

money-payment to Nizam Ali "should not appear to be by virtue of the Company's holding the Circars from the Nizam, but only in consideration of the friendship existing between them."

tidings yet more unpleasant were on their way home. Haidar's overtures for peace with the English, made more than once in 1768, had come to nothing; mainly, it seems, through his own fault. For some months longer the war raged with varying fortune. Fresh negotiations opened in the following February were soon broken off —this time by the Madras Council. By the middle of March Haidar found himself hard pressed by his old opponent, Colonel Smith, near Chingalpat, about forty miles from Madras. Suddenly, turning southward, he drew Smith after him in slow and vain pursuit. Then, leaving his infantry and guns in the hills near Pondicherry, the wily freebooter with six thousand of his best troopers turned back upon his steps, and swept past Chingalpat almost up to the very walls of Fort St. George. Smith hastened after him, but it was too late. The bold invader was already master of the position. At Haidar's own request Du Pré was sent by his trembling colleagues to the camp on Mount St. Thomas, which overlooked the city and suburbs of Madras. Smith's homeward march was stayed by an order to halt his troops. On the 3rd of April, 1769, five days after his sudden appearance before Madras

Haidar signed a treaty of his own dictating, which restored to him all his former possessions, and bound each party to help the other against all assailants. Want of money and the cowardice of their native allies were the excuses pleaded by Palk's Council for this lame sequel to their former menaces.

CHAPTER III.

1769—1772

As second in the Madras Council to its new President, Dupré, his new colleague at once joined the Select Committee which had been entrusted with the task of restoring peace to the Carnatic, of putting the Nawáb's affairs into better order, settling all disputes with the Rajah of Tanjór, and reforming certain abuses in the Company's own service. Hastings found the Carnatic already at peace, and the disputes with Tanjór seemed to be on their way to a fair adjustment. But in other directions the work cut out for the Committee was all to do. In all the business of the Council Hastings bore due part; and his mild influence made itself felt in the troubled dealings of the Madras Government with the intriguing ruler of the Carnatic, and the high-handed envoy who, in an evil hour, had been sent from England to his Court, in utter disregard of the Company's rights and interests.

But the task to which Hastings' time and energies were mainly devoted, was one which specially devolved upon him as second in Council. To this post were attached the duties of Export Warehouse Keeper. Unlike his predecessors, Hastings declined to discharge by deputy the work entrusted to his own hands. And at that work he laboured with successful zeal. The Company's investments in silk and cotton goods had been of late so carelessly overseen, that the roguery of native contractors had brought about a marked decline in the quality of the goods shipped to England for the Company's use. Hastings set himself to find a cure for evils which threatened the very life of an important industry.

It was a task which took him some time to accomplish. He began by checking with a strong hand the extortions practised by the native middlemen on the poor weavers, whom they had forced to work on terms that plunged them deeper and deeper into debt and misery. In the bales of silk and cotton prepared for the English markets a great improvement presently took place. In the course of time, Hastings had drawn out a scheme which won the entire approval of the Court of Directors, for placing their investments on a sound and lucrative footing. Acting on his advice, they resolved to entrust the duties of export warehouse keeper to a separate officer, specially qualified for the post, and to furnish him with a competent staff of trained clerks. In the room of contractors and middlemen, he was empowered to employ his own agents in dealing directly with the headmen of the weaving villages, who should bind themselves in return to work for no private masters.

In the midst of these and other useful labours, Hastings learned that the Court of Directors had marked their high appreciation of his deserts, by offering him the post of Second in Council at Calcutta, with the right of succeeding Cartier in the Government of Bengal. The welcome news reached him about the end of 1771. In spite of some natural regret at parting from the friends among whom he had been living "with much comfort," and from colleagues of whom he had nothing but good to say, Hastings avowed to his friends at home the great pleasure which either his pride, or his "partial attachment to Bengal," aroused within him at the thought of returning to the scene of his former services. His fortune, as he wrote to his friend, Mrs. Hancock, was "not worse" than when he landed at Madras, but he was "not certain that it is better;" and perhaps the hope of bettering it formed one strand in the rope of circumstances that drew him back to Bengal.

Be that as it may, his letters of this date to friends and placemen at home, evince alike his pleasure at the new turn thus given to his prospects, and his gratitude to those who had used their influence on his behalf. "I could not lose," he writes to Francis Sykes, on January 30, 1772, "the first occasion to tell you how much joy it has given me to learn that I am much indebted to you for my late appointment. . . . . You are the friend you have always professed yourself and you shall always find me your most warm, and hearty friend." Two days later, he writes to thank Sir George Colebrooke, then Chairman of the East India Company. for this fresh instance of his confidence, and to ask for his friendship as well as his support. Laurence Sulivan, a Director of the Company, meets with a like return of thanks and promises for his share in forwarding "this very unexpected change" in his friend's fortunes. That prudence may have helped to point some of these expressions of seeming gratitude, we need not greatly care to question. It would be rash indeed to deny some mixture of motives in the conduct even of the most single-minded of men. But that Hastings was no hypocrite, the whole story of his life, if studied fairly, ought to place beyond a doubt.

The very letters to which I have been referring speak loudly in their writer's favour, as a man of warm heart, of a nature at once gentle, sensitive, and kindly, of frank yet winning manners, and upright aims. Through the veil of a somewhat stately diction, these pleasant traits reveal themselves. He has "cased a pipe of old Madeira" to be shared between his brother-in-law and Mrs. Hancock. He tells the latter to kiss his dear Bessy for him, and make her "remember and love her godfather, and her mother's sincere and faithful friend." His colleagues at the Council Board will ever have his kindest remembrance, for he "never did business with men of so much candour, or in general of better disposition." To another friend he writes of his happiness in leaving Mr. Du Pré still in the chair, and hopes the Directors "will encourage him to continue in it." In a farewell letter to Du Pré himself, he says, "I on my part shall never forget the many instances which I have received of your kindness, nor yet the very great and amiable qualities which eminently distinguished your character, especially the sincerity and candour of your expressions, and the gentleness of your manners." His friend Sykes is to have another pipe of Madeira by the next ship; "old wine and the pipe cased." To Mr. and Mrs. Woodman he writes in the following strain:—

> "I cannot answer your letters, for I am at a distance from them. I remember they told me you were all well; that Tommy was become a great scholar, and my niece a most thriving and fine child—indeed, I have letters that speak wonders of her accomplishments. May every year bring me the same glad tidings; I wish not for better, and would compound for many a misfortune to be sure of such an annual present. I leave this place in health and spirits, except what I feel in parting from it. Accept the repeated assurance of my affection, of my warmest wishes for your long, long continued happiness, my dearest brother and sister, aunt, Tommy, Bessy; may God bless and protect you is the prayer of your most affectionate
>
> WARREN HASTINGS."

On the 2nd February, 1772, Hastings set sail from Fort St. George for Calcutta. During a voyage of nearly three weeks, he wrote to Sulivan and Colebrooke long letters on the recent course of affairs in Southern India. From these we learn how cruelly the free action of the Madras

* Gleig's "Warren Hasting's," Vol. 1, Chap. vi.

Government had been hampered by the unwise interference of the English ministry, who had sent out Sir John Lindsay, armed with powers that clashed directly with those of the Company's agents. While Dupré and his colleagues were trying to steer their way through the difficulties that beset them after the peace with Haidar Ali, Sir John was sowing the seeds of future mischief with both hands. He encouraged the Náwab of Arkot to break loose from his old dependence on Fort St. George, and gratify his hatred of Haidar Ali by a league with the Maráthas, whose growing power the Government of Fort St. George regarded with just misgiving. In vain had the hard-pressed ruler of Maisúr entreated help from his new English allies, under the treaty of 1669. They could not help him if they would, and Haidar had to pay a heavy price for the deliverance of half his country from Marátha rule. If they could not help him in his need, the Madras Council steadily refused to take part with his assailants. But Lindsay's rash proceedings were destined to bear much fruit for evil. Haidar never forgave the English for what he regarded as a breach of faith, although his vengeance seemed to slumber for several years.

Sir John Lindsay's successor in the command of the fleet, Sir Robert Harland, had been enjoined by the Ministers of George III. to act in all harmony with the Madras Government.* But the post he held at the Court of Mohammad Ali, the Nawab of Arkot, gave him an authority which he too could not help wielding against the Company, whose "honour and importance" were to have been his chief concern. It seemed to Hastings an evil day for his countrymen in India, when a King's minister came out to thwart the best efforts of the Company's officers, and to sow dissention between the Madras Council and the Prince who owed his well-being to their support.

He saw nothing but mischief in the "unnatural powers" entrusted to Sir Robert Harland; "powers given, not to extend the British dominion, or increase the honour of the nation, but surreptitiously stolen out for the visible purpose of oppressing the King's subjects, and weakening the hands by which his influence is sustained in India." The Company's affairs, he wrote, "will never prosper, till the King's minister is recalled. His presence can do no good. He alienates the Nabob from the Company, and

* Auber's "British Power in India," Vol. 1, Chap. vi.

is the original cause of all the distress which you have suffered, and are like to suffer in your finances."

In the same strain Hastings proceeds to urge on Sir G. Colebrooke the need of removing the King's minister, as the only way of restoring to the Madras Government "that authority which it always exercised, till lately, in the administration of the affairs of the Carnatic." His removal is needed in order that the Company may secure a share in all the advantages gained by their arms: "at present the risk is almost wholly the Company's, and the fruits entirely the Nabob's." To Sulivan he complains of the troubles brewed in Madras itself by the Nawáb's Scotch partisans, "who inflame his jealousy of our government, feed his resentments with every rascally tale that the idle conversation of the settlement can furnish them with, and assist him in his literary polemics, for such his letters of the last two years may be truly called."

In spite of the grievance thus vehemently urged, Hastings seems to have borne himself discreetly towards the Nawáb in the disputes that blazed between that Prince and the Madras Council. He had received at parting, "the warmest assurances of the Nabob's friendship," of his gratitude for the "moderating part" which Hastings had played in many a recent controversy, and of his entire satisfaction with "every part" of that gentleman's conduct towards himself. "This," says Hastings, "was too honourable a testimony for me to receive with a safe conscience, but I can with an unblemished one affirm that I never opposed any interest to his but that of my employers."*

* Gleig's "Warren Hastings," Vol. 1. Chap. vi.

CHAPTER IV.

1772—

THE future Governor of Fort William reached Calcuttta about the 20th February, 1772; his friends, the Imhoffs, who had sailed with him from Madras, landing in his train. It was not till April that Cartier, who had succeeded Verelst in 1770, the year of the dreadful famine, which slew millions of people in Bengal, and left half the land a desert, handed over to Hastings the keys of office, a failing treasury, and a government sadly out of gear. Ever since Clive's departure from Bengal in 1767, the Company's affairs had been going more and more amiss. The rich provinces won by his sword, had been left in the hands of native governors and agents, who fleeced their own countrymen in the name of a puppet Nawáb, living in idle state at Murshidábád on the noble income secured to him by the Company. An army of Faujdars, Amils,

Sardárs, and such like gentry preyed, like leeches, upon the people, and intercepted the revenues designed for the Company's use. The English supervisors, appointed in 1769 to check these abuses, and to look after the revenue, were, in Hastings' words, "the boys of the service," and "rulers, very heavy rulers, of the people." Against the mischief caused by their ignorance or their greed, the Board of Revenue at Murshidábád strove vainly, if indeed it strove at all.

While trade languished, and money came in slowly at Calcutta, and the Company's servants laid new burdens on a rackrented and starving peasantry, the Company itself was paying in other ways the penalty of its transformation from a trading body into a political power. Besides the heavy tribute payable yearly to the Moghal Emperor for the right of governing Bengal and Bahar, and the large sums expended in governing those provinces through native officers, the India House magnates had to reckon at home with all the forces of popular prejudice, party rancour, and official jealousy. Macaulay has

* Gleig's "Warren Hastings," Vol. 1, Chap. vii. (letter to Dupré); see also Auber's "British Power in India," Vol. 1, Chap. vi.

told us in his own brilliant periods, how the Nabobs who had grown rich in the Company's service, by means too often blamable, returned home to become the envy, the horror, or the laughing-stock of their untravelled neighbours.* The fabled wealth of Ind semed no longer a fable in view of these pushing upstarts, who bought their way at all costs into the House of Commons, and eclipsed the splendour of the wealthiest county lords. The fame of their riches gave the Ministers of George III. a handle for fresh inroads on the revenues of a Company, whose new political greatness was held to clash with the paramount rights of the Crown. In vain did the Court of Directors appeal on this point from Lord North to the Parliament. They were glad to compound the matters in dispute, by agreeing to pay the nation £400,000 a year for the privilege of holding at the Crown's pleasure the dominions they had won by treaty from Shah Alam. From these, and other causes, it happened that the Company's debts in England and India had risen to more than two millions, or little less than the whole of their actual revenue.

On the 13th April, 1772, Hastings entered

* Macaulay's Essay on Lord Clive.

formally on his new duties. For some weeks past he had been steadily engaged, as he wrote to his friend Dupré, in "reading, learning, but not inwardly digesting." It was now his turn to act. No one could have seen more clearly how much was comprehended in that word; but he had hopes of able and willing support from his colleagues, and he wished for nothing more.*

Within a fortnight, the new Governor of Bengal had taken the first steps towards effecting a noteworthy revolution in the affairs of that province. Hitherto its internal government had been entrusted to a Naib Dewán, or deputy governor, who, in the Company's name, wielded almost supreme power in almost every department of the State. He had to look after all matters concerning the revenue, the police, the law-courts, civil, and criminal, as well as the management of the young Nawáb's household. Under the nominal control of the Company, he had become, indeed, as Hastings put it, "in everything but name the Názim (ruler) of the province, and in real authority more than the Názim." The officer to whom these large

* Gleig's "Warren Hastings," Vol. 1, Chap. vii.

powers had been entrusted by Clive himself, was Mohammad Reza Khan, a Mussulman noble of undoubted loyalty and long-established worth. At the same time the outlying province of Bahar was governed, in like manner, by Shitab Rai, the brave Hindu chief who had fought under the walls of Patna in the front rank of Knox's warriors.

To this state of things, which tended to divorce the show of power from the substance, and so produce a rich growth of evils, the Court of Directors, after the famine of 1770, resolved to proclaim an end. The sad results of the famine, and the tales they heard of fraud and oppression by the Naib Dewán, gave strength and colour to their new purpose. On the 24th April, Hastings received a letter, in which the Court declared their intention to "stand forth as Dewan," and to commit to their own servants "the entire care and management of the revenues" of Bengal. Hastings was further instructed to divest Mohammad Reza Khan, and all his underlings, "of any further charge or direction in the business of the collections," and to bring that officer himself down to Calcutta, to answer to the charges that might be brought against him, "both in respect to his public administration and private conduct.*

On the very next day, Hastings set himself to carry out the Court's instructions in his own way. The needful orders were issued to a trusty agent up the country; and before Hastings' own Council knew what was doing, Mohammad Reza had quietly yielded himself a prisoner to Mr. Middleton, and was on his way, under a guard of Sepoys, from Murshidabad to Calcutta. With his wonted courtesy and love of fairplay, the Governor himself had written to assure the deposed Dewán of the deep regret with which he obeyed the commands of his masters at home, and of his readiness to help him "in his private character" as far as he honestly could. The same courtesy marked his treatment of the Rajah Shitáb Rai, who, by an order of Council, not of Hastings, was likewise arrested and brought to Calcutta. The two were kept "in an easy confinement," pending a careful enquiry into their alleged guilt. With the Council's sanction, Middleton was placed for a time in charge of the vacant Dewáni.

The progress of the enquiry was delayed for

* Auber's "British Power in India," Vol. 1, Chap. vii.

many months, by matters of yet more pressing importance. How to place the land revenue upon a sounder footing, was a question to which Hastings had busily addressed himself for some weeks before Cartier's retirement. When the new orders from England reached him, a scheme for settling the revenue for a term of years had already been laid before the Council, and a committee appointed to carry it out. Early in the heats of a Bengal June, Hastings and his committee set forth on a round of personal inspection through the various districts of Bengal. During many weeks of wet or stormy weather, they pursued their labours with much diligence, and, all things considered, with a fair degree of success.* The lands of Bengal were farmed out to the highest bidders among the Zamindárs, or landholders, who derived their right to a share in the produce of the soil from patents granted to their ancestors by the Moghals. It was left for Englishmen of a later day to accept these landlords, or rent-farmers, as real landowners of the modern English type. Hastings' committee took

* Mill asserts (Book 5, Chap. i.) that Hastings "did not proceed with the committee;" but we have Hastings' own words, quoted by Mr. Gleig (Vol. 1, Chap. viii.), to show that he did, at least for some part of their journey.

them simply as they found them, explored the records of each estate and district, and strove to adjust their demands with due regard for the interests alike of the governors and the governed. The ráyats were protected in various ways from the extortions of the Zamindárs and their agents. Some check was also placed on the power of the money-lenders to prey upon the rayats at a rate of interest ranging from three to twelve per cent. per month. Those Zamindars who bade too little for their lands, were pensioned off, and the lands put up to sale.

If the committee did not wholly succeed in the work of settling the land-revenue, if in the next five years the defaulting Zamindárs were to be counted by hundreds, and the arrears of unpaid revenue came to exceed two millions, if the country still suffered from many shapes of oppression and misrule, it must be remembered that the reformers were almost, if not wholly, new to their difficult work, that the land-tenures of India were to our countrymen a cipher of which they lacked the key, and that a body of English traders, who might be "dead hands at investments,"* would

* Kaye's "Administration of the East India Company," Part 2, Chap. ii.

take some time to learn the duties of practical statesmen in a country which had been more or less misgoverned for centuries past.

The reforms thus begun invoved others. English Collectors replaced many of the native *Amils* in the civil management of districts larger than most of our English shires. The Board of Revenue was transferred from Murshidabad to Calcutta. The magisterial and judicial powers, hitherto wielded by native Dewans, Faujdars, and Zamindars, were largely curtailed, by the creation in each district of a civil and a criminal court, in which the Collector ruled supreme. In Calcutta itself were established two Courts of Appeal for civil and criminal cases. Over one of these, the *Sadr Dewáni Adálat*, or chief civil court, the Governor himself, with two members of his Council presided. The *Sadr Nizámat Adálat*, or criminal court, was still entrusted to a native Daroga, or Judge, appointed by the Governor in Council. In each court the judges were aided by native assessors, skilled in expounding the dark points of Hindu and Mohammadan law. All these changes were effected, or set on foot, during the first year of Hastings' government.

Nor was the Governor idle in other directions.

In furtherance of the new movement for getting rid of double government in Bengal, he abolished the office of Naib Subah, hitherto held by Mohammad Reza Khan, as Vicegerent for the Nawáb himself. The Nawáb's stipend was cut down, under orders from England, to sixteen lakhs of rupees, or about £160,000 a year. The same economy was directed against the pension-list and the expenses of the Nawáb's household. As guardian of the little Prince, who had but lately succeeded to his shadowy throne, Hastings selected the Manni Begam, widow of the unfortunate Mír Jáfar. In compliance with the tenour of his instructions from the Court of Directors, he appointed Rajah Gurdás, son of his old enemy, Nand-Kumár, to the post of Dewán, or Controller of the Household. To Nand-Kumár himself, for very good reasons, he bore no love; and the misdeeds of that wily Brahman, his plots, his treasons, and his forgeries, were well known to the India-house Directors. But they had bidden Hastings make what use he could of the traitor's services, and Hastings saw his way to using them through the son.

"I expect," he wrote to Dupré, "to be much abused for my choice of the Dewan, because his father stands convicted of treason against the Company while he was the servant of Meer Jaffier, and I helped to convict him. The man never was a favourite of mine, and was engaged in doing me many ill offices for seven years together. But I found him the only man who could enable me to fulfil the expectations of the Company with respect to Mahommed Reza Cawn; and I had other reasons, which will fully justify me when I can make them known. For these and those I supported his son, who is to benefit by his abilities and influence; but the father is to be allowed no authority, lest people should be suspicious of his misusing it.

What those other reasons were may, perhaps, be gathered from Hastings' official minute of July, 1772, in which the need of employing the vigilance and activity of Nand-Kumár, to counteract the designs of his hated rival, Mohammad Reza Khan, and to eradicate the latter's influence in the government of Bengal and in the Nawáb's family, is declared to be the sole motive for the appointment of Gurdás.* Some members of the Calcutta Council at first opposed this measure, as tantamount to appointing Nand-Kumár himself. But further discussion seems to have turned their reluctance into assent, and the young man was duly installed in the post designed for him by his father's foe.

Among the matters to which Hastings set his reforming hand, were the improvement of the Company's trade, and the repression of corrupt

* Mill's "British India," Book 5, Chap. i.

practices among their servants. The Directors had enjoined him to chastise severely all who, in the teeth of their orders, had conspired to set up a monopoly of salt, betel-nut, tobacco, rice and other grains, during the recent famine. These injunctions he obeyed in the spirit rather than the letter, tempering firmness with delicacy in his arrangements for suppressing the unlawful traffic. With regard to matters of mere trade, his letters of this period show his conversance with all kinds of practical details, the keenness of his appetite for fresh knowledge, and the readiness with which he could turn from larger subjects to discuss some new method of preparing silk thread, or to give advice about the purchase of cocoons.

Of the multifarious duties which had devolved upon him, and the heavy labours which he had thus far taken in hand, Hastings himself has left us a lively picture in the following extract from a letter written in October, from Calcutta, to his friend Du Pré:—

"Here I now am, with arrears of business of months, and some of years to bring up; with the courts of justice and offices of revenue to set a-going; with the official reformation to resume and complete; with the *Lapwing* to despatch; with the trials of Mohammad Reza Cawn and Raja Shitabroy to bring on, without materials, and without much hope of assistance. . . . and with the current trifles of the day, notes, letters, personal applications, every man's business of more consequence than any other's, complainants from every quarter of the province halloaing me by hundreds for justice as often as I put my head out of window, or venture abroad, and, what is worse than all, a mind discomposed, and a temper almost fermented to vinegar by the weight of affairs to which the former is unequal, and by everlasting teazing. We go on, however, though slowly; and in the hopes of support at home, and of an easier time here when proper channels are cut for the affairs of the province to flow in. I persevere. Neither my health nor spirits, thank God, have yet forsaken me."

He goes on to say that the powers entrusted to him in these matters "tend to destroy every other that I am possesssd of, by arming my hand against every man, and every man's, of course, against me." For that present, however, Fortune smiled upon her future victim; and the praises which the new Governor received from his friends in India were ratified by the terms in which the Secret Committee at home recorded their "entire approbation" of his conduct, and assured him of their "firmest support" in accomplishing the work he had so successfully begun.*

* Gleig's "Warren Hastings," Vol. 1, Chap. vii.

CHAPTER V.

1773—1774.

It was not till the early part of 1773 that Mohammad Reza Khán and the Rajah Shitáb Rai were brought to trial before a committee over which Hastings himself presided. Neither of the prisoners seems to have felt the hardship of a delay which suited the Governor's purposes little less than their own. To them it gave time for the preparation of their defence, while it gave Hastings time to "break their influence," and to push on the great work of administrative reform in the lines marked out for him by the Court of Directors. In the pressure of public business consequent on their avowed decision to "stand forth as Dewán," he had found ample excuse for putting off the trial, until the new policy had been established on a sure foundation. "Do not impute these delays to my inattention,"—he writes to Sir George Colebrooke—"my whole time and all my thoughts, I may add all my passions, are devoted to the service of the Company; and I am sure I do not labour in vain. But you cannot form a conception of the infinite calls which I have perpetually upon me, by the greatest charge which has devolved to this government, every part of which is now full, and the channels through which the business of it should flow scarcely opened for its conveyance."*

Of Shitab Rai's innocence Hastings seems never to have felt much, if any, doubt; and the first days of the Rajah's trial left him firmly convinced that the brave Governor of Patna would "escape with credit." Hastings could "discover no defect" in his conduct, while he had certainly "shown himself an able financier." "Indeed," says Hastings in a letter to Sykes, "I scarce know why he was called to account."

The inquiry, which was virtually ended in April, issued three months later, as the Governor had foreseen, in an honourable acquittal. Under a new title Shitáb Rai was restored in effect to his former dignities; and the Governor spared no marks of respect or courtesy that might serve to atone for a wrong of which his Council had

* Gleig's "Warren Hastings," Vol. [illegible], Chap. 8.

been the real authors. In August the Maharajah set out for Patna; but, whether from the climate of Calcutta or from the forced inaction that encouraged the morbid broodings of a wounded spirit, his health was so broken that he survived the journey but a few weeks.* His son, Kaliam Singh, was at once installed by Hastings in the vacant offices of Rai-Rayan and Naib-Nazim, Chief Treasurer and Deputy-Governor of Bahár, "from an entire conviction of the merits and faithful services, and in consideration of the late sufferings of his deceased father."

The trial of Mohammad Reza Khán on various grave charges of fraud and embezzlement, lingered on until the following March. It proved to be "a tedious and troublesome business;" but Hastings never shrank from trouble in the discharge of a public duty; and in this matter, at any rate, his sense of duty did not clash with a strict regard for justice. The charges against the late Naib Dewán were investigated from day to day with unwearied patience; Hastings himself filling the twofold part of examiner and

* Macaulay, following Mill, kills him of a broken heart; but this, as Wilson justly remarks in one of his notes to Mill's "History" is "a gratuitous supposition."—(Book V., Chap. 8.)

interpreter. The result of examining scores of witnesses and hundreds of documents for either side served only to deepen his distrust of Nand-Kumár, and to convince him that even if Mohammad Reza Khán were guilty on any point, the time for proving him so had gone by. Nand-Kumár himself, the mainspring of the whole proceedings, broke down egregiously at every turn. Hastings spent hours and days, he tells us, "in listening to the multiplied but indefinite accounts and suggestions" of the man upon whose abilities and active malignity he had relied for proofs of some kind in a case of such importance. Bnt the evil old Brahman could only produce accounts that proved nothing, and reiterate charges which he always failed to bear out.

At last the long trial ended in an acquittal, and the prisoner was set conditionally free. But the question of his future disposal was referred home to the India House; and the Directors, though half unwilling to accept the issue of an inquiry ordered by themselves at the prompting of a worthless schemer, declared their approval of Hastings' conduct, and restored the victim of NandKumár's hate and their rashness not only to freedom, but ere long to much of his former eminence. More fortunate than his fellow sufferer, Mohammad Reza Khan lived to hold high office under the new Government of Bengal, and to see his old enemy undergo the death of a convicted felon.

To Hastings himself, the result of this enquiry was the removal of a heavy load of care and misgivings from a mind at once tenacious of its own conclusions, and keenly sensitive to the opinions of men in power. The despatches from the India House brought him manifest tokens of his masters' goodwill, and full assurance of their readiness to uphold and develope the new system of direct government in Bengal. On this point therefore he had nothing more to fear.

Some further changes in the machinery of govenment were soon to occupy his attention. The English Collectors appointed under the new system were found unequal to those fiscal duties of which they had no experience; and their powers were transferred, in 1774, to native Amils, or revenue officers, controlled by a Committee of Revenue, which sat daily in Calcutta to hear complaints from rayats or other aggrieved persons, and by a staff of English Commissioners, who from time to time were to "visit such districts as might require a local investigation." The Collectorates were grouped into six divisions, each administered by a Provincial Council, whose duties ranged from the hearing of appeals in civil suits, to a close inspection of revenue accounts, and a careful inquiry into land tenures.*

One especial object on which Hastings had set his heart, was already far towards accomplishment. He had given the country a judicial system which, however imperfect, aimed at dealing uniform justice, on fixed principles, to all classes alike. This great boon he hastened to better, by planning a Code of Hindu and Mohammadan Law for the guidance of the new Courts. One part of the task was comparatively easy, for a good, if lengthy, digest of Mohammadan law had been made by order of the Emperor Aurangzíb. But the Hindu laws, which concerned two-thirds of the people of Bengal, still lay embedded in a multitude of books, written in a language which only a few learned Pandits could understand. If a question of law was referred to the Pandits for their opinion, justice was often seriously delayed ; if the case at issue was decided without their aid, justice was liable to sad mis-

* Auber's "British Power in India," Vol. 1, Chap. viii.

carriages. In a long letter to the great Lord Mansfield, Hastings tells how he had invited ten of the most learned Pandits to Calcutta, "to form a compilation of the Hindoo laws, with the best authority which could be obtained," and how their labours had issued in the production of a Code which would give confidence to the people, and enable the Courts to decide with certainty and despatch.*

From its original Sanskrit, the Code was speedily translated into Persian. Mr. Halhed, of the Company's civil service, then set to work upon an English translation, which he completed early in 1775.† The result of his labours was dedicated to Hastings, by whom the work had been planned, and to whose influence its execution was mainly due. While it was still in progress, Hastings sent the first two chapters to Lord Mansfield, "as a proof that the inhabitants of this land are not in the savage state in which they have been unfairly represented."

Meanwhile Hastings employed his spare energies on other matters of more or less moment. He had to reform the police of Calcutta, to re-

* Gleig's "Warren Hastings," Vol. 1, Chap. viii.
† Auber's "British Power in India," Vol. 1, Chap. viii.

press the plague of Dakaity in the provinces, to deal with a formidable inroad of Sanyási fanatics. and to drive the invading Bhútias out of Kuch-Bahár. The Dakaits, or gang-robbers of Bengal, had driven a roaring trade in murder and rapine throughout the troubled period which, after the death of Aurangzíb, beheld the gradual disruptisn of the Moghal Empire. Like the brigands of Greece and Sicily they flourished upon the weakness, the fears, or the complicity of their peaceful neighbours. "They are robbers by profession, and even by birth;" wrote the Committee of Circuit to the Calcutta Council in 1772, "they are formed into regular communities, and their families subsist by the spoils which they bring home to them; they are all therefore alike criminal wretches, who have placed themselves in a state of declared war with Government, and are therefore wholy excluded from every benefit of its laws."* They were mostly members, in fact, of a great robber-caste, bound together by hereditary ties, by the use of a secret language and secret signs, and, like the Thags of a later day, by the common observance of religious rites.

* Quoted in Kaye's "Administration of the East India Company," Part 3, Chap. iii.

Disguised as travellers or pilgrims, they would set out in gangs of thirty or forty, with long walking-sticks for their only visible weapons. But hidden about them were sharp spear-heads, of which those sticks were the convenient handles. They had emissaries in every village, who kept them furnished with all needful information. The doomed village was always attacked by night. Awakened by the sudden glare of torches and the noise of shouting men, the startled sleepers seldom found time or courage to make a resolute defence. Merchants, bankers, peasants, all were plundered without mercy, and those were fortunate who escaped with their lives. A part, often a large part, of the booty thus gained, was set aside for the Zamindár, on whose lands, or with whose connivance, the crime had been committed. The village headman, also, and even the Thánadár, or chief constable, came in for their several shares.

Hastings saw the full extent of the evil, and prepared to suppress it with a strong hand and a stern spirit. With his Council's sanction, he decreed that every convicted Dakait should be hanged in his own village; that the village itself should be fined, each man according to his substance, and that the convict's family should "become the slaves of the State, and be disposed of for the general benefit and convenience of the people, according to the discretion of the Government."* To this last measure no objection can fairly be raised. Even in England, Wilberforce had not yet begun his long struggle against slavery; and in India, where slaves were treated as children of their master's own family, it seemed fair to argue that the well-being alike of the State and the Dakait's children, would be furthered by a measure which might deter many from a life of crime.

Hastings would have gone yet further, to the extent of holding the Zamindars themselves answerable for gang-robberies on their estates. Of their complicity he had no doubt, and the fact was proved some time afterwards on the clearest evidence. But his proposals seem to have been rejected by the majority of a Council in which he had only a casting vote. His letters of this period show how keenly he regretted the lack of that power to over-rule his colleagues at need, which was afterwards entrusted to the weakest of

* Kaye's "Administration of the East India Company," Part 3 Chap. iii.

his successors. It says much for his personal influence, that he carried his Council with him on many questions that justified debate. But on this occasion, all his tact, patience, and powers of suasion failed to win the Council over to his views; and the evil which he would have suppressed by timely measures of sweeping sternness, lived on to vex the greatest of Indian Viceroys known to this century.* In dealing with the Sanyási "bandits," as he calls them, Hastings was much more successful. He describes them as a race of wandering Fakírs, from the country lying south of the hills of Tibet. They went "mostly naked," had "neither towns, houses, or families,' but roved continually from place to place, "recruiting their numbers with the healthiest children they can steal in the countries through which they pass." The terror inspired by their courage, strength and enthusiasm, was heightened by the awe in which, on account of their supposed sanctity, these "gypsies of Hindostan" were held by Hindus of all classes.† They seem to have crossed the Brahmapútra in

* Lord Dalhousie, in 1852, complained of the prevalence of gang-robberies in the neighbourhood of Calcutta.

† Gleig's "Warren Hastings," Vol. 1, Chap. viii.

large bodies, robbing and ravaging the country through which they marched on their yearly pilgrimage to the shrine of Jagannáth, in Orissa. One of these bodies in Rangpúr defeated two small parties of Pargana Sepoys—"a rascally corps," says Hastings—and cut off the two English officers who led them. Several battalions of regular Sepoys had to be employed in fighting, or rather chasing back these hardy ruffians in 1773, and troops were afterwards posted along the frontier, to guard against future troubles from the same quarter.

At the same time, other troops were waging a harder fight against fiercer foes in Kuch-Bahár, a tract of fertile country lying at the foot of the Bhután Himalayas. In 1772, its young Rajah had appealed to Hastings for help in driving the Bhutia invaders back to their own hills. In return he offered to place his little kingdom under British rule, and to pay over half his revenues to the Government of Bengal. His prayer was granted, and a small Sepoy force hastened to his aid. The men of Bhután fought valiantly, on one occasion for seven hours, against their new assailants; but Sepoy discipline under English leading overbore the stubborn highlanders, and erelong the Deb Rajah, who had led the invasion, was glad to make peace on terms which restored to him his lost strongholds, and secured to Bhutia Merchants the right of trading with Rangpúr.

Out of this campaign arose the first British mission ever sent into Tibet The Teshu Láma, one of the two rival Lámas, or Buddhist Popes, who held sway over that unknown corner of the Chinese Empire, had written to Hastings an intercessory letter on behalf of the Deb Rajah, whose misconduct he fully admited, while pleading for merciful treatment from the Power whose wrath his unruly subject had provoked. One result of this letter, was the treaty which Hastings concluded with the Rajah in 1774. Another shortly followed in the despatch of George Bogle, a young civil servant of high promise and already proven worth, as special envoy to the Lama's court. Always zealous in the furtherance of his masters' interests, Hastings saw a good opening for friendly intercourse between India and Tibet; and his choice of fit agents for the work in hand was fully justified on this occasion, as on many others. The young envoy spoke of him to his own friends with the same warm appreciation which Lord Wellesley won from Sir Charles Metcalfe, and with which every officer of mark in India spoke of the Marquis of Dalhousie.*

Bogle set out on his journey to Tassisudon, the capital of Bhután, laden with presents for the Lama and samples of Indian goods. He was to make diligent inquiry into all matters bearing upon the special object of his mission, and to note down, from day to day, all that seemed to him "characteristic of the people, their manners, customs, buildings, cookery, the country, the climate, or the road." Nor was this the whole of his task, for Hastings wanted him to learn all he could of the course of the Brahmapútra, the countries through which it flowed, and the yet more distant regions of Tartary and China. Further, he had to send to Calcutta samples of strange plants and animals, including shawl goats, and "cattle which bear what are called cow-tails."† Curiosities of any kind that might be "acceptable to persons of taste in England," were added to the list.

* Gleig's "Warren Hastings," Vol. 1, Chap. xii. Auber's "British Power in India," Vol. 1, Chap. viii. A full account of the Mission will be found in Mr. Markham's "Narrative of Bogle's Mission." Trübner & Co., 1876.

† Now known as Yáks.

Bogle was accompanied by an assistant surgeon named Hamilton. At Tassisudon they were kindly received by the new Deb Rajah, who had replaced the defeated invader of Kuch Bahár. A long journey northwards across the Himalayas brought them to Desherigpay, in the heart of Tibet. Here the travellers found a warm welcome from the Teshu Láma, in whose train they recrossed the Tsánpu, or upper Brahmapútra, to the Lama's palace at Teshu-Lumbo. They would have gone on, as Hastings wished them, with their host's consent, to Lhása itself, but the Regent at that city proved less friendly to foreigners, or more amenable to Chinese dictation; and in June, 1775, Bogle found himself back in Calcutta, received by his patron with open arms, but regarded with coldness by the new Councillors, whose persistent efforts to thwart, to humble, and to annoy their President had already begun.

But this new chapter in the life of Hastings must for the present remain unopened. Down nearly to the end of 1774, he was still virtually his own master in the government of Bengal. He had made his influence felt, on the whole for good, in every branch of the public service. His zeal for the Company's interests had always been tempered by the prudence of a statesman, the shrewdness of a man of business, and the humanity of a just and kind-hearted ruler. The trade of the country had been stimulated by the removal of local imposts, and the adoption of a low uniform customs duty. The weavers were left free to make their own bargains for the goods supplied to the Company; a bank was started in Calcutta for the public benefit; the opium trade was brought under Government control; and, what Hastings reckoned no small boon to his people, the old duties on marriage were wholly swept away.

CHAPTER VI.

1773—1774.

"THE new Government of the Company consists of a confused heap of undigested materials, as wild as the chaos itself." So wrote Hastings to his colleague, Barwell, in July, 1772. We have seen how far in the next two years his government had succeeded in evolving order out of that chaos. If his efforts to improve the Company's revenues had borne but little immediate fruit, he had done his best at any rate to keep down the public debt, to encourage thrift in every department, and to increase the balances in the Calcutta exchequer. In retrenching the military outlay, he found himself engaged in "a violent squabble" with the general commanding the Bengal Army, Sir Robert Barker,* a brave but hot-tempered officer of the Royal Artillery, who had served

* Stubbs's "History of the Bengal Artillery," Vol. 1, Ch. i. note A.

with credit against Lally in 1758. It need hardly be added that the violence of the squabble was all on one side. Sir Robert's angry remonstrances against economies which seemed to him unwise were met by Hastings with courteous answers, regretting the strong language provoked by his reduction of three hundred black troopers, and pleading his earnest desire to "live in peace with all men."

In the midst of his peaceful labours, the Governor's attention was continually called away to matters of foreign policy. In the troubles brewing outside the Bengal frontier he saw signs of danger to the peace of his own provinces. The restless Maráthas had already recovered from the blow inflicted on their power at Pánipat. Alike in Southern and Northern India their successes and their ambition seemed to foretel the establishment of an empire wider than that of the Moghals. In 1769 Mádhu Rao, the Peshwa of Puna, sent forth a mighty army to despoil the princes and ravage the populous plains of Hindustan. After levying black mail on the Játs and Rájputs, the invaders swept over Rohilkhand, threatened Oudh, and, driving the Moghals before them, entered Delhi in the winter of 1770.

The new masters of that imperial city, at once invited Shah Alam thither from his temporary capital of Allahabad. That weak but ambitious scion of the house of Bábar, caught with pardonable eagerness at the prospect of revisiting the home whence he had fled, in 1757, to escape the murderous clutches of the ruffianly Ghazi-ud-din.* In spite of the dissuasions of the Calcutta Council he set forth, in 1771, with his little army from Allahabad; and Christmas Day of that same year saw him escorted into Delhi by Sindhia's horsemen, and installed on the throne of Akbar by the men whose fathers had so rudely shaken the empire of Aurangzíb.

Early in the next year, he set out, in company with his new allies, to reconquer some of his ancestral domains lying to the north of Delhi. The campaign finished to their common satisfaction, he returned to his capital at the beginning of the rainy season. But the burden of his new alliance sat heavy on the restored monarch, who found, or deemed himself a mere cipher in the hands of his overbearing patrons. The booty which they had promised to share with him, they

* The Vizier, and afterwards the murderer of Shah Alam's father, Alamgír II.

kept entirely for themselves. They fomented disturbances around his capital, and attacked the forces which he sent against the insurgents.* His best general, Mirza Najaf Khán, was beaten by the hosts of Túkají Holkar; before the year's end, Delhi was entered by the booty-laden victors; and the helpless monarch was forced to purchase a brief rest from trouble, by agreeing to surrender into Maráthá hands those provinces of Korah and Allahabad, which Clive had made over to him in 1765.

The English, however, were not prepared to see these provinces, which linked Bengal with Oudh, pass into the hands of their most formidable foes. On this point, Hastings and his Council were soon of one mind. If the Company were strongly set against any further enlargement of their possessions, might not these provinces be restored for a handsome money payment to the Nawáb-Vazir of Oudh, from whom they had once been wrested by our arms? Of late years the Nawáb had shown himself our firm ally, while Shah Alam had not only flung himself into the hands of our enemies, but had even intrigued against his English friends by sending an envoy

* Keene's "Fall of the Moghul Empire," Book 2, Chap. iii.

to the King of England, to treat for the transfer of Bengal from the Company to the Crown.* This, and some other acts of unfriendliness, may have been provoked by the recent failure of the Bengal Government to pay Shah Alam his yearly tribute, on account of the losses entailed by the famine of 1770, and of his own withdrawal from Allahabad. Hastings himself, at first, made light of the danger which threatened his own provinces from the arrangement made between the Emperor and the Maráthas. Naráyan Rao, a youth of nineteen, had just succeeded his brother, Mádhu Rao, as Peshwa, and the Maráthas, reduced in number, were "sick of a long campaign." In the first days of 1773, Hastings saw "no good cause to interfere." But the Council voted promptly for interference, and Hastings clinched his adhesion to the policy thus ordained with the utterance of a wish that "it could with honour and safety have been avoided."

The Company's troops were at once ordered to occupy Korah and Allahabad. These provinces the Governor would still have held for Shah

* Major John Morrison, formerly a Company's officer, who afterwards took service with Shah Alam. Gleig's "Warren Hastings," Vol. 1, Chap. viii.

Alam, if that prince would only have agreed to follow the Governor's counsel. But he would listen to no advice or offers from Calcutta unless his arrears of tribute were promptly paid. To all such demands Hastings turned a deaf ear. To pay the Emperor his arrears would be tantamount to enriching the ravenous Maráthas, whose tool and accomplice he had become. His desertion of us," wrote Hastings to Laurence Sulivan, "and union with our enemies, leave us without a pretence to throw away more of the Company's property upon him, especially while the claims of our Sovereign are withheld for it." To prevent all further misunderstanding on this score, Hastings informed the Emperor that he must look for no more tribute from Bengal. This step was greeted with hearty approval by the Court of Directors, who some years before had suggested it as a fitting punishment for any attempt of the Emperor to "fling himself into the hands of the Maráthas, or any other power."

Hastings owns that this seeming breach of faith was regarded "in the most criminal light" by many persons, both in India and at home. But it must be remembered that he had better means of threading the maze of Indian politics, than any of those who found fault with him. Shah Alam had broken away from his English friends and thrown himself into the arms of their most dreaded enemies. Hastings had watched the gradual resurrection of the Marátha power after the rout of Pánipat; and he looked upon Shah Alam as something more than a mere tool in the hands of his new patrons. In surrendering to these the provinces which Clive's bounty had bestowed upon him, the Emperor had broken the contract which entitled him to receive tribute from Bengal. Hastings may have judged his conduct too harshly; but against the error of judgment, if such there were, may be set the necessities of a position which left him no choice between acting harshly for the public good, and endangering the Company's rule by strict adherence to the letter of a covenant.

The next step he took in furtherance of the new policy, was destined to bring down upon him a yet wider and fiercer storm of reprobation. Shujá-ad-daula, the Nawáb-Vazir of Oudh, had already proposed, not only to buy back the provinces forfeited by the Emperor, but to purchase the aid of our troops in conquering Rohilkhand, the fruitful, well-wooded and well-watered province which lay between Oudh and the northern Himálayas. This tract of country had been conquered, early in the century, by bands of Rohilla Patháns, a tribe of plundering, war-loving Afghans, who, under the Moghal standard, carved out broad fiefs for themselves on the rich plains eastward of the Upper Ganges. On the bloody field of Pánipat, they had fought with their wonted courage on the side of Islám and the Empire against the hosts of the infidel Maráthas. Since then, they had carried their arms across the Ganges, had quarrelled with each other at home, and otherwise helped to increase the chaos of fighting, intrigue, plunder, and perfidy, which obscures the history of the following decade.

At last the time came, when the Pathán lords of Rohilkhand found themselves powerless to withstand the flood of Marátha invasion. Their leader, Háfiz Rahmat Khán, appealed for help to Shujá-ad-daula, the son of their old foe. The crafty ruler of Oudh agreed to furnish it, if Rahmat Khán would pledge himself to pay his new ally the sum of forty lakhs of rupees—about £450,000—for driving the Maráthas out of Rohilkhand. A treaty to this effect was signed in July, 1772. In May of the following year, the

Maráthas withdrew to their own country before a combined movement of troops from Oudh and Bengal. The Náwab-Vazír claimed from Háfiz Rahmat the fulfilment of his bond. On one plea or another, the Rohilla leader evaded the claim. His wily creditor, forgetful of the kindness shewn him in his hour of need by Rahmat's countrymen,* caught at so good a handle for carrying out his father's schemes against Rohilkhand. He had already persuaded the Emperor to bestow upon him the office of Protector,† which Rahmat Khán had assumed without warrant. It only remained now to secure the countenance, if not the active aid, of his English allies.

In answer to his proposals Hastings, with his Council's consent, agreed to an interview with the Nawáb-Vazír. The meeting took place in August at Banáras. To the Nawáb's overtures Hastings listened with no unwilling ear. His fear of the Maráthas, who would retire only to renew their raids on the first opportunity, his deep distrust of Shah Alam, his belief in Shuja's

* When Shuja fled, in 1765, before the English advance into Oudh, after the battle of Baxar, the Rohillas sheltered him and his family, and placed 3,000 of their troops at his command. Keene's "Moghul Empire," Book 2, Chap. i.

† "Hafiz" means "Protector."

usefulness, and his zeal for bettering the Company's finances, all conspired to lead him in the direction pointed out by his able but unscrupulous ally. For the sum of fifty lakhs—more than half a million—he agreed to make over to the ruler of Oudh the provinces of Korah and Allahabad. For the services of a British brigade, whenever needed, the Nawáb-Vazír bound himself to pay the Company 210,00 rupees a month, besides forty lakhs at the end of the campaign. The important fortress of Chunár on the Ganges, a little above Banáras, was likewise ceded to the Company.

In the middle of September, Hastings set out again for Calcutta. Of the twelve members of his Council, only one, Sir R. Barker, found any fault with the Treaty of Banáras. Among other arguments based on that officer's reading of the Treaty of 1765, it was urged that the Emperor might transfer to other hands the powers which he had then bestowed upon the Company. Hastings boldly declared that the rule of the Company rested on no *Sanads*, or letters-patent, issued by the Moghal. "The sword, which gave us the dominion of Bengal, must be the instrument of its preservation; and if (which God forbid) it shall ever cease to be ours, the next proprietor will derive his right and possession from the same natural charter."*

What Hastings said was the simple truth. It may have suited the views of Clive and the Court of Directors, to obtain from a titular King of Dehli a formal grant of provinces won by the valour of their own troops. The same show of respect for legal sanctions marked the Company's later policy, down to the close of the great Sepoy War. But the fact remains, that our rule in India rests ultimately, as it did at first, upon the sword; and Hastings was fully justified in laying so much stress upon a truth which no English Government can ever afford to overlook. Dealing with the case before him as a statesman rather than a moralist, he saw the advantage of strengthening the Nawáb of Oudh by an arrangement which would replenish the Bengal exchequer, and raise up a new bulwark against Marátha aggression. The Rohillas he regarded as a weak yet troublesome race of adventurers, who had no special right to govern a country which they had shown themselves unable to defend. To him, therefore, it seemed a thing of

* Auber's "British Power in India," Vol. 1, Chap. vii.

course, that the task to which they had proved unequal, should be entrusted to stronger hands

The true key, perhaps, to Hastings' policy, may be found in that want of money which continued to vex the masters of Bengal. He owned himself doubtful of the judgment which might be passed upon his acts at home, where he saw "too much stress laid upon general maxims, and too little attention paid to the circumstances, which require an exception to be made from them." But he rejoiced to think that "an accidental concourse of circumstances," had enabled him to "relieve the Company in the distress of their affairs." by means which seemed to him altogether harmless. "Such," he writes to Laurence Sulivan, "was my idea of the Company's distress at home, added to my knowledge of their wants abroad, that I should have been glad of any occasion to employ their forces, which saves so much of their pay and expenses."*

This was not a very lofty motive for a course of action which has often since been denounced, by none more eloquently than Macaulay, as a wanton aggression upon the innocent rulers of a

* Gleig's "Warren Hasting's," Vol. 1, Chap. x.

prosperous and well-governed land. But the Court of Directors were loudly calling for "ample remittances" from Bengal, and for large retrenchments in their military outlay.* The innocence of the Rohilla chiefs had just displayed itself in negotiations with the Maráthas for objects dangerous to the peace of Oudh. Instead of paying their debt to the Nawáb-Vazír, they were already planning a raid across the Ganges into the country about Cawnpore. Instead of thriving in almost Arcadian bliss, the people of Rohilkhand were a rack-rented peasantry, living amid scenes of lawless strife, and doomed to suffer alike from the exactions of their own masters and the raids of ubiquitous Maráthas.† There was disunion also among the Rohilla chiefs, some of whom openly sided with the ruler of Oudh, while others either stood neutral, or against their better judgment, espoused the cause of Rahmat Khán.

In March, 1774, Colonel Champion's brigade crossed the Káramnása. The Emperor of Dehli, who had confirmed the grant of Allahabad and Korah to the Nawáb-Vazír,‡ sent a body of Moghal troops to aid that prince in his campaign.

* Mill's "British India," edited by Wilson, Book 5, Chap. i.
† Hamilton's "History of the Rohillas."
‡ Keene's "Moghul Empire." Book 2, Chap. iii.

In April the allied forces entered Rohilkhand. On the 23rd of that month the Rohillas, fighting bravely, were routed near Katra with heavy slaughter by Champion's disciplined troops. Charge after charge was broken by the fire from his well-served guns, and 40,000 Rohillas turned and fled before the bayonets of his advancing infantry. Among the slain was Rahmat Khán himself. When the issue of the fight was no longer doubtful, the Nawab Vazír, who had hitherto looked on from a safe distance, let his own soldiers loose for the work of pillage, which they accomplished in a style that provoked loud murmurs from their disgusted allies. "We have the honour of the day"—they said to each other—"and these banditti the profit."

If Shujá-ad-daula left his brave allies to do all the fighting, he did not forget to reward their services with a handsome share of the profit thence accruing to himself. At the end of the campaign, which lingered on fitfully to the close of the year, Champion's brigade received a donation of ten lakhs and a-half, equal at that time to £130,000, a very fair allowance for so small a force.*

* So thinks Major Stubbs: "History of the Bengal Artillery," Vol. I., Chap. ii.

After the 23rd of April, however, there was no more fighting for our troops in Rohilkhand. Faizulla Khán, who had unwillingly taken part in the war, withdrew the wrecks of his beaten army towards the hills. Some months of inaction caused by the rains passed over before Champion was ordered to follow up his first successes. But the Rohillas, straitened for food and disheartened by defeat, were in no mood for further resistance. The Vazír had already offered them terms of peace. These were at last accepted by Faizulla Khán, who, on payment of a heavy fine, was allowed to retain his father's fief of Rámpur.* His followers, to the number of eighteen or twenty thousand, were compelled or allowed to migrate across the Ganges into the districts around Meerut, which had been granted to the Rohilla, Zábita Khán, as a reward for his adherence to the Oudh Vazír.

That the conquest of Rohilkhand was marked by some of the cruelty and injustice so common in Eastern warfare it is needless to deny. But the tale of horror which Macaulay's eloquence has burned into the popular mind has small foundation in recorded facts. Some villages may have been plundered and burned, some blood

* Keene's "Moghul Empire," Book 2, Chap. iii.

shed in pure wantonness, some part of the country laid waste. Shuja-ad-daula was neither worse nor better than the average of Eastern rulers. But it was not likely that the new master of Rohilkhand would turn a rich province into a desert, or exterminate the very people to whose industry he would look for increased revenues. At one elbow he had Colonel Champion, at the other Hastings' own accredited agent, Middleton, both empowered to remonstrate freely, and the latter even to use threats, on the side of humanity and fair play. Colonel Champion was a good officer, but his feelings often ran away with his judgement, and his jealousy of Middleton sharpened his readiness to believe whatever he heard told against the Nawab-Vazír. The complaints which he forwarded to Calcutta were often at variance with the reports which Hastings received from Middleton. Hastings could only remind the Colonel that, up to a certain point, he had ample means of inclining the Nawab towards the side of mercy, if he chose to employ them. In his letters to Middleton the Governor enjoined him to use all his influence in behalf of the family of Háfiz Rahmat, to remonstrate with the Nawab-Vazír against every act of cruelty or wanton violence to his new subjects, to impress him with the English abhorrence "of every species of inhumanity and oppression," and, if need were, to work upon his fears of losing the future countenance of his English neighbours.*

Few men have ever suffered so cruelly as Hastings, from the malice of his enemies and the mis-statements of one-sided critics. A pamphleteer of his own day coolly affirmed that 500,000 Rohilla families were driven across the Jamna, and that Rohilkhand was a barren and unpeopled waste. Mill asserts that "every one who bore the name of Rohilla was either butchered or found his safety in flight and in exile." And Macaulay, improving on Colonel Champion, tells us how "more than a hundred thousand people fled from their homes to pestilential jungles," rather than endure the tyranny of him to whom a Christian Government had "sold their substance, and their blood, and the honour of their wives and daughters;" Hastings looking on with folded arms, "while their villages were burned, their children butchered, and their women violated." The truth, as I have shown, was widely different. The "extermination" of

* Gleig's "Warren Hastings," Vol. 1, Chap. xii.

the Rohillas meant the banishment of a few Pathan chiefs with seventeen or eighteen thousand of their soldiers from the lands which they or their fathers had won by the sword. Some thousands of them stayed behind with Faizulla Khán and other chiefs of the same stock. Behind also remained nearly a million Hindu husbandmen, who were "in no way affected" by the change of masters,* but would certainly have starved if the whole country had been laid waste. Instead of looking carelessly on at scenes of unparallelled outrage, Hastings did all he fairly could to stay the hand of a conqueror, whose carelessness for others' sufferings was tempered by a keen regard for his own interests.

After all, however, it must be admitted that this Rohilla campaign is one of the few passages in Hastings' career on which no impartial critic can look back with much complacency. Even the Court of Directors qualified their entire approval of the Treaty of Banáras by demurring to the employment of their troops in a war waged by a foreign ruler. The misdeeds of Shuja-ad-daula have cast their shadow on the memory of him whose policy ensured the conquest of Rohilkhand.

* Hamilton's "History of the Rohilla Afghans."

BOOK III.

CHAPTER I.

—1774.

Thus far the Governor of Fort William has been sailing along through waters seldom ruffled by an adverse breeze. His work has indeed been heavy; but its progress has been hampered by few collisions, whether with his colleagues in India or with the Company at home. With the means allowed him, within the limits prescribed by the Court of Directors, he has succeeded in laying fast the foundations of civilised rule over the provinces won by the sword of his old master, Clive. In the prime of manhood, for he was barely forty-two at the close of the Rohilla War, he was still apparently in vigorous health after many years of constant toil in a tropical climate, to which so many Englishmen have owed an early death or a life of prolonged suffering.

Of his private life at this period Mr. Gleig can tell us nothing; but it may be assumed that he had his moments of recreation among his favourite books, his friends of whom he counted many, and in the company of her whom he would soon be free to make his wedded wife. Nor were those dear ones at home forgotten, whose lives his bounty had so long helped to cheer. If the good will of his employers—the esteem of friends—the gratitude of kinsfolk—coupled with the near prospect of wedded happiness and a pleasing sense of great power successfully wielded for the general good, could make a man happy in the midst of many cares and trials, Hastings at this moment had little cause for murmuring at his lot.

But evil days were already in store for him. In 1773 Parliament passed a Regulating Act which revised the whole machinery of the Company's affairs. It was ordained that each Director should retain his post for four years instead of one. The qualification for a vote in the Court of Proprietors was raised from £500 to £1,000 stock, and no Proprietor could claim more than four votes. The Governor of Bengal was transformed into Governor-General of British India; his Council was reduced from twelve members to four; and under their joint control were placed the Governments of Madras and Bombay. The Governor-General was to receive a salary of £25,000 a year, and each Councillor £10,000. A Supreme Court of Justice, consisting of a Chief Justice and three other judges, was to be established at Calcutta to administer English law for all British subjects in Bengal, Bahar and Orissa. The loud remonstrances of the Company against these new encroachments on their chartered rights were answered by the concession of powers to borrow £1,400,000 from the British Treasury.

Of the new Councillors, one only, Mr. Barwell, belonged to the former Council. The other three, General Clavering, Colonel Monson, and Mr. Philip Francis, were appointed in England by Lord North's ministry for the manifest purpose of shaping the policy of the Indian Government in accordance with the views of Parliament and the Crown. Hastings might stand forth as Governor-General, and Barwell's Indian training and growing friendship for his

Chief, might lead him to vote with Hastings in the future as well as the past. But the nominees of the Ministry might safely be trusted to outvote the other two in a Council where each member would have an equal voice. If Hastings had hitherto managed to win his own way, as a rule, in a council of thirteen composed of Company's servants, a very different prospect awaited him now. The new Councillors were of course enjoined to cultivate harmony and good-will in the discharge of their appointed duties. But Lord North at any rate knew what he was about; and the sequel will show what sort of value they attached to a form of words so little in harmony with their own prejudices and the manifest object of their errand.

Of the three who sailed for India in the following year, Clavering was an honest, hot-headed soldier, who had risen into favour with the king and his ministers. "He brought," says Hastings, "strong prejudices with him, and he receives all his intelligence from men whose aim or interest it is to increase those prejudices." Of the Hon. George Monson, who had served in Indian campaigns on the coast, and gained much renown in the conquest of Manilla in 1762,* Hastings spoke at first as "a sensible man," who had received wrong impressions from the party opposed to himself. He appears to have been a man of small intellect, arrogant, rash, self-willed, yet easily led by those who paid him the needful deference. Last of the triumvirate, but far the first in intellect, boldness, ability, and force of character, comes Philip Francis, sometime clerk in the English War Office, and since identified by competent judges with the author of the famous "Letters of Junius," those masterpieces of spiteful satire clothed in racy and powerful English. His malignant nature, his crafty daring, his freedom from all vulgar scruples, his fierce hatred of opponents, his wrong-headed zeal in any cause that took his fancy, all these qualities marked him out as a leader in the long and furious struggle into which his party was about to drag the Governor-General of Bengal.

In the same ship with these three sailed the judges of the new Supreme Court, at the head of whom was Sir Elijah Impey, the Governor-General's old school-fellow and fast friend. Friendly letters from Hastings awaited each of

* See Grose's "Voyage to the East Indies, Vol. 2."

the party at Madras. Whatever doubts he had concerning some of his new colleagues, he kept to himself. To Impey he wrote without reserve, as one who rejoiced at "the prospect of seeing so old a friend," and who looked to that friend for help in the "peculiar circumstances" of his new position.*

On the 19th of October, 1774, the whole party landed at Calcutta under a salute of seventeen guns. Some of them had expected a salute of twenty-one guns, the number reserved for the Governor-General alone. An officer of Hastings' staff conducted them to Hastings' own dwelling, where the Governor-General and his old colleagues stood ready to greet them with all needful courtesy. But to all such marks of outward respect the new Councillors made but a cold return. Because no guard of honour had met them on the beach, and their landing had been proclaimed by only seventeen guns, they chose to sulk over the fancied indignity, and retired in no pleasant mood to the lodgings which had been secured for them in the suburbs. They had come all that way from England, not to exchange civilities with the Governor-General, but to

* Gleig's "Warren Hastings," Vol. 1, Chap. xiii.

reform after their own fashion the Government of which he remained the nominal head.

It does not appear that the new judges shared in the angry feelings of their late shipmates. Impey, at any rate, was received by Hastings with the warmth of an old friend; and the good understanding then established between them outlived the storm of untoward circumstances which forced them for a time into outward antagonism.

On the following day the new Council, with the exception of Barwell who had not yet returned to Calcutta, met for the first time to hear the commission read, which set aside the former government, and defined the powers, aims, and responsibilities of its successor. The new Councillors were enjoined to act harmoniously together for the preservation of peace throughout India, for the safeguarding of the Company's possessions, and the due advancement of their interests, financial and political. A separate Board of Trade was to be established. The military outlay was to be kept within certain limits—an inquiry was ordered into past abuses—the land-revenue system, as worked by Hastings, was to be let alone—and all correspondence with the "country powers" was to be carried on by the Governor-General, on condition that each letter received or sent by him was duly laid before the Council.* In issuing these instructions, the Court of Directors seem to have hoped that the new Government would work as smoothly as its predecessor, with results still happier for the general good. But they had reckoned without the new conditions under which the Government was to be carried on.

The Council adjourned till the 25th of October, when Barwell also took his seat among them. On that day Hastings laid before his colleagues a clear and carefully-written statement of the policy pursued by his government during the last two years and a-half. The first part of the Minute was received with quiet approval, or at least without dissent. But the story of the Treaty of Banáras and the Rohilla War at once evoked the latent hostility of Francis and his two allies. Then, indeed, there burst forth on Hastings' head a storm which was destined to rage against him long after the death or the retirement of its first fomenters. Monson called on Hastings to produce all the letters which had passed between him and his agent at the Court of Oudh. The

* Auber's "British Power in India," Vol. 1, Ch. ix.

Governor-General refused for good reasons to violate private confidences in obedience to some *ex post facto* law. All pertinent passages in those letters he was ready to produce, but "no power on earth could authorise him" to give up the letters themselves. His old friend, Barwell, manfully supported him, but in vain. The new triumvirate marked their displeasure at Hastings' refusal by at once decreeing Middleton's recal from Lucknow.

This was the first blow struck in a quarrel forced on the ablest of Anglo-Indian statesmen by the tools and emissaries of Lord North; a quarrel which, in Macaulay's words, "after distracting British India, was renewed in England, and in which all the most eminent statesmen and orators of the age took active part on one or the other side."

Middleton was recalled, and presently his place was filled by Bristow, the nominee of the triumphant majority in Council. Colonel Champion received orders to withdraw his brigade forthwith from Rohilkhand, and to enforce the payment of all monies due from the Nawab-Vazír under a threat of withdrawing his troops from Oudh itself. The same men who had just denounced the Treaty of Banáras, and inveighed in unmeasured terms against the abettors of the Rohilla War, saw no inconsistency in reaping the solid fruits of the bargain they professed to abhor. It was useless for Hastings to bring all the weight of his reasoning and his practical knowledge to bear against measures which tended to upset his best-laid schemes, to destroy his influence with neighbouring princes, and to dishonour him in the eyes of his own subjects. His opponents, with the reins in their own hands, were in no mood to behave with common fairness, or even with common decency. Hastings and Barwell might plead never so earnestly for delay, for further inquiry, for some deference to their own judgment; they might record their solemn protest against the acts of colleagues whose ignorance was equalled by their self-conceit. But Clavering, Monson and Francis paid little heed to arguments which commanded but two votes out of five. Mercy and modesty were equally alien from the nature of Philip Francis; and the other two, while deeming themselves inspired by a noble zeal for humanity and the public service, were little more than clay in the hands of that unscrupulous potter.

The struggle thus begun in the Calcutta council-chamber was carried on by the triumvirate with a bitterness which reminded Hastings of the trials which his old chief Vansittart had from like causes undergone. "But, I trust," he writes to Lawrence Sulivan, "that, by the benefit of his example and my own experience, and by a temper which, in spite of nature, I have brought under proper subjection, I shall be able to prevent the same dreadful extremities which attended the former" quarrel. The insults which almost daily awaited him rankled deep in a nature alike proud, sensitive and amiable; and at times he thought of leaving the field to Francis and his followers. But his very pride strengthened his resolve to abide by a post which he well knew that none of his adversaries, perhaps none other of his countrymen, had so clear a title from past services and proven deserts to fill. Conscious of his own fitness for that post, and still believing in Lord North's friendliness and sense of justice, he determined to indulge his avowed ambition to win his sovereign's favour, by "conducting the great and important affairs committed to my charge to the best of my abilities, for his honour and the advantage of his people"*

To trust in Lord North, however, was but trusting in a broken reed. If Hastings fancied

* Gleig's "Warren Hastings," Vol. 1, Chap. XIII.

himself in the Minister's debt for his new appointment, he had to thank him also for sending out three such thorns in the Governor-General's side as Clavering, Monson and Francis. But the noble weakness which so often made him think the best of a man until he had learned to suspect the worst, proved in this instance a fortunate thing for Hastings' countrymen, perhaps in some ways for Hastings himself. If he had thrown up his thankless office at the end of 1774, the whole, or at least the greater part of India, would in all likelihood have become the prize of Marátha ambition; and the history, not only of Hastings' proudest achievements, but of our Indian Empire whose growth they assured, would have been a tale untold.

* Sir E. Impey took up his abode in the suburb of Chowringhee, on the eastern edge of the Maidan or plain which stretches across to Fort William, the building of which, begun by Clive in 1757, was finished in 1773. At the latter date Chowringhee, now indeed a city of palaces, contained only two good houses, in one of which Impey was afterwards lodged. Hastings himself appears to have lived at Belvedere in the Alipore suburb, a house which has since become the official residence of the Lieutenant-Governors of Bengal. A lady described Belvedere in 1780 as "a perfect bijou, most superbly fitted up with all that unbounded affluence can display," while the gardens were "said to be very tastefully laid out." Close by in the same quarter lived Imhoff and his wife. Francis also lived in Alipore. The Government House was then in Fort William.—Newman's "Handbook to Calcutta." On the site of the old fort and its "black hole" now stands Dalhousie Square, formerly known as Tank Square, from a large tank dug by order of Government to provide the citizens with sweet water. The tank was cleansed and completely embanked in Hastings' time.

CHAPTER II.

1774—1775.

If Hastings had by nature a quick temper, his self-control must have been sorely tried by the council-meetings which came off under the new rules twice a week. At these meetings every act of the late Government would be reviewed in a spirit more or less unfriendly by his three opponents, whose zeal for redressing wrongs and discovering abuses seemed to spend itself on their President alone. Whoever else was right, he at least was always held to be in the wrong. "We three are king," said Francis, and very loudly did the fact proclaim itself to the astonished citizens of Calcutta. The new Chief Justice complained bitterly to Lord Thurlow of "the *hauteur*, insolence, and superior airs of authority, which the members of the new Council use to the Court."* Hastings fought them as he best could in speeches,

* "Memoirs of Sir E. Impey," Chap. iii.

minutes, and earnest letters to the Court of Directors, to Lord North, and his own friends on the India House Board. When the violence of his colleagues passed all bounds of endurance, Hastings and Barwell would save their dignity by leaving the council-chamber for that day. But nothing could shame or check the rampant insolence of the triumvirate. They never lost a chance of wounding the President's pride, ignoring his authority, or undoing his work. His management of the revenue—his dealings with the ruler of Oudh—his commercial and fiscal reforms, every detail of his past policy, was brought up against him as a crime or a blunder by the men who had been specially enjoined to work harmoniously for the peace and well-being of the Company's dominions.

The extent of their rancour against the Governor-General may be gathered from their mode of pressing the inquiry into the circumstances of the Rohilla war. If they could not undo the conquest of Rohilkhand, they might yet succeed in branding their President with lasting infamy, for his share in that awkward-looking business. Officers of Champion's force were invited to bear witness against the man who had sold their services to a ruthless tyrant. Colonel Leslie, however, declined to answer for the opinions of the army as to the moral character of the late war. Baffled at one point, the inquisitors attacked another, but always more or less in vain. There was no evidence of the cruelties alleged against Shuja-ad-daula. Of the Rohillas, their history, and their real character, they learned many things which ought to have shamed them out of conclusions founded on utter ignorance of the facts. But no amount of facts could stay them in their wild career. They even fastened on the liberal present which the Nawab-Vazír had bestowed on Champion's troops, as if that was another of Hastings' crimes. And, in spite of all evidence, they proceeded to denounce him as one who had waged war with an "innocent nation," and covered with ruin the smiling valley where the people had hitherto dwelt in peace under their noble Afghan masters.*

To Shuja-ad-daula the recal of Middleton seemed like the rending of all the ties that bound him to his English friends in Bengal. For some years past he had shown himself a faithful ally of the power to which he owed the retention of his

* Auber's "British Power in India," Vol. 1, Ch. ix.

dominions after the peace of 1765. For Hastings he had conceived a strong personal attachment, which reflected itself in his intercourse with Hastings' confidential agent at Lucknow. When Middleton showed him his letter of recal, the Nawab-Vazír burst into tears over an act which seemed to betoken a hostile purpose towards himself. It is said that his death was hastened by this and the subsequent measures of the Calcutta triumvirate.* Be that as it may, he died in January of the following year, leaving behind him a letter in which he implored the Governor-General to extend to his son the friendship he had always shown for his father.

With these last wishes of the dying prince Hastings tried his best to comply. But the foreign policy of the Government had wholly passed out of his control. Francis and his colleagues hastened to set aside the existing treaties with Oudh, and to force new and harder conditions upon the new Nawab-Vazír, Asaf-ad-daula. Their agent, Bristow, with whom they carried on the same kind of secret correspondence which

* Mr. Keene ("Moghul Empire," Book 2, Ch. iii.) refers without accepting it to a story current in those days, that Shuja-ad-daula died of a wound inflicted with a poisoned knife by a daughter of Hafiz Rahmat Khan.

they had condemned in the case of Hastings, threw himself with unquestioning zeal into all their plans. In vain did Hastings and Barwell plead for fairer treatment of the young Nawab, in accordance with the treaties of Allahabad and Banáras, and with his obvious rights as heir to his father's throne and property. In vain did the young Nawab protest against the injustice of conditions which involved his State in fresh burdens, and robbed him of the very means of carrying on his government. Before the end of May, 1775, he had signed a treaty which transferred to the Company the revenues of Banáras, and which raised by Rs. 50,000 a month the subsidy his father had agreed to pay for the British troops quartered in Oudh.

At the same time he bound himself to make good with all due speed the balance of his father's debts to the Company. In the face of these exactions and demands, with his own army clamouring for long arrears of pay, the helpless young prince was forced to surrender to the Begam, his father's widow, nearly the whole of the two millions which Shuja-ad-daula had stored up within his palace, as a fund on which he or his successors might draw in time of need. It was money collected from the public taxes, and meant to be employed for the public benefit. The Begam herself was already rich in the possession of a *jaigír*, or landed estate, which yielded fifty or sixty thousand pounds a year. But she claimed the two millions also under a will which was never forthcoming; and her son was coaxed or frightened by Bristow into signing away his right to three-fourths of the disputed treasure.

Hastings steadily refused his sanction to acts which he yet was powerless to forbid. Even the Court of Directors at first demurred to the notion that their treaties with Oudh had expired with the death of the last Nawab.* But their sense of justice speedily gave place to the pleasure derived from the new improvement in their financial prospects. In a letter of December, 1776, they recorded their "entire approbation" of the new treaty which seemed to promise them "solid and permanent advantages." Among the first-fruits of the hard conditions thus forced upon Asaf-ad-daula was an alarming mutiny of his unpaid troops, which was not quelled without heavy slaughter.

The Governor-General strove earnestly to set

* Mill's "British India," Book 5, Chap. ii.

himself right with the powers at home. He sent Lord North a copy of all his private correspondence with Middleton. To his friends at the India House and in the Company he wrote in a strain of undisguised bitterness at the malice of his foes in India, and of anxious pleading for the support of his masters and friends at home. "There are many gentlemen in England"—he writes to Messrs. Graham and Macleane—"who have been eye-witnesses of my conduct. For God's sake call upon them to draw my true portrait, for the Devil is not so black as these fellows have painted me. . . . . If I am not deceived, there is not a man in Calcutta, scarce in Bengal, unconnected with Clavering and his associates, who does not execrate their conduct, and unite in wishes for my success against them." This was written on the 29th of April. A month earlier he had announced to these two gentlemen his firm intention to return home in the next cold season, unless the Directors approved of his policy towards Shah Alam and the late Nawab of Oudh. In that event, he would await the issue of his further appeals.* The approval reached him soon afterwards, and other events were already

* Gleig's "Warren Hastings," Vol. 1, Chap. xiv.

happening which encouraged him to stay on and fight his enemies to the last. What use was afterwards made of the letter entrusted to Macleane, we shall see presently.

In due time Hastings was to learn new lessons of distrust in seeming friends. Meanwhile, his position at the head of a government in which he had no real voice, grew daily harder to bear. His opponents had stripped him even of his patronage. Beyond the management of the revenues and such other business as he alone was still found competent to discharge, he was little better than a clerk in his masters' service. The English in Calcutta looked on with wondering sympathy at the political effacement of their nominal head. Many of the natives, with an instinctive readiness to insult the fallen, began to play into the hands of Francis and his allies, who were bent on raking up, as Hastings said, "out of the dirt of Calcutta," any information which might serve to blacken his fair fame, and undo all the good which he had accomplished. Every one who sought to curry favour with the triumvirate, or to pay off a grudge against the Governor-General, found in Hastings' new colleagues greedy listeners to his tale. Nothing was too absurd for their belief—no informer too vile for a careful hearing—no means too paltry or crooked for the end desired.

Had these self-chosen inquisitors known anything whatever of Indian usages, they would have known how easy it was in India to get up any amount of false witness against any great personage fallen into disgrace. "An Indian Government"—says Macaulay—"has only to let it be understood that it wishes a particular man to be ruined; and in twenty-four hours it will be furnished with grave charges, supported by depositions so full and circumstantial, that any person unaccustomed to Asiatic mendacity would regard them as decisive. It is well if the signature of the destined victim is not counterfeited at the foot of some illegal compact, and if some treasonable paper is not slipped into a hiding-place in his house." In view of this picture, as true to the present as to the past, there is no need to accuse Francis and his colleagues of wilfully suborning false witnesses against their Chief. It is enough to know that, from whatever motive, they threw themselves without a scruple into the game which native roguery was prepared on the slightest encouragement to play.

Foremost among the crows who now began pecking at the wounded eagle was Hastings' old enemy, Nand-Kumár. That wily Brahman, whom Clive and Hastings had both called the worst man they knew in India, who was to other Bengalis what the Bengali is to other Hindus, whose whole life had been spent in plotting against the English or his own countrymen, now saw an easy opening for revenge on the man who had so often exposed and thwarted his mischievous intrigues. It is hardly possible to suppose that the Francis faction were wholly ignorant of the evil odour in which this man had long been held, even by the Court of Directors. But, in their blind hatred of the Governor General, they clutched at any tool which might help to complete his ruin. In the early days of March, 1775, the plot was already ripening. On the 11th Nand-Kumár delivered into Francis' hands a letter in which Hastings was plainly charged with various acts of fraud, embezzlement, corruption and oppression. This letter, whose purport he knew already, Francis hastened to lay before the Council.*

In this precious document Hastings was accused, among other things, of taking bribes

* Gleig's "Warren Hastings," Vol. 1, Chap. xiv.

from the Manni Begam, of sharing in the plunder amassed by Mohammad Reza Khan, and of procuring that officer's acquittal in return for a further large bribe. He met this new attack upon him with becoming scorn, and indignantly denied the right of the Council to enter into charges coming from a source so foully tainted. Barwell supported him, and the meeting broke up after a fierce debate. Two days afterwards Francis laid before the Council another letter from Nand-Kumar, bringing fresh charges against the Governor-General, and asking leave to address the Council and bring up witnesses in their support.

The triumvirate insisted that he should be heard. Hastings warmly protested against such a course. His colleagues, if they chose, might form a committee of inquiry; but he refused to accept them as his judges, or to sit as president of a Board before which the dregs of the people would appear, at Nand-Kumar's prompting, to give evidence against the head of the Government. Barwell demanded that the whole question should be referred to the Supreme Court. But the Francis faction were deaf to all argument. At length Hastings broke up the meeting and left the council-chamber, followed by his friend Barwell.

The rest of the Council at once voted Clavering into the chair, and summoned before them the Rajah Nand-Kumar. That consummate scoundrel, prefacing that his character was as dear to him as his life, produced a letter seemingly written by the Manni Begam to himself, in which Hastings figured as the receiver of presents from that lady through the agency of Nand-Kumar. The signature of this letter was shown at the time to differ widely from that of a letter which the Begam had sent a few days before to Sir John D'Oyley, of the Secretariat. But the Council of Three cared nothing either for counter-evidence, or for Nand-Kumar's collusion, if the letter were genuine, with the man whose conduct he now sought to expose. The seal, at any rate, appeared to be the Begam's own. Without waiting for further evidence, they proceeded, in spite of the late hour and of Hastings' absence, to pass judgment on the case before them. They declared that Hastings had secretly taken gifts from the Begam to the value of about £35,000, which belonged of right to the Company; and they ordered him to repay that sum forthwith into the public treasury.*

The Governor-General of course refused to obey an order issued by a court which had no conceivable right to adjudge the case, or even to hear it. He pronounced the letter a palpable forgery, and this fact was erelong attested by the Begam herself. The mystery of the seal was finally cleared up after the death of Nand-Kumar. Among the Rajah's effects was found a cabinet, which contained exact counterfeits of the seals used by almost every native of rank in Bengal.

Meanwhile fresh charges against the Governor-General were laid before "King Francis" by the Rani of Bardwan, by an emissary from the young Nawab of Bengal, and other worshippers of the rising sun. Some of those struck at Hastings through his own English subordinates Three only of his countrymen, Mr. Grant, an accountant, and the two Fowkes, father and son, seem to have joined in this cowardly game. One obscure native accused him of embezzling about two-thirds of the salary payable to the Faujdar, or military head-constable of Húgli. No evidence

* Auber's "British Power in India," Vol. 1, Chap. ix.

worth considering was adduced in any instance, none at all in the last-named. And yet the triumvirate recorded their firm belief that there was "no species of peculation from which the Honourable Governor-General has thought it right to abstain;" * and deliberately charged him with having in this way amassed a fortune of forty lakhs of rupees—more than £400,000—in two years and a-half.

In his letter of March 25 to Mr. Graham and Colonel Macleane the long-suffering statesman describes the various processes employed for his undoing:—

"The trumpet has been sounded, and the whole host of informers will soon crowd to Calcutta with their complaints and ready depositions. Nund Comar holds his durbar in complete state—sends for zemindars and their vakeels—coaxing and threatening them for complaints, which no doubt he will get in abundance, besides what he forges himself. The system which they have laid down for conducting their affairs, is, as I am told, after this manner:—The General rummages the consultations for disputable matter, with the aid of old Fowke. Colonel Monson receives, and I have been assured descends even to solicit, accusations. Francis writes. Goring is employed as their agent with Mahommed Reza Cawn; and Fowke with Nund Comar."

"Was it for this," he asks, "that the legislature of Great Britain formed the new system of government for Bengal, and armed it with powers extending to every part of the British Empire in

* Auber's "British Power in India," Vol. 1, Chap. ix.

India?" Strangely enough, he still seems to make less account of his worst enemy, Francis, than of Colonel Monson, whom he regards as 'the most determined' and dangerous of the three. He had yet to learn the full significance of his own expression, "Francis writes." While Clavering and Monson were blindly doing the rougher part of their prompter's work, the pen of Junius was already weaving the web of lies, innuendos, and assumptions, in which Francis sought to ensnare and ruin the great proconsul, whose place he wanted for himself.

Writing two days later to Lord North, the harassed Governor-General earnestly entreats his Lordship to free him from his present state, "either by my immediate recal, or by the confirmation of the trust and authority of which you have hitherto thought me deserving, on such a footing as shall enable me to fulfil your expectations, and to discharge the debt which I owe to your Lordship, to my country, and my Sovereign." This was the very day on which he wrote to warn Macleane and Graham of his resolution to return home in the event of disagreeable news from England. No wonder that

Hastings felt disheartened, even to the verge of despair. Wave after wave of misfortune had dashed against him, and as yet no gleam of daylight could pierce the dense folds of storm-cloud overhead. But the light behind the clouds was to shine out freely before long.

CHAPTER III.

1775—1777.

WHILE Francis was revelling in the near success of his schemes for supplanting his great rival, and Nand-Kumar was tasting the sweets of gratified revenge, they little knew what an undercurrent of disaster was about to drag the latter down into its most fatal depths. Scorning defeat at the hands of such assailants, Hastings turned for help to the Supreme Court. On the 11th of April a charge of conspiracy was lodged in that court against the villainous Brahman, the elder Fowke, and one or two of their abettors. They were accused of suborning one Kamal-ud-din, a revenue-farmer, to bear false witness against the Governor-General. After an inquiry prolonged through several days, the judges ordered Fowke and Nand-Kumar to give bail for their appearance at the next assizes, and bound Hastings over to prosecute them. In the teeth of such a decision,

Francis and his colleagues hastened to show their rancour against the head of the Government by paying Nand-Kumar the compliment of a formal visit at his own house.

But Nemesis was approaching him from another quarter. About five years before Impey's arrival in India, one Mohan Prasád, a native merchant, had brought a charge of forgery against the Rajah before the Mayor's Court in Calcutta. In due time Nand-Kumar was committed for trial under the English law, which made forgery a capital offence. He was still a prisoner awaiting his trial, when Hastings succeeded to the Government of Bengal. Needing him, as we have seen, for his masters' purposes, the new Governor obtained the prisoner's release. But the fatal charge still hung over him, for the written evidence of his guilt was retained in the Mayor's Court. When the records and papers of that court were afterwards handed over to the new Supreme Court, the new judges gave the forged deed back to Mohan Prasad.*

Natives of India have long memories, especially when they are driven by a thirst for revenge mixed up with a fear for their own safety.

* Impey's "Memoirs of Sir E. Impey," Ch. 3.

Mohan Prasad had doubtless very good reasons of his own for helping in the downfal of the man who had wronged him; and he chose his time well for following up the blow which Hastings had already struck against their common enemy. On the 6th of May the old action for forgery was renewed before the Supreme Court. Ere long Calcutta was startled to hear that the man whom Francis and his colleagues held in so much honour, had been arrested and thrown as a vulgar felon into the common gaol.

That Hastings had any hand in this new move, none but "idiots and biographers," says the polite Macaulay, can help believing. Biographers are sometimes foolish; but so are critics, who jump to rash conclusions. Small blame indeed would rightly have attached to Hastings, if he had in any way encouraged this new attack upon the villain who had turned and stung him. But besides the fact of his own action for conspiracy, some weight is surely due from any sober-minded critic to Hastings' own statement, as solemnly made on oath before the judges who tried Nand-kumar. He then swore that he had never, directly or indirectly, countenanced or forwarded the prosecution for forgery against the Rajah. To suppose that he swore falsely is to fling a whole mud-heap at the memory of a statesman among the most upright of his day. Either Macaulay has done this, or else he has proved his utter ignorance of a fact which tells most strongly against his own theory. Beyond the coincidence of the two charges following each other so closely, there is simply no ground whatever for his assumption, that Hastings was "the real mover in the business."

During the month which elapsed between the arrest and the trial of Nand-Kumar, his patrons in the Council displayed their partisan spirit on his behalf. They visited him in prison; they demanded that he should be enlarged on bail; they encouraged him to complain to the judges of the wrong done to a man of his caste, by locking him up in a place where he could not wash as became a Brahman, before eating his food. The judges refused to let him out on bail, and they found on inquiry that his scruples about his caste were a mere pretence. At the same time the triumvirate discovered an excuse for raising Nand-Kumar's son Gurdas to the post hitherto held by the Manni Begam, and for reinstating Mohammad Reza Khan in the obsolete office of Naib Subah.

On the 8th of June the trial began, after a true bill had been found against the prisoner by a grand jury of the leading merchants in Calcutta. The four judges, headed by Impey, tried the case, and a jury of twelve Englishmen followed the evidence. Two English barristers acted as counsel for Nand-Kumar. There was no lack of witnesses for the defence; there never is when a wealthy native has to stand a trial, especially a trial for life and death. But the evidence against the Rajah was too clear for much question, and the jury found him guilty without reserve. With the entire concurrence of his fellow judges Impey condemned the wretched man to the death awarded him by law.*

It might have been expected that some of his powerful friends would have made an effort to save him from the doom which no man better deserved. Ten years before, another native of rank condemned to death for the same crime had been pardoned mainly in answer to the earnest prayer of his fellow-citizens. But now not a finger was stirred in Nand-Kumar's behalf, either by his native or his English friends. Days passed, and weeks; but no prayer for his life

* Impey's "Memoirs of Sir Elijah Impey," Chap. 4.

went forth to the Judges or the Council. One petition indeed from the convict himself was handed to Clavering on the 4th of August, but he took care to know nothing of its contents until after the sentence had been carried out. And when he laid the petition before the Council, it was Francis who proposed and his colleagues who demanded that the paper should be burnt by the common hangman, as containing libellous matter against the Judges of the Supreme Court.*

In the early morning of the 5th of August Nand-Kumar was hanged. He was not the first native who had paid the penalty enforced by the savage old laws of England for a crime which his own countrymen regarded only as a finer form of swindling. He had been fairly tried and sentenced, as a British subject, under a law which twice at least in the last ten years had been carried out against his own countrymen. His death on the Maidan, or plain outside the city, was certainly witnessed by a crowd of curious spectators; but few, if any, gave vent to loud wailings or any other token of grief and dismay. Most of them watched his last struggles with quiet indifference, while not a few were heard to

* "Memoirs of Sir E. Impey," Chap. 4.

say among themselves, that "the worst man in India" had met with the punishment he richly deserved.*

But the evil spirit which dwelt in the heart of Francis was one day to forge out of this simple affair a whole armoury of lies and slanders against Impey and his friend Hastings. Many years afterwards a letter said to have been written at the time by his brother-in-law, the Sheriff of Calcutta, but bearing manifest traces of the Roman hand of Junius, furnished Burke with a theme for one of his fiery invectives, and became the groundwork of some splendid passages in Macaulay's memorable and misleading essay. In that writer's pages Nand-Kumar figures as the interesting victim of a plot laid by Warren Hastings, and helped forward by Sir Elijah Impey. Of the latter, especially, he speaks in language of weighty scorn, whose only fault lies in its astounding injustice. He records it as his "deliberate opinion that Impey, sitting as a judge, put a man unjustly to death in order to serve a political purpose." Impey acted unjustly, it seems, in refusing to respite a Hindu forger, whom he had unjustly condemned to be hanged.

* "Memoirs of Sir E. Impey," Chap. 12.

The short answer to these absurd charges, worthy of the writer who assumed that young Impey at Westminster was young Hastings' fag and tool, may be gathered from the foregoing pages, which show that Impey was merely one of four judges concerned in the trial of a man whom an independent jury found guilty of a capital crime. He never refused to respite the prisoner, for the simple reason that he was never asked to respite him.

In after years it suited the enemies of Hastings to declare that he and Impey had joined in murdering Nand-Kumar. But while his doom was yet hanging over the latter, neither Francis nor his colleagues made any effort to save his life. Instead of rescuing Nand-Kumar at the foot of the gallows, Clavering took care to let him die before bringing his petition to the Council's notice. How that petition was received, we have already seen. It was not likely that Hastings himself would come forward to plead for the scoundrel, whose punishment might deter others from playing a game which for him had ended so disastrously. If the triumvirate would do nothing for their friend in need, why should Hastings go out of his way to hinder the exit of his worst foe from the scene of his many villainies?

To him, indeed, that "bad man's" fate must have brought a feeling of temporary relief from the strain of prolonged anxiety and vexation of spirit. It may even be, as Francis presently hinted, and Macaulay afterwards declared, that "the voices of a thousand informers were silenced in an instant." Cheered by the support of his own countrymen and the good will of the leading natives in Calcutta, the harassed Governor could take breath to renew the struggle with his factious opponents. Two days after the death of Nand-Kumar, he found time to write to Dr. Johnson a letter thanking him in the friendliest terms for the copy of "Mr. Jones's ingenious book" which he had lately received through Mr. Justice Chambers, one of the new Calcutta judges.* He tells the great English scholar of his own efforts to promote research into the history, traditions, arts and natural productions of India; of the success achieved in compiling "an abstract of the Gentoo law;" and begs him to accept a copy of Bogle's journal of his mission into Tibet. He could have wished, indeed, that a portion of the spirit displayed in the Doctor's own "Tour to the Hebrides" had animated the

* Probably Sir William Jones's "Persian Grammar."

author of the journal; but "I flatter myself"—he adds—"that you will find it not unworthy of your perusal."

To Lord Mansfield in the following January he sends a complete copy of "Halhed's Code," and a plan drawn by himself and approved by his friend Impey, for defining and regulating the respective powers of the Council and the Supreme Court. In spite of the vague language of the Regulating Act, his own relations with the new judges still worked easily. "I have a pleasure"—he writes—"in declaring that on all occasions it has been his [Impey's] aim in particular, and in general that of the other judges of the Supreme Court, to support the authority of Government, and temper the law of England with the laws, religious customs and manners of the natives." *

Meanwhile the triumvirate still took their own way in Council. The Bombay Government had in September, 1774, entered into an alliance with Ragunath Rao, commonly called Ragoba, a Maratha leader of old repute, and uncle to the young Peshwa, Narayan Rao, who died, it was said, through Ragoba's agency in 1773. His reputed murderer at once got himself installed as

* Gleig's "Warren Hastings," Vol. 2, Chap. i.

Peshwa; but a rival party, prompted by the able Nana Farnávís, ere long set up against him a posthumous son of the late Peshwa, under the title of Madhu Rao II. The chief Maratha leaders took different sides, according as their interest or their jealousies might prompt them. Defeated in the field by his opponents, Ragoba in 1775 turned for help to the English at Bombay. The Court of Directors had lately been hankering after Salsette and Bassein, an island and a port near Bombay itself. In hopes of gratifying their wish, the Bombay Government agreed to help Ragoba with a body of troops in return for the cession of those two places, and the payment of a large yearly sum of money.

But they had reckoned without the Government of Bengal. Hastings objected to the Treaty of Surat, but he was not for setting it rashly aside. Neither was Barwell. But the Francis faction were inexorable. In spite of the successes already won by our troops and sailors, they declared the treaty annulled—ordered the withdrawal of Keating's victorious soldiers to Bombay—and sent Colonel Upton to Púna to negotiate a peace on their own account.

After some show of insolence and menace, the

Púna Regency at length agreed to the compromise offered by the English envoy. By the Treaty of March, 1776, the English retained possession of Salsette, which they had already won; their claim to the revenues of Baróch was granted; and twelve lakhs of rupees were promised them, "as a favour," towards the costs of the war. But their other conquests were to be given back, and the rest of their agreement with Ragoba was formally annulled, in exchange for the pension secured to their late ally. By this Treaty of Puranda the interests of the Company and the good faith of the Bombay Government were alike sacrificed to the ignorant self-conceit of Clavering and his two colleagues.

New causes of quarrel with the Púna Government soon arose. A despatch from the India House, received in August, confirmed the former treaty with Ragoba, and directed the Supreme Government to aid in carrying it out. Neither at Bombay nor at Púna was the new treaty carefully observed. Troops were sent from Bombay to garrison Surat, and the Bombay Council invited Ragoba to their own capital as their pensioned guest. In March of the next year, 1777, a French adventurer arrived at Púna, as envoy from the king of France, who was on the point of declaring war with England. Nana Farnavís, who had now become the foremost man at Púna, received the Frenchman with open arms. The Treaty of Puranda was openly deplored by the Court of Directors; and Hastings, who by this time had become in effect his own master, waited only for some decent pretext to set it aside.

How Hastings became his own master, must now be told. After the death of Nand-Kumar his enemies in the Council still pursued their old course of obstruction. They thwarted him, as we have seen, in his dealings with the Bombay Council. They accused him of overtaxing the Zamindars and oppressing the Rayats, while they opposed his best efforts to redress the evils of which they complained. They refused to aid him in protecting natives of rank from arrest and imprisonment for debt by order of the Supreme Court.* The very loyalty which led him, often against his better judgment, to work with the triumvirate rather than against them, failed to shame the latter into more conciliatory moods.

Meanwhile, their friends at home were muster-

* Gleig's "Warren Hastings," Vol. 2, Chap. ii.

ing for fresh attacks upon the Governor-General. While Hastings still looked for help, or at least for fair play from Lord North, every influence of his Lordship's Government was brought to bear upon the Court of Directors in order to bring about the recal of Hastings, and the appointment of Clavering in his stead. Colonel Macleane's letters to Hastings reveal the progress of a plot which, but for Hastings' firmness and the loyalty of his friends at home, would have been crowned with full success. The Minister's first attempt to secure a hostile vote from the India House came to nothing; but a second, made in May 1776, resulted in eleven votes for the plotters against ten. Fortune, however, still smiled upon the brave. In the Court of Proprietors Hastings had a large number of devoted friends. They flocked to the meeting summoned for the 15th of May, and, after a debate of many hours, carried by a large majority a vote in favour of the Governor-General. Lord North's soreness at this defeat vented itself in strong language against the victors. A few weeks later the Court of Directors rescinded their former vote by a majority of two.*

* Gleig's "Warren Hastings," Vol. 2, Chap. iii.

Things however still looked so dark for Hastings, that some of his friends deemed it prudent to make the best terms they could with a Ministry whose power for further annoyance they had reason to fear. What if Lord North were to carry out his threat of calling Parliament together to abolish the very existence of the Company as a political power? Would it not be best, in Hastings' own interests, to secure such terms as might enable him to retire with all dignity from a thankless post? Clavering had powerful friends at Court and in the House of Commons, and Lord North seemed bent on making him Governor-General. Prompted by these and such-like considerations, Macleane strove to bring about a compromise based on the Governor-General's retirement. By the end of October the negotiations to that end had been completed, in supposed accordance with Hastings' own desires.

But only a few days afterwards Clavering was gazetted a Knight of the Bath. To Macleane and his colleague, Stewart, this seemed like a breach of the covenant so lately made; and they wrote out to Hastings, counselling him not to resign until he had been assured of a baronetcy or an Irish peerage. And yet we find Macleane a month later placing his employer's resignation in the hands of the Court of Directors, on the strength of a letter written by Hastings twenty-two months before, and virtually cancelled about six weeks afterwards. During the past twelve-month Hastings had repeatedly declared that he would only quit his post at the command of those who had placed him there. His letters to Lord North and the Court of Directors alike pointed clearly to the same conclusion. In the face of these the Court hastened, after brief inquiry, to accept an offer which Macleane no doubt honestly deemed himself empowered to make. In their eagerness to save themselves by throwing over their ablest servant, they acted on the assumption that Hastings would confirm his agent's doings. The atmosphere of the time was thick with delusions. Hastings clung to the belief that Lord North was still his friend. Macleane fancied that the friend for whom he had worked so zealously would gladly accept of any compromise which enabled him to retreat with honour from his trying position. And the Court of Directors were glad to seize at any fair pretext for recalling a Governor whose chances of success they underrated, and whose plans for increasing the Company's power in India they utterly misunderstood. They had been taught by his enemies to regard their best friend as a secret enemy to the maintenance of their rule, because he aimed at bringing "the country powers" into closer relations with the British Crown.

A new prospect had lately opened to Hastings through the death of Monson in September, 1776. For some months, at any rate, he would possess the casting vote in Council. His hands were thus strengthened at a timely moment for the work of revising the land settlements of 1772. "This measure"—he writes to his friend Graham—"will oblige me to new model all the provincial councils, for I will not leave such wretches as Goring, Rosewell and James Grant (names that I blush to write) in the power to render my designs abortive; but shall think it incumbent upon me to choose my own agents for the charge of my own plan, especially as so much will depend upon it." In order to provide materials for the new settlement, he appointed a special commission headed by Messrs. Anderson and Bogle, two of the ablest civil officers in Bengal. A few weeks later his friend Nat. Middleton was sent back to his old post at Lucknow, in the room of Bristow. The younger Fowke was recalled from Banáras. All these measures were as gall and wormwood to Clavering and Francis, who blustered, talked about jobs, wrote sharp minutes, spread false stories; but in vain. Hastings knew his power, and calmly defied them from behind the bulwark of his casting vote.

Early in 1777 his busy mind was employed in shaping out a scheme to "extend the influence of the British nation to every part of India not too remote from their possessions, without enlarging the circle of their defence, or involving them in hazardous or indefinite engagements, and to accept of the allegiance of such of our neighbours as shall sue to be enlisted among the friends and allies of the King of Great Britain."* To this end he sought to renew his old relations with the Nawab of Oudh, and to form an alliance with the Rajah of Berar. By such means he hoped to counteract the designs of the Marathas, whose intrigues with the French and the Nizam of the Dakhan boded no good to the English rule. In a letter to his friend Alexander Elliott, Hastings

* Gleig's "Warren Hastings," Vol. 2, Chap. iv.

gives a detailed sketch of that subsidiary system to which our Indian Empire owes so much of its present greatness. But before this scheme could be carried into effect, it was needful for him to know how he stood with the arbiters of his fate at home, whether they meant to retain him at his post, and what kind of councillor would come out to replace Monson.

The turning-point of his career was now close at hand. On the 19th of June the newly-arrived despatches from England were opened and read in Council. Hastings learned that Macleane's offer of his resignation had been accepted, and that a new Councillor had been appointed to the vacant seat. Little as he relished the use to which his agents had turned the trust confided to them, in spite of his recent letters and avowals, and of the "public contest" to which they had committed him, Hastings was not prepared to disavow their act. "I held myself bound by it"—he wrote to Lord North—"and was resolved to ratify it."* But Clavering's hasty violence defeated its own end. On the very next day that hot-headed officer installed himself as Governor-General, and directed the troops in

* Gleig's "Warren Hastings," Vol. 2, Chap. IV.

Fort William and the neighbouring stations to obey no other orders than his own. From Hastings he demanded the keys of the Treasury and the Fort. Needless to say that Francis supported his colleague and tool in this course of lawless usurpation.* But Hastings had no mind to throw up the game under such conditions. In the army and the civil service he could still count upon many friends. His counter-orders to the troops were cheerfully obeyed. Colonel Morgan closed the gates of Fort William against his own Commander-in-Chief; and a like answer came from Barrackpore. An appeal from Hastings to the Supreme Court resulted in a fresh victory for the Governor-General. All four judges ruled that Clavering had no power to assume an office which Hastings had not yet formally resigned.†

Hastings and Barwell were for going yet further. They carried in Council a vote that Clavering had by his own act vacated his seat as senior member. But here the judges interposed with their opinion that Hastings had no legal power to declare such vacancy; and they advised

* When the game was clearly lost, he came forward as a mediator!—Auber's "British Power in India," Chap. 10.

† See letters to Sykes and Lord North in Vol. 2, Chap. iv. of Gleig's "Life."

a reference of that and other questions to the home government. While still holding to his own view on this point, Hastings cheerfully bowed to the decision of judges who had little cause to love his defeated rival, but were unwilling, as Impey said, "to thwart the measures" of the English Ministry.*

On the 29th of August Sir John Clavering died of dysentery. Hastings had steadily refused to resign his office to the man who, by illegally claiming it, had to his thinking forfeited the seat he still retained. Monson's successor, Wheler, did not arrive before December. Hastings, therefore, would for some months remain supreme in his own Council, and free to carry out his own plans. From the day of Clavering's defeat, indeed, to that of his own retirement, he never lost the ascendency which the folly of his enemies and his own firmness had combined to guard for him at the most critical moment of his career. New councillors might come to help or hinder him; his enemies might weave new plots against himself or his friends; but thenceforth he never loosened his hold on the reins which Clavering's violence had saved him from yielding up to Macleane's indiscretion.

* "Memoirs of Sir E. Impey," Chap. 6.

CHAPTER IV.

1777—1784.

Shortly before Clavering's death Hastings found himself free at last to marry the lady for whom he had so long waited. Baron Imhoff went back to his fatherland, and the accomplished Marian became the wife of the man whose heart she had won eight years before on board the *Duke of Grafton.* Among the guests at the wedding feast was Clavering himself, whom Hastings, prompted by the kindliest motives, carried off against his will to the scene of rejoicing at Government House. What his vanquished rival may have felt, as he joined "the gay circle which surrounded the bride,"* we cannot tell; but there is no warrant for connecting his after illness with the events of that particular day. He was taken

* Macaulay's Essay on Hastings.

ill in fact on his way home from a visit to Sir Elijah Impey.*

The old man's death, however—as Hastings wrote to a friend in November—"has produced a state of quiet in our councils, which I shall endeavour to preserve during the remainder of the time which may be allotted to me. The interests of the Company will benefit by it; that is to say they will not suffer, as they have done, by the effects of a divided administration." Francis of course pursued the crooked tenour of his old ways, still blinding Hastings to the full strength of his evil nature by the "levity" with which he made and revoked his promises of support to this or that measure proposed in Council But he always found himself in a minority of one, and neither of his colleagues gave any signs of failing health.

Wheler's arrival in December brought Francis a new ally, whom Hastings vainly tried to conciliate. But Barwell's steadfast loyalty ensured to his old friend the casting vote. "The two junior members"—wrote the latter to Lawrence Sulivan—"may tease, but they cannot impede

* Impey's letter to Lord Bathurst ("Memoirs of Sir E. Impey.")

business;"* and the Governor-General took all fair advantage of so encouraging a fact. The commission he had appointed to revise the land-settlements pursued its work without further hindrance. In the following year he turned Mohammad Reza Khan out of the office which Clavering had revived for him; and he relieved the Nawab of Bengal, now twenty years old, of the guardianship which he no longer required.

At the same time Hastings encouraged the Government of Bombay to form a new alliance with Ragoba and other Maratha leaders against Nana Farnavís and the French. In May 1778 a force commanded by Colonel Leslie was dispatched from Bengal towards the Narbada, and two months later his beloved friend, Alexander Elliot, left Calcutta to negotiate an alliance with the Rajah of Berar.† By that time he knew that war with France had already begun; and the Government of Madras was speedily empowered to make common cause with Haidar Ali against all enemies. Nine battalions were added to the

* Gleig's "Warren Hastings," Vol. 2, Chap. v.

† "For once," Hastings writes to Impey, on July 20, "I am pleased with Francis. Elliot is gone. A most critical service, and likely to prove the era of a new system in the British Empire in India, if it succeeds."—MS. Letters in the British Museum (the Impey Collection).

Bengal Army, and other measures of defence were taken betimes against the coming storm, from whatever quarter it might blow. Chandarnagar was promptly occupied by our troops. About this time our countrymen in Calcutta had heard not only of the war with France, but of the disastrous issue of General Burgoyne's campaign against the revolted colonists in North America; and Francis made the news of Burgoyne's surrender a plea tor urging the recal of Leslie's column, "lest it should undergo the same fate." But Hastings was not the man to abandon lightly a scheme which he had not lightly undertaken.

His temper had been sorely tried in May by the wavering conduct of the Bombay Government, at the moment when his efforts on their behalf seemed ripe for a happy issue. He had encouraged them in every way to carry out their own scheme for replacing Ragoba at the head of the Maratha power. "We promised to support it," he writes to Impey, in June, "with our influence, our treasure, our army. We realised our promises. We sent them an instant supply of ten lakhs of rupees. We formed a powerful detachment to march to their assistance. We urged (for we could not command), we urged the Government of Fort St. George, by the strongest arguments that we could use without authority, to supply them with a military force. We have finally engaged the Intermediate Powers of Indostan in their cause." Governor Hornby, "not a social man," drank success to the undertaking at a public dinner in Bombay. A sufficient force of Europeans and Sepoys was got ready to escort Ragoba to Puna as soon as his partisans might give the word. But the Governor of Bombay took sudden fright at the non-arrival of reinforcements from Madras, and at the resistance offered by two members of his Council to any movement on behalf of Ragoba. Leslie's column was ordered to halt on its westward march; and the disappointed Governor-General gave free vent to his annoyance in the letter from which I have just quoted. "Is this," he exclaims, "ingratitude, envy, stupidity, or pusillanimity, or all together? . . . . What to do I know not. I feel myself on this occasion as I have often done at chess, when my adversary, by giving his Tower the oblique movement of a Knight, has placed the game in a position for which I had never made provision."*

* MS. Letters in the British Museum

In a long letter he entreated Hornby not to abandon one who had rendered him no common service; and the appeal, as events showed, was not made wholly in vain. For his own part, indeed, he knows what ought to be done. "The eyes of all Indostan are turned upon this great enterprize, and expect great things from it." Of its success he is morally certain, "if it is prosecuted, and the people of Bombay do not counteract us; but I fear they will, and I fear my own want of credit at home." He will pause, however, so he tells Impey, "till other lights break in upon me, either from Bombay, or perhaps from England."

It was not long before some new light broke in upon him. The Bombay Government once more turned for help to Bengal. Hastings himself, like a good chess-player, planned a happy move in a new direction. He would secure the friendship of Múdají Bhosla, the Rajah of Berár, by favouring his claims, as a descendant of Sivají, to the nominal sovereignty of the Marátha race. On the 13th of July he writes to Impey, "I am prepared for the worst that can befal me, but shall not part with my place with quite the unconcern in which I should have resigned it in a time of peace. Yet I am grievously shackled, and I feel it. I am busy drawing up Elliot's instructions. If he gets safe to Naugpoor, and Leslie to the banks of the Nerbudda, my mind will be quite at ease." His colleagues seem for once to have agreed in forwarding their President's purpose. Pleased with them, with himself, and confident in the envoy of his own choosing, in his next letter to Impey, on the 17th, the Governor-General rises into a firmer and happier tone. Elliot's commission, he says, "promises well, and I am sure he will execute it well. His instructions will be opposed. Let them."*

Elliot's death in September on the road to Nágpúr proved to Hastings a bitter sorrow and "an irreparable loss." In October he was about to recal Colonel Leslie, who had been loitering away four precious months in Bundalkhand, when Leslie's death at once cleared the field for his destined successor, Colonel Goddard, "one of the best executive officers," wrote Hastings, "in the service."† Before the end of January 1779 the new commander had carried his little army without a check across India as far as Burhánpúr. But the main purpose of his march had already been frustrated by the disastrous blundering of

* Ibidem. † Gleig's "Warren Hastings," Vol. 2, Chap. vi.

those whom he had been sent to aid. The Bombay column, which set out from Panwell, full of confidence, on the 25th of November, took nearly a month to crown the Gháts beyond which lay the Peshwa's capital. On the 9th of January it lay only eighteen miles from Púna. But a strange panic beset the commanders. A retreat was ordered; the heavy guns were thrown into a pond; and nothing but the cool courage of Captain Hartley and his faithful Sepoys saved from destruction a force which, properly handled, might have driven the enemy before it like chaff, and borne Ragoba in triumph to Púna. On the 13th of January, 1779, the English leaders crowned their disgrace by the Convention of Wargaum, which surrendered to the Marathas all that our arms had won in Western India since 1765.

Neither at Bombay nor Calcutta was any respect shown for so disgraceful a compact. The officers who signed it were dismissed the Company's service. Goddard was ordered to insist on a new treaty with Nana Farnavís. Ragoba with Sindia's connivance made his way to Surat. Nana Farnavís demanded his surrender, and invited Haidar Ali to join him and the Nizam in a league against the English. In

January 1780 Goddard once more took the field. In the course of a few weeks he captured Ahmadabad, the stately capital of Gujarát, and twice defeated the combined forces of Sindia and Holkar.

Meanwhile another Bengal column, which Hastings had sent across the Jamna under the daring Popham, drove Sindia's Marathas before them, and stormed the fort of Lahár on the road from Kalpi to Gwáliár. In August two companies of his Sepoys under Captain Bruce,* aided by twenty English soldiers, carried by escalade the rock-perched fortress of Gwaliar itself, which the veteran Sir Eyre Coote, the new member of Hastings' Council in the room of Clavering, had pronounced it madness to attack. Before the year's end Bassein had surrendered to the victorious Goddard; and the dashing Hartley crowned his former achievements by utterly defeating 20,000 Marathas, who had been vainly attacking him for two days.

These successes, in no small measure due to Hastings' well-laid plans and his happy choice of competent officers, were followed in March 1781 by the surprise and rout of Mahdaji Sindia at the

* Brother of the famous African explorer.

hands of Popham's successor, Colonel Camac, during his retreat from Sironj. In the west, however, Goddard was less fortunate. A mighty gathering of Marathas under the Nana himself barred his advance to Púna, while Parasrám Bhao was already harassing his rear. To march back over the Ghats in the face of 60,000 pursuers, keen for his destruction, was all that he could do; and, thanks to his own skill and the courage of his soldiers, his little force arrived at Panwell safe, but sadly reduced in numbers, before the end of April.

By this time events had happened in Southern India which threatened to undo all that English arms and statesmanship had achieved elsewhere. Ever since 1772 Haidar Ali had lost no opportunity of strengthening himself and enlarging his boundaries at the expense of his weaker neighbours. The conquest of Kurg was followed by the recovery of the districts lately torn from him by the Marathas. Before the end of 1778 he had pushed his frontier northwards to the Kistna, and carried his arms westward over Malabar. More than once his dread of the Marathas had tempted him into making overtures to the English at Madras. But the latter, full of their own quarrels, schemes, perplexities, gave little heed to the wooings of a neighbour whose friendliness they had some reason to distrust. After Dupré's departure from Madras, the affairs of that Presidency fell into ever worse confusion. One Governor was sent home in disgrace, for allowing the ruler of the Carnatic to conquer and annex Tanjór. Another, Lord Pigott, quarrelled with his Council about the claims of some English creditors against the revenues of the restored Rajah of that country, and was held prisoner by his colleagues for eight months until his death. And his successor, Sir Thomas Rumbold, an old Bengal civilian, became from the hour of his arrival at Madras, in 1778, a mark for the many slanders and unjust reproaches which were destined long to survive him.

Hardly had Rumbold entered on his new office when the tidings of war between France and England pointed to the necessity of a prompt attack on the French possessions in Southern India. After the fall of Pondicherry in October, Mahé alone on the western coast remained in French hands. In March 1779 that place also fell to our arms. Haidar's wrath at the capture of a town which some of his own troops had helped to defend was presently inflamed by the march of a British force through a strip of his own territory into the Gantúr Sarkár, a province which the ruler of Maisúr had long been coveting, but which Basalat Jang, the Nizam's brother, had lately rented to the Government of Madras in return for the use of a British contingent.

In his anxiety to conciliate the ambitious sovereign of Maisúr, Rumbold would have suspended the movement against Mahé. But Sir Eyre Coote, who was then at Madras on his way to Calcutta, made use of his power as Commander-in-Chief and *ex officio* member of the Madras Council, to overrule the Governor's pleadings for delay.* Rumbold's dealings with Basalat Jang seem at first to have been sanctioned by Hastings himself. They were justified by the conduct of Nizam Ali, the ruler of the Dakhan, who took into his own pay the French troops dismissed by his brother. This was a clear breach of his treaties with the Madras Government. That Government, on the other hand, owed him some arrears of tribute for the other Sarkars, which they had promised to pay up "as soon as they were in cash." They now offered

* Appendix to Marshman's "History of India," Vol. 1.

to pay up as soon as he could fully satisfy them regarding the French troops.

No offer could have been more reasonable. But the Nizam, who had already been plotting against his English allies, easily caught at any handle for shifting to others the blame of his own hostile acts. The support which the English had given to Ragoba, and the prospect of an alliance between Hastings and the Rajah of Berar, had lately tempted him to concoct a grand league with Nana Farnavís and Haidar Ali against the British power. But Haidar's treachery was even then at work against his fellow-plotter. The wily Sultan of Maisúr had obtained or tried to obtain from the phantom king of Delhi a formal grant of sovereignty over all the Nizam's dominions. Nizam Ali deemed it prudent to pause betimes on the brink of an open rupture with his old friends. His agents seem to have succeeded in putting Hastings on the wrong scent. In his eagerness to detach the Nizam from a formidable confederacy, the Governor-General was led to believe that the Nizam's quarrel with the English concerned only his arrears of tribute and the occupation of Gantúr. Nizam Ali was therefore soothed with timely assurances that the Madras troops should be recalled from Gantúr, and that his tribute should be paid.

Haidar for his part would take no excuse for further delaying the fulfilment of his long-hoarded revenge. Deaf to the overtures now made by Rumbold, both through his own agent and the famous missionary, Swartz, the fierce old monarch prepared in his seventy-eighth year for a campaign which might end in driving the Farangi unbelievers into the sea. His own army, well equipped and trained by French officers, would be supported by the yet more numerous hosts which Nana Farnavís had promised to launch against the common foe.

In the middle of 1780 the storm burst. Neither Hastings nor the Madras Council had clearly foreseen the moment of its coming. Just before his retirement in April, Rumbold recorded his belief that Southern India would "remain quiet." Earlier in the year Hastings had written to Rumbold—"I am convinced from Haidar's conduct and disposition that he will never molest us while we preserve a good understanding with him." Even Sir Hector Munro, the head of the Madras Army, seems to have scouted the notion of impending danger from the highlands of

Maisúr. On the 19th of June it was known at Madras that Haidar had begun his march from Seringapatam ; yet even then, and for some weeks afterwards, Munro and Whitehill, the new Governor, refused to believe that trouble was near at hand.

At last about the 20th of July the hosts of Maisúr, ninety thousand strong, poured like a lava-flood through the mountain passes into the plains of the Carnatic ; and the smoke of burning towns and villages erelong told its tale of horror to scared beholders on the heights near Madras.

In order to meet this formidable inroad Munro set out for Kanjeveram a month afterwards, with about 5,000 men and forty guns. Colonel Baillie with half that number was marching thither from Gantúr. Had Munro on this occasion proved equal to his old renown, a great disaster would have been avoided. But of him it might truly be said, *Quantum mutatus ab illo Hectore*—how changed from the Hector Munro who in 1764 had routed the formidable hosts of Shuja-ad-daula at Bakhsar ! By the 9th of September Baillie had fought his way to a place within easy reach of the main body. The next morning he had gained a point whence the great pagoda of

Kanjeveram could be clearly seen rising above a broad belt of verdure. Munro himself advanced a few miles towards his fellow-commander. Haidar's army, which still lay between them, was on the very brink of retreating, lest it should find itself placed between two fires. But Munro came to a sudden halt. Not an inch further would he move, in spite of the heavy firing which soon began to deal havoc in Baillie's ranks. Late in the afternoon a wounded Sepoy brought him the first news of Baillie's ruinous defeat after a long and heroic struggle against hopeless odds.

Returning at once to Kanjeveram, Munro was soon to learn that the wrecks of Baillie's column, about 300 officers and men, nearly all wounded, had surrendered to the ruthless victor, whose French officers alone saved them from being slaughtered where they stood. Pressed for supplies and stunned by a disaster which he might have prevented, Munro threw his heavy guns into a tank, left much of his baggage behind him, and hurried back to St. Thomas's Mount near Madras. Haidar meanwhile proceeded at his leisure to waste the Carnatic with fire and sword.

In that hour of his country's need, when the Madras Council knew not which way to turn for help against the ravening Tiger of Maisúr, when the war in Western India still raged as fiercely as ever, and the Rajah of Berar seemed likely to turn against his English friends, Hastings' courage rose at once to the occasion. His old enemy, Francis, whom he had wounded in a duel a few weeks before, might still oppose him, and his old friend Barwell had sailed home. But the brave though headstrong old warrior, Sir Eyre Coote, was prompt in answering the call of manifest duty; and even Wheeler had sometimes voted with the Governor-General. On the 25th of September—two days after receiving the news of Baillie's surrender—Hastings carried through Council a vote for the immediate despatch of troops and money to the seat of war.* He was also empowered to treat for an alliance with the Maráthas through the Rajah of Berar. A few days afterwards he issued an order removing Whitehill, the acting Governor of Madras, from his post, for refusing to restore Gantúr to Basalat Jang. The Company's remittances were kept back for that year, and a war-loan was speedily raised in Calcutta. On the 14th of October a small but well-equipped force of Europeans and Lascars

* Gleig's "Warren Hastings," Vol. 2, Chap. viii.

dropped down the Húghli for Madras. A few days later Coote himself sailed from Calcutta to command the army which was destined to retrieve in many a hard fight and perilous march the disasters and disgrace of the past September.

About the same time Hastings ventured on another of those "frantic military exploits" which his short-sighted critics were so ready to condemn beforehand. Mindful of Goddard's daring march across India, he prepared to send another Sepoy column overland from Bengal to the scene of danger; a distance of seven hundred miles. Early in the following January Pearse began his memorable march southwards into Orissa, a province already occupied by troops from Berar, whose Rajah had just declined to mediate with the Court of Púna. But Hastings was not to bo daunted by a show of unfriendliness which meant only a prudent care for the Rajah's own well-being. "Acts"—he wrote—"that proclaim confidence and a determined spirit in the hour of adversity, are the surest means of retrieving it. Self-distrust will never fail to create a distrust in others, and make them become your enemies; for in no part of the world is the principle of supporting a rising interest and depressing a falling one more prevalent than in India."

Pearse was ordered to march on in the teeth of all opposition, but to avoid, if he could, any hostile encounter with the Berar troops. Meanwhile Hastings smoothed the way for his advance by deputing Anderson, one of his trustiest subalterns, to purchase the cooperation of the Maratha general with offers of money and promises of help.* Anderson's errand was crowned with complete success. Two thousand Maratha horse gave Pearse the strength he needed in that arm; and the Rajah of Berar himself was converted, in Hastings' words, from "an ostensible enemy into a declared friend;" while Bengal was saved "from a state of dangerous alarm, if not from actual invasion and all the horrors of a predatory war."

At Ganjam, on the southern border of Orissa, Pearse's column encountered that deadly foe, the cholera, with whose ravages the world has since become but too familiar. In a few weeks nearly a thousand of our brave Sepoys died of this new and fearful scourge, which presently reached Calcutta, and made, says Hastings, "an alarming havoc for about ten days," in the month of April, 1781.

* Hastings himself furnished three lakhs of rupees out of the sixteen thus offered.

On the 5th of the previous November Coote landed at Madras, only to find matters in the worst possible plight. The Government was paralysed. Haidar's cavalry had swept the surrounding country for supplies and plunder, and the people themselves were ill-disposed to their feeble protectors. Arkot had already fallen, and one of Haidar's generals was besieging Wandiwash. As soon as he could gather a few thousand troops with the needful supplies, Coote on the 17th of January 1781 hurried off towards the scene of his great victory won about twenty-one years before over Bussy. The mere news of the veteran's approach frightened the enemy away from Wandiwash, which young Flint, aided by 300 Sepoys, had defended with the courage of a second Clive. After the relief of another stronghold and the capture of a third, Coote struck off southward for Kadalór. The supplies which he expected from the fleet were long in coming, and it was not till the middle of June that he found himself able to make a bold but fruitless dash at the fortified pagoda of Chilambram on the Kalarún.

While Coote after this repulse was resting his troops at Porto Novo, he learned that Haidar with an army ten times his own numbers sought to bar his return to Kadalór. This was all that Coote wanted. On the 1st of July the fiery veteran launched his eight thousand men against the myriads of Maisur with a skill and resolute courage that nothing could long withstand. After six hours of hard fighting and steadfast waiting, Coote struck his crowning blow; and the enemy fled, carrying off all their guns, but leaving thousands of dead and wounded on a field which Coote had won with the loss of only three hundred men.* This victory secured our hold upon Southern India, and set Coote free to join hands with the Bengal column under Colonel Pearse.

In August the two armies clashed again at Haidar's challenge near the scene of Baillie's great disaster; but the victory of Palilór proved less decisive than that of Porto Novo. On the 27th of September, however, Coote surprised and utterly routed his great antagonist at Sholingarh. By this time the Dutch also had joined the war against England. But, thanks to Hastings' influence and Coote's strategy, bolder counsels were prevailing at Madras. The Nawab of the

* Stubbs's "History of the Bengal Artillery," Vol. 1, Ch. iii.

Carnatic had been relieved of all control over the revenues he had hitherto squandered on himself. In November Negapatam was captured from the Dutch by a force which Lord Macartney, the new Governor of Madras, had sent against it under Sir Hector Munro, aided by the fleet of Sir Edward Hughes. This was followed, early in the next year, by the capture of Trincomalí, the finest harbour in Ceylon.

Still the war went on with varying fortune throughout the year 1782. The relief of Vellór by the aged and war worn Coote was counter-balanced by the destruction of Colonel Brathwaite's column in Tanjór at the hands of Tippu, after a fight prolonged with matchless heroism for twenty-six hours. A timely reinforcement from Bombay enabled the brave defenders of Talicharri in Malabar to rout the army which had besieged them for eighteen months. But Kadalór was taken with the help of Haidar's French allies; and Sir Edward Hughes was too late to save Trincomalí from the fate designed for it by the brilliant Suffrein, the Nelson of France. The fleets commanded by these two great sailors never met without doing each other the utmost damage, at the smallest possible gain to either side.

Coote's tireless energy once more rescued Wandiwash, and dealt Tippu another hard blow near Arni in June. But the ill-timed absence of the fleet baffled his attempt to regain Kadalór by surprise; and later in the year his health, broken down by prolonged toil, anxiety, and more than one fit of apoplexy, drove the old warrior back for a few months' rest to Calcutta. On the Malabar coast our troops and garrisons were hard beset by the hosts of Tippu, on whom one or two repulses made but small impression. In spite of his successful struggle against heavy odds, Humberstone was well nigh driven into a corner, when the news of Haidar Ali's death sent Tippu off with the bulk of his army in hot haste to the camp at Chitúr, where his famous father had breathed his last on the 7th December at the age of eighty, weary of waging war, as he said at last, "with a nation whom he might have made his friends, but whom the defeat of many Baillies and Brathwaites would never destroy."

At that moment, indeed, things looked dark enough for our countrymen in Madras. Refugees from the wasted plains of the Carnatic were dying in the Black Town at the rate of fifteen hundred a week. The monsoon gales on the eastern coast had been playing sad havoc with English merchantmen and native coasters. Hughes's fleet, on which so much depended, was disabled by sickness and much fighting. A strong French force, under the renowned Bussy, was hourly expected to land at Kadalór from the fleet which Suffrein was waiting to lead thither. In Coote's absence, the chief command in Madras devolved upon General Stuart, an officer whose unfitness was soon to reveal itself. And to crown all, Nana Farnavís still hung back from ratifying the treaty by which Hastings hoped to detach the whole Marátha power from its alliance with Maisúr.

But with the news of Haidar's death, the indecission of the Court of Puna· passed away. Early in 1783 the crafty minister affixed the Peshwa's seal to the memorable Treaty of Salbai, which had been signed by Mádhaji Sindia for himself and fellow princes in the previous May. By this treaty Hastings wisely surrendered much to gain a good deal more. If Sindia recovered all his lost possessions save Gwaliar, and Bassein with some other districts was made over to the young Peshwa, the Marathas on the other hand were pledged to aid Hastings' Government, should need arise, in its further dealings with Maisur.

One dangerous thorn was thus removed from the great proconsul's side, and his countrymen in India were already discounting the prospects of a speedy issue to the war in the south. But the snake, though scotched, was not yet killed. Trusting in the support of his French allies, Tippu prepared to carry on the war with all his father's energy, if not with all his father's genius. For a time Fortune still seemed to favour him. Haidar's stoutest foe, Sir Eyre Coote, died in April, two days after his landing at Madras. Bussy's troops had already been disembarked at Kadalor; but Coote's successor, the feeble Stuart, wasted some precious weeks in his march towards that stronghold, although he knew that Tippu had gone off westward to avenge himself on Matthews for the loss of Bednór. In three months Bednór's new master was forced to surrender on terms which Tippu took care to violate. Mangalór was closely besieged. Meanwhile Stuart's army, having at last encamped on the 6th June before Kadalór, carried the outer line of Bussy's defences after a hard day's fighting on the 13th. But Suffrein presently grappled with his old antagonist Hughes, and another drawn battle resulted in the latter sailing off to repair damages at Madras. Reinforced by Suffrein's sailors, Bussy made a strong sortie on the 25th against his besiegers; but his signal repulse by a regiment of Bengal Sepoys did little to mend Stuart's prospects. His fine array was fast dwindling away from sickness and short supplies, when the news of peace between France and England came just in time to mar Suffrein's schemes for our undoing, and to rob Tippu of his last and doughtiest allies. In accordance with the Treaty of Versailles, Bussy withdrew his troops from Tippu's service, and Stuart's army returned in safety to Madras.

Erelong a powerful force, under Colonel Fullarton, was marching up into the highlands of Maisur. Before the end of November, Seringapatam itself lay almost within his grasp, while Tippu's army was still engaged at Mangalór. But the Governor of Madras, unheeding the counsel and the commands of Hastings,* had already begun to treat with Tippu for the peace which Fullarton would have dictated under the walls of Seringapatam. That brave officer was

* It was Hastings' aim, among other things, to bring about a treaty in which the Nawab of Arkot should appear as a principal, backed by the Marathas and the Nizam.

ordered to fall back in compliance with a truce which the wily Sultan was openly breaking. Not till Mangalór had surrendered in January, 1784, did Tippu deign to admit the envoys from Lord Macartney into his camp, and to discuss the terms of a treaty which flattered his own pride at the expense of those who had brought him to the brink of ruin. On the 11th March the insults and indignities which he had heaped on the heads of British envoys, were crowned by the sight of two English gentlemen standing bareheaded for two hours, beseeching him to sign the treaty they held in their hands. At the intercession of envoys from Puna and Haidarabad, he at length agreed to ratify a peace which restored to each party their former possessions, and rescued more than a thousand Englishmen—the surviving witnesses of Haidar's savagery—from the slow torture of prison life in Maisur.

CHAPTER V.

1779—1780.

In the foregoing chapter we have followed the stream of war through many windings to its two-fold outlet in the Treaty of Salbai and the peace concluded with Maisur. Throughout that chequered story, the slender form of Warren Hastings rises clear in the background, as of England's guardian angel, foreshaping and ever trying to help forward the policy which other hands, not always the most capable, must be left to execute. To his influence were largely owing the great *things done or attempted by Goddard, Popham,* Pearse, and the veteran Coote himself. He had saved Madras in spite of its own weak and wayward Government; he had greatly strengthened the hands of Governor Hornby at Bombay; he had taught the ablest of Indian statesmen to acknowledge English excellence in diplomacy as well as arms. The credit of saving British India during a crisis, in many ways more formidable than the Great Mutiny of 1857, belongs especially to Hastings, if not to Hastings alone.

But we must now return to his own personal history and the affairs of Bengal. For some time after Clavering's death, the Governor-General had the casting-vote in his Council. But Barwell's loyalty to his friend could not be expected to hold out for ever against his natural craving to return home. Enough that it held out till 1780, the year after Sir Eyre Coote's arrival in Calcutta. That brave, but irritable and wayward officer, voted in a fitful sort of way with Hastings rather than Francis. Anxious to relieve his friend of a burden that grew daily less bearable, Hastings came at last to a truce with his old opponent, on terms which, for the moment, satisfied him that Barwell's absence would not mar his plans for the public good.* In February a bargain was formally concluded, by which Francis pledged himself to give Hastings' policy a general support for a given period, in return for a few concessions to the claims of Francis on behalf of his own friends. Fowke, for instance, was to resume his old post

* Sir John D'Oyley, the Company's Advocate, was the chief author of this arrangement.

at Banaras, and an office of higher dignity under the Nawab of Bengal was to be found for Mohammad Reza Khan. Hastings' pleasure at this seeming reconciliation left no room for latent misgivings. His reliance on "Francis' faith and honour," as well as on his own discretion, was freely expressed in a letter to Laurence Sulivan. "Francis," he added, "has behaved so openly, and with so little of the reserve and caution of a man actuated by indirect views, that I am certain, and venture to promise you, that I shall suffer no loss of power or influence by Mr. Barwell's departure, ... and that I shall find Mr. Francis both true to his engagements, and ready and willing to give me his support and assistance, to the period destined for our acting together as joint members of this administration."*

Wheeler also exchanged with Hastings the most cordial pledges of future goodwill. Barwell bore himself and his wealth home to England with a mind, perhaps, all the easier for his timely escape from another quarrel in which he had thus far stood neutral between the Council and the Supreme Court.

* Gleig's Warren Hastings, Vol. ii. Chap. 6.

This quarrel, which went very near to estrange Hastings from his old friend Impey, arose out of the new jurisdiction created by the Regulating Act of 1773. The large and vague powers thereby entrusted to the Judges of the Supreme Court were pretty sure to bring them, sooner or later, into disastrous conflict with the local Government. For some time, thanks to the good sense of Hastings and the judges, little harm ensued. Had Hastings' scheme for removing the friction between those rival powers been adopted by the home Government as readily as it had been endorsed by Impey and his brother judges, the scandals which furnished Macaulay with materials for one more savage outburst against the modern Jeffries, would never have occurred. In 1776, Hastings had proposed to invest the Supreme Court with "an unlimited, but not exclusive authority," over all the Company's Courts, reserving for the latter their special jurisdiction in cases which specially concerned the Government itself.* But his scheme was shelved by the English Ministry, and the violence of his own colleagues thwarted his efforts to adjust the new machinery to the facts and conditions of our rule

* Gleig's "Warren Hastings," Vol. ii. Chap. 2.

in India. "It seems," he wrote in 1776, "to have been a maxim of the Board to force the Court into extremities, for the purpose of finding fault with them." The spirit of discord in his own Council let loose the waters of strife among the most litigious people in the world.

Violence on one side begat violence on the other. The authority of the Crown Judges was defied at every turn, on pretexts often of the hollowest kind. Impey and his colleagues would have been more or less than human, had they always foreborne to assert their lawful powers on behalf of those who claimed their protection. Hastings himself had borne witness to many "glaring acts of oppression" committed by the Company's servants, and their underlings, in the process of collecting the Company's revenues. Two of these cases, as related by Impey in a letter to Lord Weymouth,* suffice to show in what quarter the reign of terror, as described by Macaulay, really began. It was not "Impey's alguazils," but the agents, white and black, of the Calcutta Council, who ought to have furnished the great essayist with fit themes for eloquent in-

* Memoirs of Sir E. Impey, Chap. 5.

vective. One poor lady, widow of an Amrah, or Moghal nobleman, had been driven, it seems, to the verge of suicide, through the indignities heaped upon her by the underlings sent to execute an unjust decree of the Patna Council. The Supreme Court took up her cause, and an appeal against their sentence was afterwards dismissed by the King in Council.

"The vultures of Bengal," as the Chief Justice called the authors and abettors of such wrong-doing, loudly objected to all interference with their high-handed or predatory ways; and Francis, as a thing of course, took their part. Impey and one or two of his colleagues strove, for a time successfully, to keep such interference within due bounds. If they stood between the *rayats* and their alleged oppressors, they left the Company's Courts to deal with all questions of mere revenue. But the zeal of Mr Justice Hyde outran discretion. During Impey's absence in the latter part of 1779, he issued a writ against the Rajah of Kásijura. A sheriff's officer, with a band of armed Sepoys and sailors, entered the Rajah's house, and sequestered all his property, including an idol, which was "packed like a common utensil in a basket, and scaled up with the other lumber."* Happily his women and children had saved themselves, by timely flight, from that worst insult to an Indian gentleman, the violation of his zenana.†

This was more than even Hastings could well bear. A party of Sepoys were at once ordered off to capture the whole posse of Hyde's followers, and escort them to Calcutta, where they were sent about their business. Similar steps were taken to protect the Rani of Rajsháhi and other Zamindars from the pains and penalties threatened by the Supreme Court. For several months of 1780, the province was kept in turmoil by the conflicting claims of its political and judicial chiefs. A war of writs on the one hand, of proclamations on the other, raged with increasing violence, until at last the Calcutta Judges issued a summons against the Government itself; a proceeding which the latter, strong in its temporary union, laughed to scorn. It seemed as if the whole machinery of government in Bengal were fast approaching a dead lock.

* Hastings' letter to Baber (Memoirs, Vol. ii., Chap. 6).

† The women's apartments, screened off by a Pardah, or curtain, from the rest of the house.

At last the long quarrel was allayed by one of the wisest measures which Hastings ever planned or carried through; a measure for which Impey has been loaded with undeserved infamy by hasty and misinformed judges of his Indian career. Before the end of October, the Presidency of the Sadr Dewani Adalat—the Company's chief civil court in Bengal, which Hastings had remodelled some months earlier—was conferred on Impey by the Governor-General. The Chief Justice, in all sincerity, accepted the olive-branch held out to him by his old friend. This arrangement, which brought peace and civil order to Bengal, Macaulay, with more than his usual rashness, represents as the offering and taking of a bribe. Bengal was saved, he says, and the Chief Justice "was rich, quiet, and infamous." The atrocious language used by the essayist on this occasion, can hardly be palliated by the false estimate which he had formed of Impey's character from the first. Long before his own death, Macaulay had the means of knowing that this particular charge was absurdly untrue. There would have been nothing wrong or strange in the acceptance of a special salary for a separate office involving added work. The Court of Directors were quite willing to give the new judge £5,000, or even £8,000 a-year.* One of his colleagues, Sir Robert Chambers, was presently drawing a large addition to his salary, from an office held by him under the Government of Bengal. But it remains an undoubted fact that Impey, for various reasons, declined the £5,000 a-year which the Calcutta Council offered him for his new post.

That the new arrangement was a good stroke of policy on Hastings' part, the result made sufficiently clear. An able lawyer, an upright judge, and a painstaking reformer, Impey began by drawing up a plain and serviceable code of rules for the guidance of the courts placed under his control. The young English judges in the country courts soon learned to mend their ways, and to shape their judgments in accordance with the principles laid down by their new Mentor. The old broils between rival authorities disappeared; law and order erelong reigned once more throughout Bengal; waste lands were brought under the plough; and revenue began to flow with its former freedom into the Company's treasury.†

* Memoirs of Sir E. Impey, Chap. 10.

† Hastings' work was erelong undone by the Court of Directors, and it was not till 1860 that the Crown's and Company's chief Courts were finally amalgamated.

Before the year's end, Francis had set out on his voyage home, bearing with him a large fortune, not all fairly won,* and an undying grudge against Impey and the Governor-General. The former had once cast him in heavy damages, on an action brought by the husband of a lady whose character Francis had blighted by a love-intrigue.† To Hastings, on the other hand, he owed not only many a thwarted scheme, but the crowning mortification of a wound received in a duel of his own seeking.

How Hastings came to appear, as he himself said, "in the odious character of a duellist," must now be explained. His new understanding with Francis soon shared the fate of all compacts in which bad faith or a defective memory plays any part. Two months had hardly passed, before Francis showed signs of relapsing into his old obstructive ways. Various measures proposed by Hastings for carrying on the campaign against Sindia, were rejected by his old rival on pretexts manifestly unfair. Sir John D'Oyley once more essayed the part of mediator; but Francis shuf-

* Memoirs of Sir E. Impey, Chap 12.

† Nicholl's "Recollections and Reflections," Vol. 1. Mrs. Legrand afterwards married the famous Prince Talleyrand.

fled out of his pledges with Protean cunning, and an effrontery all his own. Devoid of the military genius which enabled Hastings to achieve great results with means seemingly inadequate, he insisted on recalling Popham from the scene of his impending victory at Gwáliár, and did his worst to hinder the advance of Camac's column into Malwa. "I am not Governor," wrote Hastings to Sulivan, with a bitterness easy to understand: "all the powers I possess are those of preventing the rule from falling into worse hands than my own." Fortunately his opponent's temporary illness left Hastings free to save India in his own way. Popham was not recalled; and the brilliant capture of Gwaliar bore timely witness alike to Popham's soldiership, and the happy daring of the Governor-General.

But it only added fresh fuel to the flame of Francis' rancour. He complained that Hastings had taken unfair advantage of his absence from Calcutta, and coolly denied the fact of any concessions made by him during his illness to Sir John D'Oyley. This was more than the patience even of Hastings could digest. On the 15th August, in reply to one of Francis' minutes, he used these words in Council—"I do not trust to his promise of candour, convinced that he is incapable of it. I judge of his public conduct by my experience of his private, which I have found to be devoid of truth and honour."*

No wonder that he should have lost his temper at this new evidence of his opponent's treachery. At the very moment when our rule in India depended upon the energy, foresight, and firm courage of his own government, he found himself once more baffled and befooled by the man, whose promises of support had alone emboldened him to dispense with Barwell's aid. No wonder that Hastings taxed his old enemy with repeated falsehoods, and wilful breaches of faith. It is easy to say that this new quarrel arose from mutual misunderstandings; but all the evidence and likelihoods go to fasten the whole blame of it on Francis himself. To take his word in this matter against that of Hastings and Sir John D'Oyley, would be an act of simple injustice to the two latter. From all we know of Francis, it is far more probable that he lied of set purpose, than that he and Hastings had merely misunderstood each other.

* A copy of the minute containing these words had been forwarded to Francis by Hastings the evening before.

Be that as it may, it seemed impossible for a man of honour, however small his regard for truth, to overlook the insult which Hastings had so publicly offered him. When the Council was over, Francis called Hastings into a side room, and there challenged him to fight a duel on the 17th. About sunrise of that day the antagonists faced each other, pistol in hand. They fired together. Happily for India Hastings remained unhurt. Francis fell with a bullet in his left side. Two hours later, Hastings learned that his rival "was in no manner of danger;" the shot having travelled round the backbone without injuring it.*

Of the spirit in which Francis went forth to fight his rival, a characteristic story was afterwards told by one of his contemporaries, a lady who died some twenty years ago at a great age.† On the morning of the 17th August, Francis was sipping coffee in the verandah, when a crow hopped invitingly near him. With a well-aimed-shot from his pistol, he laid the intruder dead, exclaiming, "If my hand will only be as steady an hour hence, I shall be Governor-General of India to-

* Gleig's "Warren Hastings," Vol. ii., Chap. 7. "Memoirs of Sir E. Impey," Chap. 8.

† Her name, I believe, was Mrs. Ellerton, who died about 1857.

morrow." Whatever truth there may be in this story, it is certain that Hastings' advances to his wounded foe were not met by the latter in a forgiving spirit. On the day of the duel, the former sent his secretary to see Francis, and to express the Governor-General's desire to see him also as soon as he was better. Some days afterwards Francis sent a message declining the proffered visit, "not from any remains of resentment, but from the consideration of what he owed to his own character." He would treat Hastings with all respect, but their future intercourse must be confined to the Council table.

Before the end of August, Francis was already preparing a reply to the minute which had provoked the duel. To that reply Hastings drew up a rejoinder, and the war of minutes went on between them until December, when Francis, after firing a last shot of ink and paper at his successful rival, sailed homewards, to brew, in due time, fresh schemes of vengeance against the author of his past mishaps and disappointments.

With his departure Hastings once more breathed freely. After six years of conflict, he could "enjoy the triumph of a decided victory." There was, indeed, "a war, either actual or impending, in every quarter, and with every power in Hindostan." He saw before him "an exhausted treasury, an accumulating debt," a costly and vicious system of administration, corruption rife in high places, trade impoverished, and "a country oppressed by private rapacity, and deprived of its vital resources" in order to feed the war, to furnish help of all kinds to the other Presidencies, and to meet the call for private remittances to England. But Francis was gone at last, and with him all the worst evils of the moment. "I shall have no competitor," wrote Hastings, "to oppose my designs, to encourage disobedience to my authority, to write circular letters with copies of instruments from the Court of Directors proclaiming their distrust of me and denouncing my removal; to excite and foment popular odium against me; to urge me to acts of severity, and then abandon and oppose me; to keep alive the expectation of impending changes; to teach foreign states to counteract me, and to deter them from forming connexions with me. I have neither his emissaries in office to thwart me from system, nor my own dependents to presume on the rights of attachment. In a word, I have power, and I will employ it during the interval in which the credit of it shall last, to retrieve past misfortunes, to remove present dangers, and to re-establish the powers of the Company, and the safety of its possessions."*

There was no idle boasting in this language, nothing mean or selfish in the exultation thus expressed. It was the unchained eagle taking his first flight upwards into the free air. "To reign is worth ambition" for purposes such as those which Hastings set himself to accomplish. The self-confidence which comes of self-insight, bade him rejoice in the prospect of wielding unfettered power for great and patriotic ends. His term of office, which expired in 1778, had since been prolonged from year to year by a reluctant ministry and a hostile Court of Directors. They knew that England, begirt with enemies, could ill afford to loose so useful a leader at such a time. Hastings knew it also, and the knowledge gave him strength to discharge his duty to his country and his employers in the way that to him seemed best, with small regard for the clamour raised against him at home. How greatly he succeeded during the next three years in fulfiling his pledge to save India we have already seen.

* Gleig's "Warren Hastings," Vol. ii., Chap. 8.

CHAPTER VI.

1781—1783.

THE year 1781 opened for Hastings on a troubled sea of dangers, difficulties, and distress. Haidar Ali was raging in the Carnatic, Goddard and Camac were still fighting the Maráthas, and French fleets were cruising in the Bay of Bengal. When he had sent Camac to look after Sindia, had shipped off Coote's soldiers to Madras, had started Pearse's Sepoys on their march through Orissa, and completed his bargain with the Rajah of Berár, Hastings found the Bengal Treasury running very low. It was no time for standing upon trifles. Money must be raised somehow, if British India was to be saved. Among other sources of supply, he turned to the Rajah of Banaras. Chait Singh was the grandson of an adventurer, who had ousted his own patron and protector from the lordship of the district so named.* In 1775, his fief had been transferred

* "Debates of the House of Lords on the Evidence delivered in the Trial of Warren Hastings," p. 61.

by treaty from the Nawab of Oudh to the Company. As a vassal of the Company he was bound to aid them with men and money in times of special need. Five lakhs of rupees—£50,000—and two thousand horse was the quota which Hastings had demanded of him in 1780.*

In spite of a revenue of half-a-million, of the great wealth stored up in his private coffers, and of the splendid show which he always made in public, the Rajah pleaded poverty, and put off compliance with the demands of his liege lord. Hastings, for his part, would take no denial from one whose word could not be trusted, and whose recent acts seemed to betoken a spirit wholly disaffected to our rule. Chait Singh had repeatedly delayed the payment of his ordinary tribute; his body-guard alone was larger than the force which Hastings required of him; he was enrolling troops for some warlike purpose, and Hastings' agents accused him of secret plottings with the Oudh Begams at Faizabad. Fowke himself had complained of the Rajah's rudeness and evasions.† Markham, who replaced Fowke as Resident at

* The first demand for five lakhs was made and long evaded in 1778.

† "Debates of the House of Lords," p. 61.

Banaras early in 1781, charged by Hastings to treat the Rajah as kindly, mildly, and civilly as he could, in vain entreated him to "make a show of obedience, by mustering even five hundred horse." In vain did Hastings himself reduce his demand to one thousand.* Chait Singh still sent evasive answers, and never furnished a single horseman.

The Rajah, in fact, like a shrewd, self-seeking Hindu, was waiting upon circumstances, which at that time boded ill for his English neighbours. The Marathas, the French, or some other power might yet relieve him from the yoke of a ruler who restrained his ambition, and lectured him on the duty of preserving law and order among his own subjects. Of his self-seeking, Hastings had learned a lesson in 1777, when the Rajah sent off a special messenger to worship, as he thought, the new-risen sun, in the person of Sir John Clavering. But before the messenger got near Calcutta, that sun had proved but a passing meteor, and Hastings' star once more ruled the Eastern sky.

It has often been argued that, in his stern dealings with the Rajah of Banáras, Hastings was

* "Debates," p. 30.

impelled by malice and a desire for revenge. But the subsequent verdict of the House of Lords on this point, justifies itself to all who have carefully followed the facts of his life. Francis gloried in treasuring up a grudge, and repaying it with interest whenever he had a chance. Hastings, on the contrary, never knowingly let his private feelings warp his public policy. No paltry personal motives seem to have entered into his treatment of Chait Singh. As a matter of policy, he determined to make an example of a contumacious vassal, whose conduct in that hour of need added a new danger to those which surrounded the English in India. A heavy fine would teach the Rajah to obey orders, and help betimes to fill his own treasury with the sinews of war. Such in other words was the purpose avowed by Hastings himself in the paper which records his journey to Banáras, and what came of it.

Chait Singh had already tried upon the Governor-General those arts which in Eastern countries people of all classes employ against each other without a blush. He had sent Hastings a peace-offering of two lakhs—£20,000. Hastings took the money, but reserved it for the Company's use.* Presently he received an offer of twenty lakhs for the public service. But Hastings was in no mood for further compromise in evasion of his former demands. He would be satisfied with nothing less than half a million in quittance of all dues. In July, 1781, he set out, with Wheeler's concurrence, for the Rajah's capital; his head full of schemes for the salvation of British India, and the punishment of all who thwarted his efforts to that end.

His wife accompanied him as far as Monghír on the Ganges. Leaving her to recruit her health in that pleasant spot,† he went on towards the Holy City of the Hindus. Travelling, as he preferred to do, with a small escort and as little parade as possible, he arrived on the 16th August at the populous and stately city which overhangs, with a rich confusion of temples, palaces, and ghâts, or bathing-stairs, one of the noblest reaches of the great Indian river. On his way thither, at Baxár, the recusant Rajah had come

* Wilson's Note in Chap. 7, Book v. of Mill's History.

† "Monghir stands on a rocky promontory, with the broad river on both sides, forming two bays, beyond one of which the Rajmahal hills are visible, and the other is bounded by the nearer range of Curruckpoor."—Heber's Indian Journal, Vol. 1, Chap. x. The place is noted for its cutlery and firearms.

to meet him, with a large retinue, in the hope of softening the heart of the great Lord Sáhib. He even laid his turban on Hastings' lap. But no such display of real or seeming contrition could now turn the latter aside from his fixed purpose. With the haughtiness of an ancient Roman, Hastings declined his prayer for a private interview. On the day after his arrival at Banáras, the Governor-General forwarded to Chait Singh a paper stating the grounds of complaint against him, and demanding an explanation on each point. The Rajah's answer seemed to Hastings "so offensive in style and unsatisfactory in substance;" it was full, in fact, of such transparent, or, as Lord Thurlow afterwards called them, "impudent" falsehoods,* that the Governor-General issued orders for placing the Rajah under arrest.

Early the next morning, Chait Singh was quietly arrested in his own palace. Hastings received from the prisoner a submissive message; and Markham, who had gone to visit him, brought back a favourable report. But the Rajah was neither submissive nor asleep. That very day he sent off messengers to the Begams at Faiza-

* "Debates of the House of Lords, &c.," p. 31.

bad.* Meanwhile his armed retainers were flocking into the city from his strong castle of Rámnagar, on the opposite bank. Mixing with the populace, they provoked a tumult, in which the two companies of Sepoys guarding the prisoner were cut to pieces. With unloaded muskets and empty pouches—for the ammunition had been forgotten—the poor men fell like sheep before their butchers. Two more companies, in marching to their aid through the narrow streets, were nearly annihilated. During the tumult Chait Singh quietly slipped out of the palace, dropped by a rope of turbans into a boat beneath, and crossed in safety to Rámnagar.

Hastings has been blamed for rashness in entering the Rajah's capital with so small a force. But "the best-laid schemes of mice and men gang aft agley," and the massacre of the Sepoys was obviously due to the fault of their own officers. His position, however, was critical enough. If Chait Singh's followers had not shared betimes their master's flight across the river, Hastings, with his band of thirty Englishmen and fifty Sepoys, might have paid very dearly for the sudden miscarriage of his plans. But the rabble

* "Debates," p. 52.

of Banáras had no leader, and troops from the nearest garrisons were already marching to the rescue of a Governor whom the whole army regarded with loving pride. Among the first who reached him was the gallant Popham, bringing with him several hundred of his own Sepoys. Trusty messengers carried the news of Hastings' danger, and orders for help to Chunár, Lucknow, and Mirzápúr. In other letters he assured his wife of his own safety, and told Wheeler all he had done, and was doing, to bring matters to a prosperous issue.

In the midst of his danger, increased as it was by risings in Oudh, and the murderous defeat of Mayaffre's headlong attack on Rámnagar on the 17th, Hastings quietly wrote off to Colonel Muir his last instructions concerning the treaty which he was then negotiating with Sindia. Finding himself still in danger, he withdrew by night to the river-fortress of Chunár.* Meanwhile Colonel Morgan was hurrying down without

* This flight gave rise to the following well-known couplet.—

"Ghoré par haudah, háthi par zín,
Jaldı bhág gaya Warren Hastín."

Which may be rendered—

"Saddle on elephant, howdah on steed,
Rode Warren Hastings away with speed."

orders from Cawnpore, and the Nawáb of Oudh made large offers of help, which Hastings proudly declined. In the same spirit, he "rejected every advance from Chait Singh, even when he had 40,000 men in arms, and I had not 2,000 to oppose them."

At one time the Rajah's forces were only a few miles from Chunár. But the beginning of September found Popham strong enough to open a campaign, which speedily avenged the slaughters at Banáras and Rámnagar, and carried Hastings back into the full stream of richly-earned success. Before the end of September the Rajah's troops had been routed at every point, and he himself had fled for shelter to his last stronghold at Bijigarh, on the hills overlooking the Són. Seeing no safety for himself even there, he escaped, with the bulk of his treasure, into Bundalkhand. The capture of Bijigarh on the 10th November, closed the brief but brilliant campaign. The booty, amounting to £400,000, was at once divided among the captors; and Hastings lost his only chance of replenishing his treasury at the expense of Chait Singh.* He consoled

* Stubbs's "Bengal Artillery," Vol. 1, Chap.ii Some handsome presents which the officers forwarded for Mr. and Mrs

himself and improved the Company's finances, by bestowing the rebel's forfeit lordship on his nephew, and doubling the tribute hitherto exacted.

He was more successful in accomplishing another object of his journey up the country. Owing partly to his own misconduct, but chiefly to the hard conditions imposed by Francis and his colleagues in 1775, the Nawáb-Vazír of Oudh was sinking deeper and deeper into the Company's debt. In six years, that debt had grown to a million and a half, chiefly on account of the British garrisons which, in the face of passing dangers and probable needs, could not with safety be withdrawn or reduced. The Governor-General was in sore want of money for a war on which hung the fate of British India. Asaf-ad-daula for his part saw no way but one out of his growing difficulties. If Hastings would not relieve him of the burden of maintaining even one brigade, he might perhaps agree to the Nawáb's proposals for recovering some of the estates and treasures, which Hastings' old colleagues had unfairly withheld from him.

Hastings, were sent back by the former. Gleig's "Warren Hastings," Vol. 2, Chap. ix.

While he was yet at Chunár, Hastings received a visit from the Nawáb. He listened to the Nawáb's proposals with a readiness sharpened by his financial straits, and by his knowledge of the active part which the Oudh Princesses had taken in the rebellious movements of Chait Singh.* Their intrigues had furnished him with a good excuse for repairing, to the Company's advantage, the injustice done by his council six years before. With a sense, it may be, of grim satisfaction at the prospect of undoing the work of his old enemy Francis, he agreed to sanction the arrangement once more proposed by his embarassed ally. He even promised, if all went well, to relieve the Nawáb of all charges for the maintenance of an English brigade.

The course adopted, says Macaulay, was "simply this, that the Governor-General and the Nawáb-Vizier should join to rob a third party; and the third party whom they determined to rob, was the parent to one of the robbers." To this neat epigrammatic statement of the case it is enough to say in answer, that the robbery was

* Soldiers of the Begams had been found among the prisoners taken at Patna, and the country around Faizabad was openly hostile to the English.

committed in 1775, by the parent upon the son. What Hastings agreed to do, was simply to encourage the person robbed in his schemes for recovering the stolen goods. Neither in law, nor in fact, had the Begams any right to the property which Asaf-ad-daula had been compelled by the Calcutta Council to leave in their possesion. His obligations under the compact of 1775 were cancelled by their recent plottings with Chait Singh, if not by the absolute failure of his financial resources.

After his return to Lucknow, the Nawáb-Vazír began to shrink from carrying out against his mother and grandmother an agreement which affected his own favourites also. But the Governor-General pinned him to his promises by threatening to withdraw his Resident and the English troops from Oudh, and to leave the Nawáb entirely to his own devices.* Middleton, who had once more replaced Bristow at Lucknow, was ordered to stand no more nonsense from our weak-minded but cunning ally. Hastings had already learned enough to convince him that the Begams deserved no special mercy at their kinsman's hands. It was shown by evidence, which

* "Debates of the House of Lords," &c., p. 119.

afterwards satisfied his judges in the House of Lords, that they had helped the Rajah of Banáras with men and money, and had otherwise abetted his revolt against the English. In order that the evidence might be duly attested, Impey, who was leisurely travelling with his wife up country, partly for his health, partly in discharge of his duties as Judge of the Sadr Dewáni Adálat, proceeded at his friend's request to Lucknow. The taking of affidavits in support of Hastings' "Narrative" of the late rebellion was a simple process conducted by Impey in the character, not of a judge or a magistrate, but merely of an Englishman acquainted with the simplest forms of law.* Being near the spot, for he had already reached Banáras, the Chief Justice readily agreed to oblige his friend, and see something of India beyond Bahár, by extending his travels into Oudh. With the contents of the affidavits he had nothing to do. His only care was to see the documents regularly attested before one who claimed "some reputation as a lawyer," and knew the difficulties which surrounded Hasting both in India and at home.

Readers of Macaulay will do well to mark the

* "Memoirs of Sir E. Impey," Chap. ix.

astounding folly which turned this act of extra-judicial courtesy into one more evidence of Impey's shame. The essayist's picture of the Chief Justice hurrying to Lucknow "as fast as relays of palanquin-bearers could carry him," and taking a host of affidavits which he did not, and some of which he could not, read, in order that "he might give, in an irregular manner, that sanction which in a regular manner he could not give, to the crimes of those who had recently hired him," is drawn entirely from that warm Celtic imagination which its author shared with Burke and Sheridan. It differs as widely from the plain truth of the matter, as a novel by Victor Hugo differs from the facts of ordinary life.*

On his return to Calcutta, before the end of 1781, Impey was thanked by the Supreme Council for the trouble he had incurred; and Hastings himself, who with his wife returned thither some weeks later,† received from his colleagues an address of congratulation for the results achieved by him at Banáras, Chunár, and Lucknow.

By that time—February 1782—the Nawáb of

* Let me remark by the way, that Impey was a good Persian and Arabic scholar, spoke Bengali if not Hindustani fluently, and took his Múnshí with him. (Memoirs of Sir E. Impey).

† They had remained at Banaras from October till January.

Oudh had been induced to carry out the pledges given under his hand in the previous September. His English troops had entered the palace at Faizabád, and the two eunuchs who managed the Begams' affairs had been compelled, by hunger and confinement in chains, to disgorge some part of the wealth entrusted to their keeping by the late Nawáb. Of the money thus obtained, more than half a million was at once paid into the Company's treasury, and the balance still due was presently recovered out of the revenues of certain Jaigírs or fiefs, which Asaf-ad-daula at length took courage to reclaim from their former holders for the good of the State.

For some months longer the hapless eunuchs were kept in bondage by their own master, in the hope of squeezing more money out of their sufferings, and their fears of yet harsher treatment to come. The Begams, also, were carefully watched, and their freedom limited to the palace precincts. Some further payments were thus extracted, by a process which seemed humane in comparison with the usual practice of Eastern princes. The ladies in the palace suffered no real hardship, and even the eunuchs were free to receive visitors, to walk in their own garden, and to eat without stint of the food their servants cooked for them. After a few months their fetters were taken off.* At last, the Governor-General himself interfered to stay all further proceedings on the Nawáb's part; and early in December, 1782, the prisoners were finally set free. The Begams lived to send Hastings "strong letters of friendship and commiseration," says Mr. Gleig, during his subsequent trial before the House of Lords. The younger of them was "alive and hearty, and very rich," when Lord Valentia visited Lucknow in 1803. "Well, fat, and enormously rich," are the words he uses in describing one of the eunuchs, on whose sufferings Búrke had descanted with his wonted eloquence many years before.†

In the whole course of these transactions, no just ground can be alleged for the blame which was afterwards imputed to the Governor-General, as if he was answerable for the means adopted by the Nawáb-Vazír to carry out the agreement signed at Chunár.

The resumption of the Jaigírs, was a stroke of

* Wilson's Note to Mill, Book 5, Chap viii.

† Lord Valentia's Travels, quoted in "Memoirs of Sir E. Impey," Chap. ix.

policy demanded in the interests of Oudh itself, and effected under conditions which left no room for just complaint. The sanction which Hastings gave to the spoiling of the Begams, might offer his enemies a new handle for reviling, and furnish casuists with a theme for endless debate. But he can hardly be held accountable for "tortures" which were never inflicted, or which impartial persons would describe in milder terms. The Kingdom of Oudh had not yet become a British Province, nor was it the part of a wise statesman to meddle with every detail of the measures adopted by his ally.

On one point only in this connexion does Hastings seem to have, for a moment, overstepped the bounds of a wise forbearance. In 1780, Faizulla Khan, the Rohilla Nawáb of Rámpur, had been required, at Hastings' suggestion, to furnish 5,000 horse for the general defence of the Nawáb's and our frontiers. Displeased at an offer of only 3,000 from a chief so prosperous and powerful, Hastings agreed at Chunár to the Nawáb-Vazír's proposal that Faizulla Khan should be dispossessed of his Jaigír. He afterwards owned that, in a

* Jaigírs were estates held upon condition of military service, and liable at any moment to be resumed.

moment of great alarm and anxiety, he had too readily assented to the Nawáb's request. His assent, however, had at least been guarded by an express provision that the Nawáb's plans should stand over for execution at some future date. In spite of impatient letters from Asaf-ad-daula, he still sought for a compromise which might secure his retreat from a false position, and enable the Nawáb-Vazír to pay another instalment of his debt to the Company. At length, in the beginning of 1783, his envoy, Major Palmer, carried through an agreement which secured the *jaigír* to Faizulla Khán and his heirs for ever, free of all liability to furnish troops for his master's service, in return for a money payment of fifteen lakhs, or £150,000.* This sum was duly paid into the Calcutta treasury, and the Nawáb of Rámpúr died in 1794, leaving rich estates and a large treasure to his heirs.

Had Hastings been half as greedy and unscrupulous as his enemies declared him to be, he might have reaped a golden harvest from the needs or arts of his native friends. He might have returned to England "rich beyond the dreams of averice," far richer than any of the

* Wilson's Notes to Mill, Book v. Chap. viii.

retired Nabobs, whom Englishmen had been wont to contemplate with mingled awe and derision. The Nawáb of Oudh, for instance, had lately offered him a present of ten lakhs of rupees, or £100,000. Instead of pocketing the money, Hastings informed the Court of Directors that he had kept it for their service, adding a request that he might, as a special mark of their approval, be allowed to keep it for himself. Yet even this, which ought rather to tell in his favour, was afterwards turned to his discredit. Although every anna of this money was duly expended in the public service, the fact of its acceptance formed one of the charges on which Hastings was to be impeached by the Commons, and acquitted by the Lords.

In the course of the year 1782, Hastings had to play the part of peacemaker between Lord Macartney and Sir Eyre Coote. The Governor of Madras complained of the old General's insolence towards himself and his colleagues, and Coote complained of their constant inattention to his demands for help. Hastings soothed the latter with kind words and wise counsels, and persuaded the former to sacrifice his pride to the public interest. In the midst of his efforts to secure the triumph of our arms in Southern India, to break down the last barriers of Maráthа hostility, to carry out reforms in Oudh and Banáras, to improve the salt and opium revenues of Bengal, and to inspire the people with a growing confidence in his firm yet temperate rule, he was seized for the first time in his public career with a long and serious illness, which delayed for months the completion of his schemes of administrative and financial reform. His own recovery was followed by Wheeler's illness; but the next year found him still hopeful and hard at work.*

* Gleig's "Memoirs," Vol. iii., Chaps. i. & ii.

CHAPTER VII.

1783—1785.

By this time new storms were brewing in England against the dauntless and proud-souled statesman, whose achievements in India formed the one bright spot in the picture of England's losing or unfruitful struggles with a world in arms. The rancour of Francis, who might have sat for Milton's Belial, or given Pope ideas for his portrait of Lord Henry, was already doing its poisonous work. Hastings had already heard of the censures passed on him by a Committee of the Commone, and read, with a smile of bitter scorn, the letters which told him how his enemies at the India House were engaged in driving those censures home. Early in 1873, his steady friend and fellow worker, Impey, received the order for his recal, as voted by the House of Commons in the previous May. This was another shaft from Francis' quiver. Hastings himself had just been rebuked by the Court of Directors for his treatment of Chait Singh; and they had even gone the length of recalling him, when the Court of Proprietors came once more to the rescue of their old favourite. By a large majority they forced the Directors to rescind their vote, and appointed a committee to watch over the Company's interests in the coming conflict with a hostile House of Commons.

To the strictures of the India House upon his conduct, Hastings replied in terms of just indignation and manly scorn. He had been arraigned before "the whole body of the people of England" for "acts of such complicated aggravation that, if they were true, no punishment short of death could atone for the injury which the interest and credit of the public had sustained in them." To every statement made on behalf of Chait Sing he gave a flat denial. "The man," he added, "whom you have thus ranked among the princes of India will be astonished when he hears of it—at an elevation so unlooked for; nor less at the independent rights which he will not know how to assert, unless the example which you thought it consistent with justice, however opposite to policy, to show, of becoming his advocate against your own interests, should inspire any of your own servants to become his advisers and instructors." In spite of the difficulties which, thanks to the powers at home, had beset him in the last eleven years, "I please myself," he said, "with the hope that, in the annals of your dominions which shall be written after the extinction of prejudice, this term of its administration will appear not the least conducive to the interests of the Company, nor the least reflective of the honour of the British name." He called upon the Court to attest the patience and temper with which he had borne all the indignities heaped upon him "in a long service." Gratitude to his original masters and most indulgent patrons, had hitherto kept him faithful to his trust. Now, however, in the midst of formidable dangers, which his government had thus far successfully encountered, the Directors had chosen that very season to "annihilate its constitutional powers." It only, therefore, remained for him to "declare, as I now most formally do, that . . . . it is my intention to resign your service as soon as I can do it without prejudice to your affairs, after the allowance of a competent time for your choice of a person to succeed me; and to declare that if, in the intermediate time, you shall proceed to order the restoration of Rajah

Cheyte Singh to the zemindary from which he was dismissed, for crimes of the greatest enormity, and your council shall resolve to execute the order, I will instantly give up my station and the service."*

Happily for India, the challenge thus boldly flung down in March, 1783, was not yet to be taken up. Chait Singh remained in comfortable exile at Gwáliár, and Banáras presently became a British district. Hastings staid on for nearly two years longer, chafing under new annoyances, but determined, if he could, to see the great game of Indian politics fairly played out. Of his colleagues in Council, not even Wheeler could still be trusted. to follow his lead, and the friendly understanding with Lord Macartney had already passed into a bitter feud. The Governor of Madras, perhaps with good reason, refused to reinstate the Nawáb of Arkot in the management of his own revenues, rebelled with less reason against every order received from Calcutta, and poisoned the minds of the Court of Directors with unfair complaints against the Governor-General. Hastings' own agents at Lucknow and Banáras were replaced by nominees of the India House. At home, a

* Auber's "British Power in India," Vol. 1, Chap. xi.

succession of new ministries, from that of Rockingham to that of Fox and Lord North, brought him no real increase of political strength, although for a few months his friend and schoolfellow, Lord Shelburne, guided the helm of state in the room of his late chief, the Marquis of Rockingham.

In the spring of 1783, Lord Shelburne was succeeded by the coalition ministry of Fox and Lord North, in which a secondary place was found for Burke. The conjunction boded no good for Hastings or the East India Company. But the King himself held strong opinions on the folly of recalling the foremost man in British India from a post which still demanded his saving presence. His intense dislike of Fox and his Whig followers, had much to do with the subsequent overthrow of a ministry, whose India Bill aimed at transferring the Government of India from the Company to seven Directors named by the Ministry, and irremovable by the Crown.* In spite of Burke's eloquence and a majority in the House of Commons, the Bill was rejected by

* Sir G. Lewis on the "Administrations of Great Britain," p. 68. They were to be removable by an address from Parliament only. Auber's "British Power in India," Vol. 1, Chap. xii.

the Lords in December, and the next year opened on the the long and eventful ministry of William Pitt.

In the previous November the Court of Pro prietors had carried, all but unanimously, a formal vote of thanks to Hastings for his long and invaluable services. For the moment Hastings' star was again dominant. To him and his friends the defeated Ministry gave nearly all the credit for their own downfal, and even the Court of Directors began to look more kindly on the ruler who had just brought his treaty with the Maráthas to a triumphant issue. Among the new Ministers Hastings reckoned a few powerful, and one or two staunch friends. Even Dundas seems for the moment to have been dazzled by the latest proofs of Hastings' ability in managing a great war, and winning an important peace. "His relief and support of the Carnatic, his improvement of the revenues of Bengal, his spirit and activity, claim every degree of praise that I can bestow upon him, and every support that his Majestys ministers can afford him."*

Meanwhile, in spite of many annoyances, and the effects of his late illness upon his own health,

* Gleig's "Warren Hastings," Vol. 3, Chap. iv.

Hastings worked away, as he best could, at the business which still required his care. In order to strengthen his influence at the Court of Delhi, and forestal the designs of the Maráthas in that direction, he had sent two envoys, in 1783, to the Imperial City. Their reports convinced him of Shah Alam's readiness to renew his friendship with his old allies, in preference to accepting the dangerous overtures of Mahdaji Sindia. But Hastings, once more hampered by opposing colleagues, could not interfere to any good effect; and the harassed Emperor prepared to bow down before the advancing shadow of Marátha greatness.*

Before the end of 1873, Hastings took affectionate leave of Impey, who, with his wife and children, at length set off on his homeward voyage, sped by the farewell greetings of many friends and well-wishers, high and low. Among those friends was Sir William Jones, the great Sanskrit scholar, who had only that year arrived at Calcutta to replace one of Impey's colleagues, removed by death in 1779. In the following January Hastings had to undergo the pain of parting from his own wife. Through years of incessant

* Keene's "Moghul Empire," Book 2, Chap. iv.

care and trouble, and vexatious strife, Mrs. Hastings had been the very pole-star of his being; in Mr. Gleig's own words, "his friend, his confidant, his solace, his supreme delight." During the outbreak at Banáras, his first thought had been of her, his chief anxiety to keep her from feeling anxious on his account. At that time she was still an invalid, and since then her health had continued to decline. But the war with France, and the boldness of Suffrein's cruisers, delayed her departure, as it had delayed that of the Chief Justice. With the return of peace Hastings would no longer consent to put off his wife's return home. On the 10th January, 1784, he "left the *Atlas* under sail" for England, and went back to Calcutta resolved to follow his wife before the year's end.

He had hoped, indeed, to leave India with Mrs. Hastings. But new reasons for waiting a year longer presented themselves to him in the meanwhile. The peace with Tippú was still to ratify; the quarrel with Lord Macartney still raged with small hope of adjustment; a famine had broken out in Upper India which threatened to affect Bengal; and the affairs of Oudh, mismanaged by Bristow, the Company's chosen agent, called for Hastings' further interference. Early in 1784, Bristow was recalled. About the middle of February Hastings, with the consent of his Council, started on his last tour up the country to Banáras and Lucknow. At Banáras he received an interesting report from his young kinsman, Captain Turner, whom he had despatched the year before on another mission to the Lama of Tibet. In the interval between his mission and that of Bogle, Hastings had kept up a friendly intercourse with the Tibetan Rajah of Bhután. From Turner himself, he had already learned at Patna the story of his journey to Teshu Lumbo, and of his visit to the infant Lama at the monastery of Terpaling.*

His stay at Lucknow extended from April to the latter part of August. During that time he succeeded in rescuing the Nawáb-Vazír's finances from utter wreck, and placing his government in the hands of two able and trustworthy ministers. At Faizábád he made friends of the lately despoiled Begams, by restoring them a part of their forfeited Jaigírs. Among those who sought his countenance at Lucknow, was the Shahzáda, or Prince Jawán Bakht, heir to the once honoured

* Markham's "Narrative," Introduction.

throne of Dehli. Hastings took a fancy to his visitor, and would have helped him, if he could, to rescue his father from the hands of traitors at home, and the wiles of his Marátha neighbours. But his colleagues at Calcutta still shrank from the bolder policy which would have saved the House of Bábar from final collapse. With such help as Hastings was free to give him in men and money, the Shahzáda afterwards returned in safety to his father's capital. Hastings could only advise him to look to Sindia for protection against the dangers which surrounded the Emperor in his own city.*

Early in September, Hastings was sailing down the broad flood of the rain-swollen Ganges to Banáras. In a letter to his wife, he describes the incidents of his voyage, the damage done, through careless boatmen, to his "beautiful budgerow;" the receipt of letters from England, which announced the overthrow of his enemies and the re-establishment of his own reputation; his brief stay with kind friends at Chunár; his arrival at Banáras; his state of health, bodily and mental; and the joy with which he received "a

* Keene's "Moghul Empire," Book 2, Chap. iv. Gleig's "Warren Hastings," Vol. 3, Chap. vii.

short but blessed letter," from Mrs. Hastings, written off St Helena in May. Of his way of life he says, "I eat sparingly; I never sup, and am generally in bed by ten. I breakfast at six. I bathe with cold water daily, and while I was at Lucknow, twice a day, using soorcys* cooled with ice. Though my mind has laboured under a constant and severe load, yet the business which has occupied it has been light with no variety to draw my attention different ways, and with little vexation. To these may be added, that unless everybody was in a conspiracy to deceive me, all ranks of people were pleased, not because I did good, but because I did no ill."

His references to the Shahzada, who had accompanied him so far on his way home, bear witness alike to the good qualities of a prince "whose character gains instead of losing by acquaintance," and to the deep reluctance with which Hastings had to play the part of a mere adviser. A good deal of the letter deals with "public concerns," which Hastings discusses freely with his Marian, dwelling especially on his reasons for coming home soon, even with an income barely equal to his wants. "What a letter," he adds, "have I

* Large jars of porous clay, more properly written "Sarais."

written; and who that read it without the direction would suspect it to be written by a fond husband to his beloved wife?" To this letter he adds a postscript, written some days later, in which he declares himself "the happiest man living," because he had just received another letter from his wife.

On his previous journey from Bakhsár to Banáras, he had been saddened by the traces of the long-prevalent drought, and "fatigued" by the complaints of sufferers who everywhere thronged his path. Within the City of Banáras he had found matters well ordered under the able control of Mohammad Reza Khán; but the adjacent province seemed to have suffered, not only from famine, but from official misdeeds. At the time of his next visit, things wore a more cheerful look. The bare brown fields were green with the promise of a rich harvest, and the measures he had taken to reform past abuses were already bearing fruit.

The news of Wheeler's death quickened his return to Calcutta. On the 21st October, he took leave of the Shahzáda, and set out next morning from the Holy City, reaching Calcutta on the 4th of the next month. Awaiting him was a letter from the Court of Directors, "as unpleasing as any that I ever received from that body in the time of General Clavering." They scolded him, among other things, for drawing bills upon the home treasury in aid of funds for the yearly investment.* This letter, followed by the tidings of Pitt's India Bill, decided him to leave India without more delay. He was "literally sick of suspense." His friends at home urged him to stay on for the present; but symptoms of his old fever warned him to go betimes, and a study of the provisions of Pitt's Bill convinced him that his resignation was "expected and desired." On the 26th of December he writes to tell his wife, of whose safe arrival in England he has just heard, that, as soon as his colleague Macpherson shall have pledged himself to respect his arrangements with the Nawáb of Oudh, he will prepare for his voyage home. "This point settled, it is determined absolutely. I will wait for no advices. They have given me my freedom and opened the road to my happiness."

He had taken his passage in the *Barrington* as early as November. On the 22nd of that month

* Auber's "British Power in India," Chap. xiii.

he wrote to warn the Court of Directors of his firm intention, as things then stood, to return to England, as soon as the *Barrington* could be got ready to sail. On the 10th of the following January, he informed them that he would hand the government over to Macpherson by the end of the month. His purpose of returning home had evidently been strengthened by certain hopes which his wife's letters had lately raised within him. "At this instant," he wrote to her on the 26th December, I have but one wish, and a *little one* annexed to it; and O God, grant them!" And on the 10th January, 1785, he tells her of his "desire to be gone before any advices can arrive from England, for a reason which I cannot trust to writing, but which you, my Marian, will applaud, and the public ought to applaud, if they knew it." Mrs. Hastings, he thought, was about to become a mother.

One of his last acts as Governor-General was to review the troops which, under Colonel Pearse, had borne their part so bravely in the war with Haidar. As he rode in a plain blue coat, with head uncovered, along the diminished ranks of war-worn Sepoys, dressed in motley and patched uniforms, the cheers that greeted him were among the brightest memories he carried home. The army, indeed, as Macaulay has well said, "loved him as armies have seldom loved any but the greatest chiefs who have led them to victory." Swords of honour were bestowed by him on Pearse and two of his officers; and the Colonel, whom he was "proud to call his friend," was requested publicly to thank all under his command for services which the Governor-General never could forget. Nor were the claims of Goddard's victorious soldiers, whom Colonel Morgan had led back to Cawnpore, overlooked. Every sepoy who had served in Southern or Western India received a medal, and to each petty officer and private, European or native, in either army, was granted an increase of his monthly pay.*

Amidst all the cares and difficulties of his great post, Hastings had shown himself a steady patron of the pursuit of knowledge and the arts that tend to humanise life. Under his auspices, Major Rennell and a band of able and enterprising surveyors, carried on, over a wider field, the survey work begun by Clive. Their researches were extended even to Cochin China,

* Stubbs's "Bengal Artillery," Vol. 1, Chaps. ii. and iii.

Burmah, and the shores of the Red Sea. He would have forestalled the measures taken long afterwards for making Egypt the highway from England to India. In the last year of his rule, Hastings helped to found the Asiatic Society, whose first President was the new judge, Sir William Jones. He was the first Englishman who persuaded the Pandits of Bengal to unfold to his countrymen those treasures of Sanskrit lore, which Sir W. Jones afterwards turned to such memorable use. We have already seen the success of his endeavours to enlist the Pandits in the work of codifying the native Hindu law. He encouraged scholars like Halhed, Anderson, and Hamilton to translate and arrange the chief sources of Hindu and Mohammadan law.

For the extension of learning among the Mohammadans, Hastings founded, partly at his own expense, in Calcutta, a Madrasa, or College, where nearly a thousand students now drink, more or less deeply, of the springs an Englishman opened to their forefathers more than a century ago. In the sphere of art, too, he showed himself a liberal and discerning patron. Imhoff was but one of several artists, who had reason to bless the day which made them acquainted with a ruler, whose patronage helped them further along the road his bounty had first smoothed for them.

By the ablest members of his own service Hastings was loved and served with a devotion that never faltered. One of these was the wise and good Augustus Cleveland, whom he had placed as magistrate over the wild hill-tribes of Bhágalpur. Cleveland's success in taming these naked flat-nosed savages, who had long been a terror and a nuisance to their lowland neighbours, was achieved by that kind of influence which Outram afterwards employed to like effect upon the Bhíls of Western India. He learned their language, mixed freely with them at all hazards, shared their sports, listened patiently to their grievances, and dealt even justice between them and the neighbouring zamindars. The goodwill of the chiefs he won by timely presents of clothes, money, and corn-seed. Bazaars for trade were established in their villages, and the people were secured against the inroads of Bengáli tax-gatherers. He enrolled from among them a corps of hill-rangers, who kept the peace of the district, and he encouraged the chiefs to administer justice under his direction, in accordance with certain accepted rules. His death in January, 1784, at the early age of twenty-eight, was a cause of much sorrow, alike to Hastings and to the people whose reverence he had won, both for himself and his honoured master. Two monuments were raised to his memory; one at Bhágalpur, by the hill chiefs and lowland zamindars, the other at Calcutta, by Hastings and his Council. *Hastings himself supplied the inscription*, which tells how Cleveland, "without bloodshed or the terror of authority," had tamed the lawless inhabitants of the Rájmahál jungles, and "attached them to the British Government by a conquest over their minds; the most permanent, as the most rational, mode of dominion."*

The last few weeks of Hastings' stay in India, were taken up in devising plans of retrenchment in the public service, in adjusting the public accounts, in receiving farewell addresses from all classes of his countrymen, in writing letters to the India House, and to his agent, Major

* Kaye's "Administration of the East India Company," Part 4, Chap. ii. Heber's Indian Journal, Vol. 1, Chap. ix.

Scott, the former announcing his early departure, the latter complaining of Pitt's apparent treachery to himself. Some time, of course, was devoted to his own private affairs, to the paying of farewell visits, and to the writing of farewell letters to all the native chiefs and princes with whom he had corresponded for so many years.

On the 1st February, 1785, he delivered up the keys of the Treasury and Fort William to his next in Council, Mr. Macpherson,* and expressed to his colleagues "the warmest and most affectionate wishes for the prosperity and success of their public administration, and for their private ease, credit and happiness."

A crowd of sorrowing friends and admirers stood ready to greet him, as for the last time his bearers brought him back to his own dwelling at Alipur. In returning their greetings he nearly lost his self-control. That same afternoon, he went down with three intimate friends to the ghát or quay, where lay the state-barge that would bear them down the Húghli to Kijrí,

* Macpherson had been transferred from the service of the Nawáb of Arkot to the Madras Civil Service. Returning home, he entered Parliament, but soon after went to Calcutta as second member of Council. He acted as Governor-General for about twenty months.

On the 6th, he boarded the *Barrington*, and two days later the three friends and the pilot left the good ship speeding southward, on her long voyage to the land which Hastings had not seen for sixteen years.

NOTE.—Among those whom Hastings' patronage drew to Calcutta was the painter Zoffany, who presented his "Last Supper" as an altarpiece to St. John's Church, since known as the Old Cathedral. This church replaced the older one, which had been destroyed by Suraj-ad-daula in 1756. Hastings himself took a leading part in the preliminary business, and the first stone was laid during his absence by Mr. Wheeler in April 1784. The new building was finished and consecrated in 1787. —"Handbook to Calcutta."

BOOK IV.

CHAPTER I.

1785—1788.

NOTHING of importance marked the voyage home. "I had," wrote Hastings to one of the three who saw him last at the Sandheads, "a pleasant voyage without bad weather; a clean and tight ship; officers of skill and attention, and even of science; a society that I loved; and a rapid course." He only complained that his mind was stupid, and that he never passed a night without a slight fever.* The monotony of life at sea was broken by a short stay at St. Helena, and he employed his ample leisure in writing a narrative of the last three months of his rule, and in scribbling

* Gleig's "Warren Hastings," Vol. 3., Chap. viii.

verses in imitation of Horace. On the 13th of June he landed at Plymouth, and next morning posted off to London.

The first meeting with his wife took place at Maidenhead on the 17th. The rest of the month they spent together in London, performing "all the duties of loyalty, respect, and civility," and as happy as love could make a well-matched but still childless couple. Ever since the austere and stately Queen Charlotte had smiled upon Mrs. Hastings, her reception in the drawing-rooms of the great was assured. Her husband, too, was graciously received at Court. His welcome at the India House was all that he could desire. The Directors unanimously thanked him for his great services Among the ministers, Lord Thurlow greeted him as a true friend. Even from Dundas, who under the new India Act had become President of the new Board of Control, a machine devised by Pitt for the gradual absorption of the Company's power by the Crown,* he

* Pitt's India Bill of 1784, created a Board of Control composed of six Privy Councillors, in whose hands the Government of India was virtually centred. Of the twenty-four Directors, three were formed into a secret committee, subject to the orders of the Board. The Court of Proprietors was reduced to utter powerlessness.

met at this time with nothing but the compliments due to his deserts. Hastings' friends, public and private, were numerous and powerful. In short, as he himself wrote a few weeks later, "I find myself everywhere, and universally, treated with evidences, apparent even to my own observation, that I possess the good opinion of the country."

At Cheltenham, Tunbridge, and Bath, Hastings and his wife seem to have spent the remainder of that year. Together they drank the waters of those places and enjoyed the company which they found there. Hastings' letters of this period show the interest he still took in Indian affairs, and his readiness to help the Ministry with advice on questions raised by the working of the new India Act. If a shadow of coming trouble now and then crossed his path, he soon escaped from it into the sunshine of surrounding bliss, of dreams fulfilled or still awaiting fulfilment. One of these latter now occupied his thoughts; the dream of his early childhood, the hope that he might one day become owner of the old ancestral domain at Daylesford. He had brought home no more than £80,000, after thirteen years of high office in a country where any less scrupulous governor might, in the same circumstances, have amassed a million, if not much more*. With a part of this money he made a handsome offer to the owner of Daylesford, but in vain. Mr. Knight refused to part with his property on any terms; and so, for the present, Hastings had to content himself with buying a small estate in Old Windsor, called Beaumont Lodge. His town house for the next four years was in Wimpole Street. It was not till 1788 that Mr. Knight agreed to sell him the greater part of Daylesford for about £11,424.†

By that time, the malice of his enemies and the force of party spirit had once more triumphed over the dictates of common justice and gratitude to a public hero. With a zeal which he may have mistaken for patiotism, added to the vindictive rage of an ousted placeman and a discomfited partisan, Burke had once more made himself the blind tool and ready slave of the unforgiving Francis. Under the influence of that lying Belial, he had worked himself into the belief that the saviour of India was the worst of criminals,

* "Debates of the House of Lords," &c., p. 442. Mrs. Hastings owned a separate sum of about £10,000, the proceeds of her marriage settlement.

† Gleig's "Warren Hastings," Vol. 3, Chap. xii.

an enemy to the whole human race. His rash zeal and fiery eloquence had dragged the leaders of the great Whig party, some of them against their will, into a course of action at once impolitic and cruelly unjust. As early as June, 1785, he had announced in the House of Commons his intention erelong, to "make a motion repecting the conduct of a gentleman just returned from India."

In the following February he carried out his threat.* His demand for copies of certain papers having, through Pitt's influence, been twice rejected, he proceeded, with Francis' help, to draw up a list of charges against the object of that crafty schemer's undying hate. Eleven of these were presented on the 4th April, and as many more were added later to the black account. On the 25th, Hastings obtained leave to be heard in his own defence. Five days only were granted him, "to reply to a volume that could not be read in less than two." But he worked hard, and at

* It has been argued that the rashness of Hastings' agent, Major Scott-Waring, in challenging Burke to make his threat good, provoked the issue which Burke's friends would else have shirked. This may be true, in default of evidence to the contrary; but to me it seems more probable that Burke's mind was already made up for war *à outrance* with the late Governor-General.

four p.m. on the first of May began the reading of an elaborate paper, to which the House listened, he says, "with an attention unusual in that assembly." For six hours and a half the reading went on, his friend Markham and two clerks taking their turn when he himself grew tired. The next evening he finished his task, to the great relief, we may suppose, of all who heard him; although Hastings, for his part, went home thoroughly satisfied, good easy man, with the impression which his able but long-winded statement had left upon a House accustomed to eloquence of a much more stirring sort. "It instantly turned all minds to my own way," he wrote out to his friend and former secretary, Thompson.*

From this delusion he was soon to be awakened. Burke, indeed, was defeated in the beginning of June in his attempt to prove Hastings guilty of hiring out British soldiers, "for the purpose of extirpating the innocent and helpless people inhabiting the Rohillas." Pitt threw his influence into the scale against the accusers; and Dundas himself, in spite of his share in the previous censure of Hastings on this very point, now declined

* Gleig's "Warren Hastings," Vol. 3, Chap. ix.

to join in a more serious attack on one who had meanwhile deserved so well of his country For a time it seemed as if the friends of the accused Governor were justified in crowing over their discomfited assailants. But on the 13th June, Fox opened the next charge, which branded Hastings with wanton cruelty and gross extortion in his treatment of Chait Singh. Among the leading speakers on the same side was Philip Francis, who, like many other old Indians, had easily found a seat in the House of Commons.

On this occasion Pitt spoke. The hopes of Hastings' friends ran high, as the youthful Minister disposed of all arguments founded on Chait Singh's sovereign rights, and vindicated the Governor-General's conduct in calling upon his vassal for further aid in a time of special difficulty. He declared that Hastings was right in levying a fine for the vassal's rejection of his just demands, and even, if need were, in putting the Rajah under arrest. His praise of Hastings' conduct during the insurrection was heightened by his scornful censure of the "dishonest and malignant" Francis. But just as every one felt sure of a second victory for the defence, Pitt surprised his hearers by announcing his intention to vote for the side against which he had argued. "The whole," he said, "of Mr. Hastings' conduct showed that he intended to punish Chait Singh with too much severity." That intention he held to be criminal, and on that ground alone "he should, though with extreme reluctance, vote for the impeachment of Mr. Hastings."

At this sudden change of front none were more amazed than the bulk of Pitt's own followers, who had come prepared to vote against Fox. Some of them were too honest to turn round with their leader, but Dundas, and many more, followed him into the same lobby with Fox, Burke, and Sheridan; and Hastings was condemned by a majority of forty in a House of only 198 members.

The true cause of this strange manœuvre, this seeming betrayal of a friend in need, has never been clearly explained. Was Dundas really afraid that Hastings, through his influence with the King, might yet make his way into the Board of Control, and there draw to himself the entire management of Indian affairs? He certainly told Lord Maitland that he and his friends in opposition had "done the business of the Ministry, by keeping Hastings out of the Board of

Control." It seems hardly possible to suppose that Pitt himself was moved by jealousy of a possible rival in a retired Governor of fifty-three, whose life had been spent in India, who had only just entered the House of Commons, and who knew next to nothing about home politics, about the interests of different classes in England, or the management of great political parties. It is equally hard to believe that he suddenly changed sides, as Dundas alleged, because he found "the charges so strong and the defence so weak, that the Government were compelled to give way."* Not thus, at any rate, can we hope to reconcile his speech on the Banáras charge with his vote. Did he, as others have thought, agree to the impeachment as a means of weakening the opposition, or as a sop to the clamours of a powerful and well drilled party?† Of one thing only we may be sure, that policy rather than justice drove the great Minister into a course which involved Hastings in fresh anxieties, and provoked the just indignation of Hastings' friends. Among these was Lord Chancellor Thurlow, who de-

* Sir G. Lewis's "Administrations of Great Britain," Chap. ii.

† Nicholls in his "Recollections" thinks that he consented to the impeachment, "because he saw the control which he should obtain over the Opposition by such acquiescence."

clared, with reference to Pitt's reasoning, that "if a girl had talked law in those terms, she might have been excusable." *

Hastings himself, in a letter to Thompson, thus pithily summed up the issue of the recent debate: "I have been declared guilty of a high crime and misdemeanour in having *intended* to exact a fine too large for the offence, the offence being admitted to merit a fine, from Cheyt Singh." With the Ministry and the Opposition both against him, and the newspapers filled with "wicked lies" about him and his wife, he consoled himself with the improvement of his Windsor estate, and the pleasures of a garden which he helped to stock with fruits and vegetables from India. An excellent horseman, he enjoyed his rides upon his favourite Arab, and the enjoyment was complete when his wife was able to accompany him, mounted on another Arab imported for her special use. The shawl-goats which Turner had sent him from Tibet died on their way home; but a Bhután bull reached him "in fine health." Turner had also sent him an ample supply of Himalayan turnip-seeds; and he amused himself with vain efforts to grow mangoes,

* Nicholls's "Recollections," Vol. 1, Ch. xiii.

custard apples, leechees, and other fruit dear to the memory of retired "old Indians."

Meanwhile his dear friend, David Anderson, who had followed him home from India, began to draw up a full vindication of Hastings' Indian career, from outlines furnished by his old master, to be filled in from the piles of records stored up in Leadenhall Street. In this task he was aided by other volunteers, all eager to come forward on behalf of the man they loved.

Early in the Session of 1787, the charge concerning the Oudh Begams was opened by Sheridan, in a speech six hours long, whose amazing eloquence was acknowledged, as he sat down, by such a storm of cheers and clappings as the old hall of St Stephen's had never before reëchoed. So wild was the excitement, that the debate had to be adjourned, for no other speaker would have got a hearing. When the debate was resumed, Pitt once more spoke against Hastings' and the hostile vote was carried by a majority of nearly three to one. The debates on the remaining charges ended mostly in the same way. At last, on the 3rd April, the Commons resolved to impeach the late Governor-General at the bar of the House of Lords. On the 21st May, Hastings was brought thither, in the custody of the Sergeant-at-Arms, to hear the articles of impeachment read out by Burke before the highest tribunal in the land. That done, the great prisoner was released on bail.

A Committee of nineteen managers, headed by Burke himself, was appointed by the Commons to conduct the trial of a statesman, whose services to his country ought rather to have gained him a seat of special honour among his future judges. It is sad to find on the list of managers the name of Sir Gilbert Elliot, brother of that Alexander Elliot, whose untimely death in 1781 had been to Hastings as the loss of a promising younger brother. The same man, later in the year, was active in the impeachment of Sir Elijah Impey, whose friendship for the younger Elliot had likewise been very great. Another gentleman, whom Burke strove hard to place upon the Committee, was very properly excluded by a vote of the Commons. The passionate Irishman, who, as an old East India proprietor and a friend of Philip Francis, knew more than most men about one side of Indian affairs, told his colleagues that without Francis' help the business might be damned. But the House of Commons steadily refused to give Hastings' boldest and most malignant foe any share in the conduct of a trial designed to further the ends of justice only. The managers, however, resolved to keep Francis at their elbow as long as they could. At their request he attended their meetings, and aided them largely with the fruits of his misapplied talents and his unblest experience.

The rest of the year was spent by Hastings in the needful preparations for his defence. Three eminent lawyers laboured zealously on his behalf. He had already written to his friends in India, such as Sir John Shore and Mr. Thompson, to collect testimonials in his favour from the leading natives of Bengal, and "such other creditable vouchers of whatever kind, beyond the provinces, as may refute the calumnies with which I have been loaded." In the midst of his own annoyances and his wife's distress, he takes comfort in seeing the latter "gain health and strength visibly, though of a constitution still too susceptible." In August, he assures Thompson that he has "borne with perfect indifference all the base treatment" which he has received, "except the ignominious ceremonial of kneeling before the House of Lords." In the following February, a few days before the opening of the great trial, he tells the same friend that Mrs Hastings, "in spite of some occasions on which she suffers her spirits to be affected more than they ought with the impending transactions, gains daily though but gently, both in health and the appearance of it; and I," he adds, "am well."*

Hastings' trial was fixed for the 13th February, 1788. On the 4th of that month, his friend and fellow-sufferer, Impey, was arraigned before the House of Commons on various charges, including the murder of Nand-Kumár. More fortunate than Hastings, the late Chief Justice knew how to better a good cause with an eloquent tongue. His great speech in answer to the Nand-Kumár charge, turned the tables upon his accusers, and drew from Pitt himself the admission that in like circumstances he might have acted as Impey had done.† In less than four months, Sir Elijah was acquitted on all the graver charges, and his mortified assailants threw up the game.

On the day appointed, more than two hundred of England's peers marched, in their robes of state, from their own House into Westminster

* Gleig's "Warren Hastings," Vol. 3, Chap. xiii.
† "Memoirs of Sir E. Impey," Chap. xiii.

Hall, a fitting theatre for an event of the highest national concern. In the long galleries, hung like the walls with scarlet, sat the Queen, the Princesses, the peers' ladies nearly all in mourning, ambassadors from every country, some two hundred members of the House of Commons, Mrs. Siddons, Mrs. Fitzherbert, wife already in fact of the Prince of Wales, Sir Joshua Reynolds, the learned Dr. Parr, and a number of other men and women, eminent in their day for beauty, talents, or public worth.* Gibbon himself was seated among the Commoners. Seats in the body of the noble building were reserved for the Managers, who all appeared in full dress. Outside the Hall, a curious crowd was kept in order by hundreds of the King's Guards, mounted or on foot.

Into this scene of solemn splendour, Hastings presently entered, "in a plain poppy-coloured suit of clothes."† "He looked," says Macaulay, "like a great man, and not like a bad man." His portraits show him as about this time he may have appeared; his grey hair surrounding a lofty, thoughtful-looking forehead; his arched,

* Dr. Johnson had died shortly before Hastings' return to England.

† Gleig's "Warren Hastings," Vol. 3, Chap. x.

pensive brows overhanging a pair of soft yet sad eyes; a long and sensitive nose contrasting with the firmness of his lips and chin; and an oval face, "pale and worn," says Macaulay, "but serene, on which was written as legibly as under the picture in the council chamber at Calcutta, *Mens æqua in arduis.*" His small spare figure was still upright, and his bearing full of dignity, yet marked with all the deference due to so august a Court. After standing for some time, the observed of all observers, he was allowed by the Chancellor, Lord Thurlow, to take a chair.

At noon the Court was opened, and the Sergeant-at-Arms summoned "Warren Hastings, Esquire, to come forth" and save his bail. Hastings advanced to the bar, and on bended knees awaited the Chancellor's permission to rise. That promptly granted, he listened to the Proclamation charging him with high crimes and misdemeanours, and made brief but becoming answer to Lord Thurlow's opening address.

Two days were spent in the reading of the charges and the defendant's replies. Then Burke himself, in a speech which lasted four days, and drove some of his hearers into hysterics and fainting-fits, went into a full review of Hastings'

20

career, exhausting the language of abuse, and pouring out the whole wealth of his luxuriant rhetoric in the attempt to justify the impeachment of a criminal who had betrayed the trust of the Commons, sullied the honour of the English nation, trodden under foot the rights of the Indian people, and shown himself "the common enemy and oppressor" of mankind at large. It was a masterpiece of night-mare eloquence, which carried away the whole assembly, stirring even the strong-headed Chancellor into words of praise, and tempting poor Hastings at times to deem himself the monster that Burke's violent fancy loved to paint him.

But it was after all a sad display of hysteric fury about imaginary crimes. The great orator raved and screeched like a madman, or a raging fishwife, against a gentleman whose alleged misdeeds were as nothing to his acknowledged merits. He spoke of Hastings as "a captain-general of iniquity, one in whom all the fraud, all the tyranny of India are embodied, disciplined, and arrayed." He charged him with "avarice, rapacity, pride, cruelty, ferocity, malignity of temper, haughtiness, insolence—in short, everything that manifests a heart blackened to the very blackest, a heart dyed deep in blackness, a heart gangrened to the core" Hastings "murdered Nand-Kumár by the hands of Sir Elijah Impey." He "is not satisfied without sucking the blood of fourteen hundred nobles. He is never corrupt without creating a famine. . . . . He is like the ravenous vulture, who feeds on the dead and the enfeebled." He is a "swindling Mecænas," "a bad scribbler of absurd papers, who could never put two sentences of sense together." He is "a man whose origin was low, obscure, and vulgar, and bred in vulgar and ignoble habits." Such, yelled Burke, "are the damned and damnable proceedings of a judge in hell, and such a judge was Warren Hastings." In a closing burst of Billingsgate, he denounces his victim as "a captain-general of iniquity, thief, tyrant, robber, cheat, swindler, sharper."

Such was the language in which the foremost orator, and one of the oldest statesmen of that day, vented his own spleen and the malice of Philip Francis on the man of all others who least deserved to be held up to public obloquy. How grossly he exceeded the license of fair invective, even on points that might still be open to question, the reader of these pages will have already seen. To denounce the great Proconsul as another and a blacker Verres, was even more absurd than Macaulay's subsequent attempt to prove Impey another Jeffries. Happily for Hastings, it was not on speeches, however powerful, but on the weight of evidence carefully sifted, that the question of his guilt or innocence was to turn.

The next sittings of the Court were taken up in discussing points of procedure, in hearing the speeches of Fox and Grey on the Banáras charge, in the reading of papers and the examination of witnesses. The temper of the Managers betrayed itself in their demand that each of the charges should be brought forward, sustained, and defended in its turn. Against this departure from legal usage, Hastings' counsel of course objected, and the objection was enforced by a majority of three to one. Some further attempts to embarrass the defence were equally futile. In due time, Sheridan summed up the charge concerning the Indian Begams in a brilliant and powerful speech that lasted two days, and clinched the fame he had won by his former oration on the same theme. Not long afterwards, Parliament adjourned for that session.

Meanwhile Hastings had his consolations in the endearing company of his *placens uxor*, in frequent intercourse with Impey and many other loyal friends, in the congenial pleasures of country life, in negotiating the purchase of Daylesford, and in studying or imitating the works of his favourite authors. Like most men of strong literary tastes, he wooed the Muses with a fair degree of success, throwing off copies of verses, and prose essays on all kinds of subjects which tempted his active and cultivated fancy. If the possession of a good conscience can bring balm for the wounds of undeserved obloquy, Hastings was happy in that also, even though his enemies mistook the utterances of conscious worth for so many proofs of his blindness to all distinctions between right and wrong.

CHAPTER II.

1789—1803.

THE kind of impression which Warren Hastings made at this time on the minds of witnesses unbiassed by former personal knowledge of him, is well conveyed by the author of "Recollections of the Reign of George III." * "He appeared to me"—says Nicholls—"to be a man of a strong, vigorous, decisive mind, well acquainted with the character of the natives of India, and with the views and interests of its various princes. He seemed to me to be a man capable of extricating himself from difficulties by his great resources and dauntless courage. In one word, he came nearer to the idea which I had formed of an able statesman, than any other man with whom I ever had intercourse. But he was a statesman only for the affairs of India. He knew nothing of the various parties in England, their interests, their designs, or how far they were likely to be

* John Nicholls, son of the physician to George II., sat in the House of Commons during three parliaments in the reign of George III.

influenced or restrained by moral considerations. These were subjects on which he seemed to me never to have formed an opinion."*

The impression thus made on an independent member of the House of Commons grew deeper, as the acquaintance begun in 1788 ripened into a close and lasting friendship. "I think of his memory," writes Nicholls, "with the highest veneration. I think that he was a man of the most powerful mind I have ever conversed with."

The great trial on which hung his fate was destined to drag on very slowly indeed. In 1788 thirty-five days had been spent in hearing two of the twenty charges. The king's illness in the autumn was followed by stormy debates in Parliament over the Regency, and men's minds were already engaged in watching the first throes of the French Revolution. It was not till April 1789 that the trial was resumed, with the charge concerning the receipt of presents. In his opening speech Burke denounced Hastings with having murdered Nand-Kumar by the hands of Sir Elijah Impey. Against such language Hastings and his friends appealed to the House of Commons, and Burke was formally censured for exceeding the limits of his brief. But no rebuffs

* Nicholls's "Recollections," Vol. 1, Ch. xiii.

could discourage the passionate avenger of India's fancied wrongs. Fresh attempts of the managers to warp in their own favour the rules of legal evidence were duly baffled by the Lords. In the whole of that Session only seventeen days were employed on the impeachment, and barely half the articles of the third charge had been examined, when the House once more adjourned.

In 1790 more time was wasted to as little purpose. Meanwhile Parliament was dissolved, and the friends of Hastings pleaded the dissolution as a bar to further proceedings. But the new Parliament rejected the plea, and in May 1791 the trial again went on. One more charge, that of corruption, was then brought forward; the remainder having been dropped by general consent. That year's proceedings closed with the reading of Hastings' defence. The next two years, memorable for the events which issued in the outbreak of the long war between England and the French Republic, were taken up with the speeches of counsel and the examining of witnesses for the defence. In the Session of 1794 the Managers replied upon the several charges, and produced some further evidence in completion of their case.

Seven years had now elapsed since the Peers

were marshalled for the first great gathering in Westminster Hall. Great events had happened meanwhile in Europe and Asia. In France the Revolution had not only destroyed the monarchy, suppressed the priesthood, and proscribed the nobles, but it had devoured its own children, Danton and Robespierre. The avenging armies of the Duke of Brunswick had been driven back across the French frontiers, and Prussia had been glad to sue for peace. Lord Cornwallis had come home crowned with glory from the campaign which stripped Tippu of half his father's dominions. At home Burke had quarrelled with his Whig friends for opposing the war with Republican France. A milder Reign of Terror had begun in England with the suspension of the Habeas Corpus Act. At sea a great English defeat off Cape St. Vincent had been compensated by Lord Howe's famous victory on the 1st of June. Kosciusko's gallant struggle to save Poland's freedom from utter extinction had been made in vain, and the slaughter of 30,000 Poles at Praga by the fierce Suwarrow sealed the ruin of an ill-starred cause.

During these years Hastings had spent much time and labour in the improvement of his Daylesford estate, where he took up his abode in 1791. Between that event and the sale of Beaumont Lodge in 1789, he had rented a house in Berkshire. In rebuilding the old house at Daylesford, in bringing the farm lands into working order, and adorning the pleasure-grounds with the fairest fruits of English landscape-gardening, he had laid out during his trial more than forty thousand pounds. The amount was more than doubled by common rumour, which depicted him as living at the rate of twenty thousand a year, and squandering twenty thousand pounds on the newspapers which sold their columns to his friends.* He may have been careless and openhanded with his money; but his style of living, as his friends could testify, was "rather below than exceeding the rank of life which my former station might have entitled me to assume;" and he affirmed "most positively," that his regular expenses both in town and country had not, "one year with another," exceeded £3,500 a year.

At length in January, 1795, the Lords began to take counsel together as to "the mode of giving judgement on high crimes and misde-

* Hastings' letter of September 22, 1795, to the Court of Directors. "Debates of the House of Lords," &c., pp. 436-440.

meanours." Towards the end of February, they proceeded in due form to discuss the question of Hastings' guilt or innocence. Lord Thurlow's place as Chancellor had been taken some years before by his old opponent, Lord Loughborough; but the weight of Thurlow's judgment and long experience, still gave him the lead in the business over which he had so ably presided. Seven days of March were spent in debating the grave questions involved in the first charge alone. The articles of charge concerning the Begams were duly weighed and dismissed in two days. Three more sufficed for the charge of taking presents, and two for that of corruption in the matter of contracts and appointments. Lord Thurlow's strong good sense, his perfect mastery of details, his weighty reasoning, and forcible clearness of statement, had never been shown to greater advantage than in these last days of a trial, which, as he said, "for its duration, and the immense mass of criminality imputed to the defendant, had no parallel in the history of this or of any other country."

At last the "immense quantity of rubbish and trash," as he called it, had been fairly sifted of "the very little evidence" it contained. On each count of the impeachment, the Peers who had originally formed the Court had voted, with few exceptions, in favour of the accused. On the 23rd April, the final verdict was pronounced, with due solemnity, in the Hall which seven years before had witnessed the first impeachment before the Lords. On that occasion Hastings, as the Archbishop of York declared, had been treated "more like a horse-stealer than a gentleman. His hour of triumph was now come. Once more the noble Hall was crowded with spectators. Of the peers who had figured in the former pageant, many had gone to their long rest. A few of the Managers were dead or absent, and the rest no longer met as friends. A new generation helped to fill the galleries, and the number of peers who had sat through the long trial was only twenty-nine. Those peers who, for one reason or another, were to take no part in pronouncing the final verdict, stood unrobed about the throne, spectators only of the coming solemnity.

Warren Hastings having knelt down before the Court, was then bidden to rise and withdraw. To each of the few peers who formed the Court, the Lord Chancellor then put the question, "Is

Warren Hastings, Esq., guilty or not guilty of the first article of charge?" As junior Baron, Lord Douglas was the first to make answer. Standing uncovered, with his right hand on his breast, he replied, "Not guilty, upon my honour." When each peer in his turn had declared his vote, Lord Loughborough himself, in like manner, pronounced the words, "Guilty, upon my honour."* On this article, Hastings was acquitted by twenty-three votes to six. Fifteen times was the same process repeated. On the first two charges, those namely, which concerned Rajah Chait Singh and the Begams, the same number of votes, twenty-three, was recorded in Hastings' favour. On two charges of bribery and corruption, he was acquitted unanimously. On the remaining charges, the adverse votes ranged from two to five. Eighteen of the twenty-nine, including one archbishop and two bishops, found him not guilty on any count. Lord Mansfield acquitted him on all but one, and that concerned a question rather of law than justice †

Once more Hastings came forward, knelt down, and was bidden to rise. Thereupon the Lord

* "Debates of the House of Lords."

† He allowed that the present received from Nobkissen had been "taken for the Company," but he held that in this instance Hastings had acted illegally. (Debates of the House of Lords.)

Chancellor pronounced his acquittal on "all things contained" in the articles of impeachment. "You are, therefore, discharged," he curtly added, "paying your own fees." Hastings bowed respectfully and retired; his honour vindicated, but himself, in point of wordly fortune, a ruined man. When he turned his back on Westminster Hall, he could not tell, says Mr. Gleig, "whence the funds were to come by which the weekly bills of his household were to be discharged."* He was growing old, the costs of the trial were enormous, the Company had never granted him a pension, and from neither party in Parliament could he hope for employment in the public service.

He did hope, however, that some feeling of pity for a man so cruelly wronged, some desire to atone for past injustice, might lead the Ministry to reimburse him for the heavy expenses of the late impeachment. The country, he thought, would surely defray the costs of a trial which had proclaimed his innocence to the world. But to his prayer for help in bringing his claim before Parliament, Pitt returned an ungracious answer. He "did not conceive that he should be justified in submitting the petition of the late Governor-

* Gleig's "Warren Hastings," Vol. 3. Chap

General of India to the consideration of the sovereign."

Hastings' old friends in the East India Company, were still ready and eager to help him to the best of their power. They knew that the legal charges for his defence alone exceeded £70,000, and that Lord Cornwallis, the late Governor-General, had just been rewarded with a pension of £5,000 a year. At a general meeting of East India proprietors on the 29th May, speaker after speaker, with one or two exceptions, extolled the value of Hastings' "long, faithful, and important services," and upheld the duty of rewarding those services with an annuity of £5,000, and a sum sufficient to cover the legal expenses of his defence. A general ballot, taken a few days later, confirmed the resolutions passed at the previous meeting. The Court of Directors voted, in their turn, to the same effect.

But even this act of justice to the Company's late servant was to be robbed of half its virtue by the interference of the Board of Control. After months of controversy touching the right of the Company to grant money in payment of Hastings' costs, the Directors, in the following March, had to limit their bounty to a pension of £4,000 a year for twenty-eight years and a half, dating back from June, 1785. A few days later they voted Hastings a loan of £50,000, free of interest, for a term of eighteen years.* This sum, with the arrears of pension, would at least enable him to tide over his present difficulties, if it could not altogether bar their return. It saved him, in fact, from utter ruin at a time when popular rumour, mindful of former Nabobs, and fed with the slanders circulated by his enemies, spoke of him as revelling in untold riches.

Not the least of his consolations at this time of pecuniary pressure, was the receipt of congratulatory letters and addresses from admirers of every class and race in those parts of India where he had been best known. The names of Morgan, Popham, Forbes, and other officers of renown, headed the signatures to the brief but fervent utterances of esteem and sympathy forwarded by the officers quartered at Chunar, Fathigarh, Cawnpore, Dinapore, Fort William, or presented at home by the chosen mouthpieces of every division of the Bengal army. Similar addresses, signed by hundreds of English and native residents in Calcutta, expressed in terms of equal warmth the general rejoicing at the acquittal of a statesman so justly honoured and so hardly

* "Debates of the House of Lords," &c.

used. Conspicuous among the native addresses were three signed by all the leading citizens, Hindu and Mohammadan, of Banáras.

It may, of course, be pleaded that some of these effusions, as well as the testimonials forwarded during the impeachment, are worth little as marks of genuine sympathy spontaneously offered. Everyone who knows aught of Indian ways, knows how easily such things can be made to order. An English Collector, as Macaulay reminds us, "would have found it easy to induce any native who could write to sign a panegyric on the most odious ruler that ever was in India."

But Mr. Lumsden, in forwarding the Banáras addresses to Sir John Shore, then Governor-General, shows that with these, at any rate, English influence had nothing whatever to do. When some of the leading citizens came and told him of their desire to sign the address drawn up by Bissambar Pandit, if only they were sure Government would not object, he simply told them in return that "their signing or not signing depended entirely on their own option," and that this was "a matter perfectly indifferent to Government."*

* "Debates of the House of Lords," &c.

As for the natives of Calcutta, they had already caught from their white neighbours something of that freer spirit which breathes in their descendants of to-day. Their congratulations, at any rate, as well as those of his own countrymen, fell like balm upon Hastings' spirit, consoling him, as he said, "for the want of money to throw away on the luxuries of a farm and a greenhouse, and on the tax of a town residence."

From this time forth Hastings lived the life of a country gentleman, owning an estate of 650 acres, to whose improvement he set himself with an energy unchilled by years and misfortunes. He amused himself with breeding horses, fattening bullocks, growing barley-wheat by new methods, trying new kinds of food upon his cattle, cultivating his gardens, and attempting to raise fruits and vegetables from Indian seeds. At certain seasons he took his wife to town for a few weeks, or paid a visit to Impey's place in Sussex, or to some other of his old friends. "Of the ingredients of happiness," he writes to Thompson, in 1803, "I possess all but one, and that occasionally comes and goes. . . . . My beloved wife is what she was in her moral and spiritual substance, and I should and ought to be perfectly contented, if her health (which is not worse, but rather better) was more stable. The worst is, we live too much secluded from society, excepting that of our neighbours, and too remote from our friends; but our hearts turn to them with as much warmth as ever, and with as hearty an interest in their concerns." *

In return for Hastings' visits to Newick, some of the Impey family often stayed as welcome guests at Daylesford. Sir Elijah himself had taken like his old friend to farming;† and we may imagine how their talk would sometimes turn aside from politics, literature, art, or family affairs, to a comparison of the progress made by each in his new pursuit.

True to his Indian training, Hastings always rose early and took his cold bath every morning. After spending an hour among his books and papers, he breakfasted, always by himself, in his own room on bread and butter and tea, which he would never allow to be watered twice. When Mrs. Hastings and her guests assembled for breakfast, he would come and entertain them, says Mr. Gleig, with a copy of his own verses on some topic of passing interest, with a passage

* Gleig's "Warren Hasting's," Vol. 3, Chap. xii.
† "Memoirs of Sir E. Impey," Chap. xvi.

from some favourite author, or with the latest news contained in the journals of the day. Great, we are told, was the disappointment of his friends, if no verses were forthcoming; but some of them, perhaps, if the truth were known, found greater pleasure in hearing him talk about things in general, with a gravity lightened by his playful humour and the winning courtesy of his address. Like other great men, Hastings had his little vanities; but these were clearly of a kind that only the more endeared him to those who knew him the most intimately.

He played to perfection the part of a courteous and kindly host. Whether he sat for a while among his guests in the large library at Daylesford, or shared, as he generally did, in their out-door amusements, or took his place at the head of his well-furnished dinner-table, his presence always added to the enjoyment of those around him. He adapted himself to his company and the mood of the moment, with an easy grace that never overstepped the bounds of self-respect. He could be grave without dulness, and gay without buffoonery. His own cheerfulness helped to make others cheerful. He had some turn for epigram and repartee, and a keen relish for displays of genuine wit. "He laughed heartily," says Mr. Gleig, "could trifle with the gayest, and thought it not beneath him to relish a pun; but the most remote approach to ribaldry offended his taste, and never failed of receiving from him an immediate check."

His own diet was very simple, and his great temperance in eating and drinking may have added some years to his long life. His favourite drink was water, and so nice was he about the quality of it, that, while staying in London, he would get his water from a distant spring that rose near Knightsbridge barracks. His old taste for swimming he indulged whenever he could. He was past eighty years old before he gave up his habit of daily riding. Much as he enjoyed his trips to London, and his visits to friends in the country, he was never happier than at home. In the words of one who knew him intimately during his latter years, "it was among his own guests, at his own table, in his own study, and in the bosom of his own family, that he appeared ever most like himself, and therefore to the greatest advantage."*

Of his literary tastes we get an inkling in the

* Gleig's "Warren Hastings," Vol. 3, Chap. xiii.

fact of his fondness for Lucan, from whom, like Pitt, he often quoted; and of the pleasure he took in reading Young's "Night Thoughts" again and again. The one author may have reflected his political, the other his moral and religious sentiments. Among the poets of his own day, he seems to have given the highest place to Scott, whose war-songs fired his patriotism in 1803, and whose "Marmion" filled him with just delight. "If you can borrow it," he writes to Thompson in 1808, "read above all things Walter Scott's new poem of Marmion, not for its political worth." Of Malthus, whose doctrines were just then beginning to please or shock his countrymen, Hastings at once formed a high opinion. His pamphlet on population he viewed as "one of the most enlightened publications of this and the last age." * In 1815 he read Scott's new poem, "The Lord of the Isles," through twice, "once with Mrs Hastings, who is disposed to read him once more."

Much of his daily exercise was taken on horseback. He prided himself on his good horsemanship, and delighted in taming the most refractory brutes. Mr. Gleig tells a pleasant story of his success in managing a donkey which had dis-

* Gleig's "Warren Hastings," Vol. 3, Chap. xiii.

mounted young Impey, and several other of his guests. Without saddle or bridle, the old gentleman mounted the unruly beast, and defying all his efforts to unseat his new rider, forced him at last to move on. If the boys had any turn for classic parallels, they must have regarded Hastings as a modern Chiron or another Diomed.

Among other visitors at Daylesford was his old friend Sir John D'Oyley, whose son Charles had lately gone out to India as a writer. With young people Hastings was always a favourite, for his gentle manners and the fatherly interest he took in their wellbeing. Few things pleased him more than the receipt of his first letter from the young civil servant, whom he hastened to thank for this proof of kindly remembrance. Nor could any advice have been sounder or more delicately conveyed, than the few words in which Hastings congratulated his young friend on his early escape from the perils of Calcutta society. "Against these," he writes, "your good sense would have been an insecure guard, and the goodness of your heart would but have more exposed you to them." Young D'Oyley had found a home with his father's friend, Mr. Brooke; and this protection Hastings bade him cherish while he had it. "When you lose it, as you must in the course of a few years, resolve to be in every sense your own master, nor suffer any influence but the rectitude of your own understanding to prescribe your conduct in the pursuit either of pleasure, interest or reputation."*

* Gleig's "Warren Hastings," Vol. 3, Chap. xii.

NOTE.—The following story, which perhaps refers to this part of Hastings' life, was told by Mr. Alfred Gatty of Ecclesfield in No. 80 of "Notes and Queries," for May 10, 1851.

During the latter years of his life Warren Hastings was in the habit of visiting General D'Oyley in the New Forest, and thus he became acquainted with the Rev. W. Gilpin, Vicar of Boldre and author of "Forest Scenery," &c. Mr. Gilpin's custom was to receive morning visitors who sat and enjoyed his agreeable conversation; and Warren Hastings when staying in the neighbourhood often resorted to the Boldre parsonage. It happened one Sunday that Mr. Gilpin preached a sermon on the character of Felix, which commences in words like these:—

"Felix was a bad man, and a bad Governor. He took away another man's wife and lived with her; and he behaved with extortion and cruelty in the province over which he ruled."

Other particulars followed equally in accordance with the popular charges against the late Governor-General of India, who, to the preacher's dismay, was unexpectedly discovered sitting in the D'Oyley pew. Mr. Gilpin concluded that he then saw the last of his "great" friend. But not so: on the following morning Warren Hastings came, with his usual pleasant manner, for a chat with the Vicar, and of course made no allusion to the sermon.

This was told me by a late valued friend who was a nephew and curate of Mr. Gilpin, and I am not aware that the anecdote has been put on record.

CHAPTER III.

1803—1810.

In granting Hastings a loan of £50,000 without interest for eighteen years, the Court of Directors took care to guaad themselves from ultimate loss by stopping half his yearly pension, and taking Daylesford as security for the balance of their loan. Hastings thus found himself charged with a virtual interest of four per cent., while the sum total of his debts remained nearly as large as ever, and his chances of getting clear grew daily less with the growing burdens laid on him by the war. His appeal to the India House in 1799, against what seemed to him "a direct contradiction to the declared terms of the loan," issued in a new and fairer arrangement, under which the interest on the half-yearly payments was allowed to accumulate for the borrower's benefit alone..

It was not long, however, before Hastings had

to sue the Court for some further boon. Careless and profuse he may have been, and Mr. Gleig himself owns that he "never could bring the year's income to cover the year's expenditure." The keeping of his own accounts was certainly not his forte. His long term of Indian government had given him small leisure and few inducements for the practice of household thrift; and the years of struggle at home against the authors of his impeachment, had saddled him with burdens which swallowed up two-thirds or more of his nominal income. The war, moreover, had seriously enhanced the cost of living, at the time when Hastings had least money to spare. He had no extravagant tastes; but, as he wrote to the Court of Directors in 1804, "I cannot conform to that strict line of economy which another might, who possessed by inheritance an income of the same measure as mine, and had formed the habits of his whole life to it. This was not be expected from a man who had passed all the active part of his life in the hourly discharge of public duties, which allowed him little leisure or thought to attend to his own affairs, or to care about them."* He could fairly

* "Gleig's "Warren Hastings," Vol. 3, Chap. xiii.

plead the same excuse for himself that was afterwards made for Pitt, whose debts were paid by the nation he had served so well.

Encouraged by promises of support from Addington, Pitt's successor in the Ministry, and from Lord Castlereagh, then President of the India Board of Control, he appealed to the Court of Directors not to suffer him to descend to the grave, with his "last moments embittered with the prospective horrors of an insolvent debtor." His past services, he said, had been amply rewarded by the Company. As for the sufferings he had endured on their behalf, he could claim from them no compensation for "wrongs which they had not inflicted," although to their benevolence he owed "all of compensation that had been bestowed upon him."

To this prayer for help from an old man of seventy-two, still struggling with the weight of debt which a thankless nation had steadily refused to pay, the Court of Directors gave prompt and liberal answer, by relieving him for the future of all stoppages from his pension. Their bounty would have gone yet further, had it not been checked by the Board of Control. Thenceforth, however, Hastings could look forward to an old age free from small anxieties, and fairly furnished with the means of indulging his benevolence and his social tastes.

It was about this time—in May, 1804—that Hastings, prompted whether by gratitude or public spirit, tried his best to dissuade Addington from yielding up his post in compliance with a hostile vote of the Commons, led by those erewhile rivals, Pitt and Fox. Macaulay will not believe that "a man so able and energetic as Hastings," whose politics on some grave points were not those of Addington, could "have thought that, when Bonaparte was at Boulogne with a great army, the defence of our island could safely be intrusted to a Ministry which did not contain a single person whom flattery could describe as a great statesman." He thinks that Hastings was swayed rather by resentment to Fox and Pitt, than by any regard for the public interest. But the arguments used by Hastings in his interview with Addington, afford no warrant for the imputation thus lightly made. He assures the Minister that the voice of the House of Commons "is not the voice of the people," which is very generally in his favour. During the past week he has "scarce seen a man or woman" who approved of "so unnatural a combination of discordant interests, connexions, and opinions," or failed to express indignation at "the savage attack made at such a time on the feelings, the peace, the health, and perhaps the life of the King." The people see, he added, that full provision has been made for their defence against the threatened invasion; "they see resources called forth for which no one gave this country credit; they are pleased with the economy of the public expenditure; they have proclaimed a spirit of zeal and unanimity, which they certainly neither showed or felt during the last war, nor during the last administration, they have not been intimidated by the power of arbitrary arrests and endless imprisonments; and even your enemies admit your integrity, while they profligately sneer at it." The ministry might be weak in oratory, but Hastings looked on oratory as a poor substitute for "useful matter and progressive action."

Whatever force there might be in such pleadings,* the time for urging them to any purpose had already passed. Addington might possess the confidence of his sovereign and the favour of

* Dean Milman's letter to Sir Cornwall Lewis (Administrations of Great Britain) bears out Hastings' views in this connexion.

the Court. His ministry of mediocrities might still suit the mass of those who, in 1802, had hailed with eager thankfulness the peace of Amiens, only to answer with sad but resolute defiance the challenge once more offered by the First Consul of the French Republic in 1803. But "Britain's guardian gander," as Canning called him, could make no head against the new alliance of his old patron, Pitt, with their common enemy, Fox. As the great camp at Boulogne grew more and more threatening, men's minds turned with increasing hopefulness to Pitt, as the only pilot who could guide his country safely through the storm of war. Ridicule and satire, wielded by Canning and all the wits of the day, helped to undermine the strength of a ministry which had lived from the first on sufferance, and made few powerful friends outside the Court. As soon as the king's illness took a favourable turn, the last excuse for prolonged forbearance towards his favourite had disappeared. To forestal the verdict of the next elections, Addington must resign.

Such, we may well believe, was the kind of answer which Addington gave his well-meaning visitor. From his "candid statement" of the causes that determined him to resign his post, Hastings, like a man of sense, could draw but one conclusion. "You have satisfied me," he said, "that the view which I took of the case was erroneous. I am now as thoroughly persuaded as you can be, that there is but one course open to you, consistent with your honour and your duty :—you must resign."*

Old as he then was, the master of Daylesford had been stirred to action by the appeal which the ministry had already made to the country, for help against the danger that lowered so darkly from the cliffs above Boulogne. In a letter of the 13th of September to his friend Anderson, the old warlike spirit which had fired Clive's young volunteer in 1757 breaks out afresh. He tells his friend how he had "called out the youth of Daylesford," and, with the help of his stepson, Colonel Imhoff, and an old porter from Chelsea, "taught them to march, and to carry themselves erect like soldiers." His ardour however was soon damped by a circular letter from the War Minister to the Lord-Lieutenant; and his little company was disbanded, lest he should "be thought guilty of disaffection, by teaching men

* Gleig's "Warren Hastings," Vol. 3, Chap. xiii.

the use of arms which they might possibly turn against their country, as they were precluded from the defence of it.*"

Hastings watched the struggle thus renewed against Napoleon with an interest brightened by anxiety for his friend Sir Elijah Impey, who had found himself detained at Paris, a prisoner on parole, when the war broke out in May 1803. More fortunate than most of his fellow-sufferers, Impey, who had friends in Talleyrand and Fouché, was allowed to return home in the middle of the following year.† His son Elijah, who was then a student of Christchurch, Oxford, was always a welcome guest at Daylesford. On one occasion he rode back to Oxford, mounted on a beautiful Persian mare which Hastings had given him. Not long afterwards the Dean of his college, the famous Dr. Jackson, came into his room with some Greek and Latin verses in his hand. Young Impey had sent them to Daylesford in honour of his friend's gift; and Hastings who loved all scholarly graces, and hoped to serve his young friend, had forwarded a copy to the Dean. The verses were good enough to please

* Gleig's "Warren Hastings," Vol. 3, Chap. xii.
† "Memoirs of Sir E. Impey," Chap. 18.

that awful functionary; and so there sprang up between the older and the younger scholar a friendship from which the latter was to reap no small advantage, as the years went by.*

About a year after Impey's safe return home, Hastings' heart was saddened by tidings of the untimely death in India of his godson, Hastings Impey, the fairest and best beloved of all his father's children. He had gone out as a writer but a few years before; and the blow was one from which Sir Elijah never quite recovered. Four years later the grey-haired father himself sank peacefully into his last sleep at Newick, in the house where he and Warren Hastings had so often talked together as old and tried friends. Only a few months before his death, he had accompanied Hastings from Newick to Brighton, in order to dine with the Prince Regent at the Pavilion. One of the guests was Sheridan, who had been specially invited to meet the object of his former invective. Sheridan came forward with a pretty speech concerning the part he had once taken against Hastings, as a public pleader bound by duty to make good his case without regard to his own private opinions. Hastings

* Gleig's "Warren Hastings," Vol. 3, Chap. xv

answered him merely with a low bow; and the reconciliation which the Prince had hoped fo, and Sheridan no doubt desired, seems to have gone no further. Possibly Hastings felt that the offer had come too late, for he afterwards told his friends at Newick, that if Mr. Sheridan had "confessed as much twenty years ago," he might have done him some service.

Of the Prince's personal friendliness towards himself Hastings had long since been assured. Alike from his Royal Highness and several of the Whig leaders he had often received marks of attention, which raised within him hopes that were never to be fulfilled. The untimely death of England's great Minister in the first days of 1806, left the ground clear for a coalition of Pitt's followers with the party of his great rival, Fox. Nine years earlier, Burke himself, the most prominent of Hastings' enemies, had followed his only son to the grave. Another enemy, Lord Melville, the Dundas of former days, had lately been impeached by the House of Commons. It seemed to Hastings as if the time had come when he might claim from his country some reparation for past wrongs. On the 14th March, 1806, he waited by appointment on the Prince of Wales at Carlton House.

The Prince received his visitor with that charming courtesy for which "the first gentleman in Europe" was always renowned. After the first exchange of compliments, Hastings proceeded to explain the object of his visit. His hopes of employment, either on the Board of Control or in the government of India, he had already relinquished; but he still looked, he said, to obtain some redress from the House of Commons for the injuries he had suffered through the impeachment. "Though acquitted, I yet stand branded on their records as a traitor to my country, and false to my trust." There was one other point, he added, concerning which his Royal Highness had himself raised expectations in the breast of one whose wishes Hastings had ever preferred to his own. "Though the best, the most amiable of women," Mrs. Hastings was "still a woman," whose heart was set upon a title in which she could have a share. The Prince heard him with courtly attention, reëchoed his praises of Mrs. Hastings, agreed with all he said about himself, and, taking him kindly by the hand, bade him go and talk the matter over with the Prince's chief follower and bosom friend, Lord Moira.

Nothing but disappointment came of the interview from which Hastings had expected much. He had fondly hoped that the Prince's influence would carry his Ministers along with him; but he was soon to discover his mistake. They might grant him a peerage to please the Prince Regent, but they refused to ask Parliament for a reversal of the sentence in which they had once concurred. Hastings, for his part, declined on such conditions the honour which lay within his reach. "I am content," he said to his good friend, Lord Moira, "to go down to the grave with the plain name of Warren Hastings, and should be made miserable by a title obtained by such means as should sink me in my own estimation."

Such disappointments, however, failed to sour his sweet temper, or to wring from him a word of unseemly complaint. The chief desire of his heart was to see his character cleared before the world by a formal vote of the Commons, which would cancel the vote for his impeachment passed in 1787. That piece of justice granted, he would have accepted a peerage to please his wife. or some post of dignity which would mark the Court's and the nation's estimate of his public worth. For the peerage in itself, he seems to have cared as little as a philosopher of ripe age and good social position could do. If he might not have it on his own terms, he would put the bauble aside, even at the cost of a heartache for the woman whom he loved with the fondness of a Jahángir or a Shah Jahán. The passing annoyance relieved itself in an epigram or two, and in the milder expressions jotted down in his diary;* and he went his way with a cheerful spirit, strengthened by the sympathy of many warm friends, including Lord Moira, and upheld by all the consolations of a philosophy which drew its power from sources eminently Christian. In his biographer's own words, he "found happiness himself in dispensing happiness throughout the circle which enjoyed the high privilege of being admitted to a share of his confidence and his esteem."

One of these, as the reader has learned already was Sir John D'Oyley, whom worldly misfor-

Mr. Gleig says, "I cannot discover, either in his diary or in his correspondence, one sentence, or the clause of a sentence, which the most fastidious may with propriety interpret as expressive of disgust."—Vol. 3, Chap. xiii.

tunes had lately driven back to the country where his son Charles had landed as a writer some years before. Charles himself was already married, and doing as well as his father and his father's friend could desire. A younger son, John, a sickly boy of eleven or twelve, had been left behind at school, under Hastings' special charge. Writing to Sir John in August, 1806, Hastings tells him of the bold step he had taken in removing the boy from Twyford to a smaller school, where his recovery from a long illness would be quickened by the tender nursing of the master's wife. For some years Hastings watched over his young charge with right fatherly care. He himself, or one of his friends, would go to see him while at school; and when young D'Oyley spent his holidays at Daylesford, he would examine him carefully about his studies, and send out to his father cheering reports of his son's progress.

In due time John goes to Hayleybury College, which had been founded in 1800 for the training of young men destined to enter the Company's civil service. His kind guardian, who has not lately troubled him with much advice, partly because at his age "advice is not always welcome, even when given with the kindest intentions," now writes to warn John against joining his fellow-students in acts of rebellion towards their masters. "As you value your future character and success in life, my dear Johnny, shun all such detestable cabals, and repel with firmness every advance made to you to poison your mind with their corrupt principles." By beginning early to practise obedience, he would earn a claim to the obedience of others in their turn. Mr. Lendon, adds Hastings, "delighted me in one of his letters, by telling me that *his boys looked up to you.* Be looked up to where you now are, and wherever you are hereafter. Disdain to be the tool of any one; be not a follower even of the wisest and the best; but do what is right from the impulse of your own judgment, not the example of others. In a word maintain the character given of you by Mr. Lendon. *Be looked up to*, and acquire that eminent distinction by example and conciliation."*

In the fortunes of Johnny's father, Hastings took an interest which never flagged. "I thank God," he writes to Thompson, in 1808, "that the best part of me, my affections, remains unin

* Gleig's "Warren Hasting's," Vol. 3, Chap. xii.

jured by wear; nay, I sometimes think them stronger then they were." His constancy in friendship reaped the full harvest sown by his capacity for making friends. Those whom he had once attached to himself, he never lost through any default on his part; and the love they bore him seemed to be the natural reflection of that which burned so steadily in his own bosom. His letters show him continually doing and receiving those little kindnesses which help to keep old friendships alive. In the joys and sorrows of his friends he expresses an equal sympathy, and the expression, however warm, is evidently sincere. There are some men whose tender yearnings seldom, if ever, blossom into words; but Hastings contrived, with no loss of dignity, to utter forth the promptings of a warm and sensitive heart.

The kindly grace with which he compliments Thompson on his eldest daughter, is surpassed by the tenderness of his efforts to console his friend a year later for that daughter's untimely death. "All that your best friends (and I rate myself high in that relation), can effect in this case, is to remind you that there are those who do sympathise with you. All other consolations must spring up from your own breast; its recesses alone can attemper your grief. I would not wish, if I had the power, to cure it. Sorrow for those we love is the link that extends and binds the affinities of this world to the next, and is the pledge of our reunion with the objects of it. This is not a doctrine of the moment; it is the result of the meditations of many past years. I have often and intensely dwelt upon it—I have written upon it—I have devised objections to it and refuted them—and I have imprinted it upon my heart with a holy conviction which is blended with my hopes of eternal felicity."*

And again, some three years later, in 1812, he is consoling the same friend for the loss of another daughter. To assuage his friend's grief must be the work of a "higher power," from whom only consolation can come. "In my eyes," he adds, "you are yet a happy man; happy in the contemplation of the blessings which you still possess, and happy in that of the perfected virtues of her whom it has pleased God to remove from you for a few years of separation, to be followed by a certain reunion with her for ever." Nor has the bereaved father any cause of added bitterness,

* Gleig's "Warren Hastings," Vol. 3, Chap. xii.

either on account of his own conduct, or of "some shade in the character of the lamented object" of his love. "You are conscious of having acquitted yourself of your duty; and of her you can say, in the sentiment of the Duke of Ormond, that you would not exchange your departed child, and lose your sorrow with it, to be the father, and to possess all the affections of a father, of any other daughter out of your own family that could be given you in compensation."

There was much, too, of mellow wisdom in the letter which Hastings wrote to Sir John D'Oyley's elder son, Charles, at the time of his marriage in 1803. After the usual congratulations, he entreats him "for God's sake," to avoid one rock on which many young families have been wrecked. "Avoid entertainments; keep no table; and, that you may avoid the obligation of returning invitations, accept of none, but from persons so much your superiors in age and standing as not to expect it." On all such points he was to take dispassionate counsel with his own reason, and make her answer his fixed law, from which no sneers, censures, or temptations should lead him to depart. "Be the slave of fashion," adds his Mentor, "in indifferent matters; but be your own master and independent in all such as may affect your moral character, or influence either your own happiness, or (which indeed is yours) the happiness of your family."*

If Hastings had been disappointed by the results of his interview with the Prince of Wales, he was spared the further mortification of seeing his arch-enemy, Sir Philip Francis, sent out to India as Governor-General in the room of Lord Cornwallis, who died in 1805, but a few months after his second landing in India as successor to Lord Wellesley. As soon as Fox came into power in 1806, Francis fancied that the prize for which he had so long hungered was within his grasp. He appealed to Lord Wellesley for help in gaining the support of Fox's Tory colleague, Lord Grenville. But the "glorious little man," whose Indian career had opened his eyes to the true worth of his famous predecessor, at once declined to say a word in favour of Hastings' bitterest reviler; and Francis consoled himself with unsparing abuse, not of the Marquis, nor of Lord Grenville, but of the great Whig leader in whose ranks he had always fought.† The prize for

* Gleig's "Warren Hastings," Vol. 3, Chap. xii.
† Brougham's "Statesmen of the Time of George III."

which he had humbled himself in vain, was reserved for Lord Minto, the Sir Gilbert Elliot of a former page.

It was natural that Hastings, who had been so cruelly wronged by the brother of Alexander Elliot, should deplore the selection of such a man for so important an office. He feared, moreover, for the effect which Lord Minto's feelings towards himself might work upon the fortunes of his old friend, Sir John D'Oyley. His forebodings on this point were not, perhaps, wholly groundless. for Sir John did get into trouble of some kind with the new Government. But his estimate of Lord Minto's fitness for his destined post proved on the whole as untrustworthy as such forecasts, made under like conditions, have often done. Sir George Barlow's successor in the Government of India—Sir George had provisionally succeeded Cornwallis—soon learned to tread, so far as a statesman who had the fear of Parliament and the India House before him might safely venture, in the steps of Warren Hastings and the Marquis Wellesley.

To a mind so sensitive as that of Hastings, few things could have been more welcome than the marked change which time had wrought in Lord Wellesley's feelings towards the victim of

Francis' rancour and Burke's delusions. Lord Mornington had gone out to India in 1797 possessed with that strong belief in Hasting's criminality which had led him nine or ten years before to offer himself as a Manager of the famous Impeachment. But his Indian experiences had taught him a very different lesson. The memory of the great Proconsul was still fresh in India, and the conqueror of Tippu found himself assailed and hampered at every turn by the same powers of slander, spite, ignorance, and distrust, which Hastings, with fewer means of resistance, had to encounter. Hastings' whilom censurer become his warm admirer; and when, in 1802, the Nawáb of Oudh offered to recompense his father's friend for the losses incurred through his impeachment, by settling on him an annuity of £2,000, Lord Wellesley made known the offer in one of the most flattering letters which Hastings had ever received.*

This offer Hastings seems to have declined, even before he learned, in 1804, that the pension granted him by the Company would thenceforth be paid in full. It had always been his wish to "owe his fortune" wholly to the bounty of his

* Marshman's "History of India," Vol. 2, Chap. xxvi.

former masters; and the enjoyment of that bounty once assured to him, he would gladly avoid "the weight of a foreign obligation." Careless he might be about spending money, but greedy of money for the sake of spending it on himself he never was.

In each step of Lord Wellesley's Indian career, Hastings saw the vindication and enlarged reflection of his own. The fall of Seringapatam, the treaty of Bassein, the victories of Lake and Wellesley sealed the triumph of that policy for which he had been so bitterly assailed, the policy which aimed at making the British power supreme throughout India. Nor does the resemblance between the lives of the two great Governors stop here. Each had carried out his own policy in defiance of orders and rebukes from Leadenhall Street. After his return home, in 1805, Lord Wellesley also became the mark of hostile proceedings in the House of Commons, especially with regard to his treatment of the Nawab of Oudh. But this time the Ministry stood between the accused and his assailants; and Fox himself, whom experience had made wiser, opposed the motion for his impeachment. The attacks in Parliament were signal failures; but the Court of Proprietors, which had always befriended Hastings, combined with the Directors to pass on Lord Wellesley a vote of censure which was only rescinded after thirty years.

NOTE.—It may have been about the time of his fruitless interview with the Prince of Wales, that Warren Hastings wrote the following lines concerning Francis Pacheco, whose services in Portuguese India were requited by a long imprisonment under false charges afterwards set aside, and whose sad fate was sung by Camoens in Book 10 of his *Lusiad*:—

"Yet think not, gallant Lusian, nor repine
That man's eternal destiny is thine.
Whoe'er it is the adventurous chief befriends,
Fell malice on his parting steps attends.
On Britain's candidates for fame await,
As now on thee, the harsh decrees of fate:
Thus are ambition's fondest hopes o'erreached;
One dies imprison'd and one lives impeached."

CHAPTER IV.

1810—1814.

It was in the year 1813, at the age of eighty, that Hastings once more emerged from his long retirement into the blaze of public notice. For many years past he had been leading the life of a quiet country gentleman, happy in the possession of health and worldly competence, in the love of his accomplished and gentle wife, in the fellowship of many friends, in the following of his favourite pursuits and the discharge of his daily duties, in the happiness which he conferred on all who came within reach of his unfailing bounty or his friendly services. These years, in short, as Mr. Gleig remarks, were "devoted to the well-being of his fellow-men in all ranks, ages, and conditions," from the wedded couples in whose quarrels he was asked to interpose, to the children and youths for whom distant friends claimed his kindly offices, and the widows or orphans whose wants he charitably relieved. To his nearest relatives, the Woodmans, he had always proved a helpful brother, and his wife's children had been brought up and cherished as his own.

In the spring of 1813 he was called up to London, to give evidence before both houses of Parliament on the affairs of a country which he had not seen for twenty-eight years past. The renewal of the Company's Charter was the question of the hour with all who had any voice in the management of our Indian Empire, or any interest in the growth of our Indian trade. Hitherto the great Company, if largely shorn of their political powers, had retained intact their chartered privileges in the matter of trade. But the charter of 1793 was now expiring, and the Ministry of Lord Liverpool had no mind to renew a monopoly which had already outgrown its apparent purpose. To that monopoly we may have owed our eastern empire and all the advantages that flowed therefrom. But the time was come for getting rid of a mischievous anachronism, which shut out the people of England from the free development of their commercial greatness. Napoleon's grand scheme for excluding English wares from the whole Continent of Europe had turned the eyes of our merchants to other and remoter fields of enterprise; the cotton spinners of Lancashire clamoured fiercely for the right of free trade with an English dependency; and the men of Bristol and Liverpool inveighed against the exclusive privileges enjoyed by London as the port of entry for Indian goods. The doom of the Company had in fact been sounded throughout England for several years before the Session of 1813.

The Ministers had agreed with some reluctance, that Parliament should hear the witnesses brought forward by the India House magnates in their defence. Scores of old and present servants of the Company were eager to display their loyalty to the masters in whose service they had made their fortunes or their name. Conspicuous in the one list stood the name of Warren Hastings, in the other, those of Malcolm and Munro. On the 30th March, the white-haired master of Daylesford appeared at the bar of that House of Commons, where, twenty-seven years before, he had read his answer to the charges laid against him by Burke. But the passions of a bygone day were buried in the applause which now greeted him from every side; applause such as had seldom been heard within those walls. He was at once invited to take a chair, and when, after a long examination, he was allowed to withdraw, all the members, he wrote to Charles D'Oyley, "by one simultaneous impulse rose with their heads uncovered, and stood in silence till I passed the door of their chamber."* The House at the time was unusually crowded, and it may be, as Macaulay states, that one or two of those who had taken part in his impeachment kept their seats. But the exceptions only served to emphasize the homage rendered by the rest.

His friend Thompson, who had heard the applause from the Speaker's room, in writing to Sir John D'Oyley, declares his perfect conviction that "there is not at this moment a man in England, the worth of whose private and public character is more universally and indisputably admitted than his is." The warmth of Thompson's friendship hardly overcoloured the simple truth. Nor was Hastings received with less reverence, a few days later by the House of Lords. The Duke of Gloucester took him to the House in his own carriage, waited with him in the outer room, and conducted him into the

* Gleig's "Warren Hastings," Vol. 3, Chap. xiv.

hall where the Lords sat in full committee. During his examination he enjoyed what seems to have been the rare honour of a seat, and the Lords also rose while he retired. "The most marked attention"—says Mr. Thompson—"was paid both to his person and his opinions." The same carriage which had brought him thither took him home; and when the House broke up the Duke himself—says Hastings—"came to make his report of what had passed to Mrs. Hastings, with the same kind of glee that you or your dear father would have expressed upon the same occasion."*

As the first of the witnesses called before Parliamen, Hastings not only cleared the way for his successors; he also helped to indicate new lines of inquiry to the examiners themselves. Age had not yet greatly dimmed his memory, nor weakened his powers of copious statement. His evidence turned chiefly on the settlement of Europeans in India, on the extent of India's demand for English goods, and the policy of encouraging Christian missions in a country ruled by men of Christian race. His opinions on these

* Letter to Charles D'Oyley—Gleig's "Warren Hastings,' Vol. 3, Chap. xiv.

points, however opposed to the more liberal spirit of our own day, or even to the views expressed by the leading statesmen of that time, were at least in harmony with the fruits of his old Indian experiences, and the ideas that still swayed the members of his old service. The free admission of European settlers into India he regarded as a new danger to the peace of that country, and a sure step towards the loss of our Indian possessions. He saw no advantage in opening to all England a trade which had nearly reached its utmost limits under the fostering care of its best guardians, the East India Company. And he looked with evident dislike on all schemes for encouraging missionary enterprise among a people noted for their attachment to their own ancestral creeds.

Reminded of the opinions he had once expressed against monopoly and in favour of free trade, Hastings could only answer that his opinions had undergone a change, and that he did not come there to defend his own inconsistencies. If we regret the change in his case, we must allow for the force of old official traditions, and perhaps of gratitude, working on a man of his great age. And it must be remembered that he erred in good company. Among the witnesses on the same side, was Sir John Shore, who had lately become Lord Teignmouth.* One of the foremost champions of monopoly in the House of Lords was the Marquis Wellesley, whose encouragement of "interlopers" and private trade with India had given sore offence, in the first years of the century, to "the cheesemongers of Leadenhall Street."

As for his views on the other questions at issue, they were held in common by most statesmen and very nearly all the Company's servants of his day. The mutiny of Vellor, in 1806, had taught all but a few enthusiasts a lesson of caution in dealing with the religious feelings and usages of the Indian people. The settlement of white men in India was a bold experiment, whose success has hardly yet been placed beyond a question. Few statesmen, indeed, of that day seem to have looked so far ahead as Lord Grenville, whose speech on the Indian question in the House of Lords foreshadowed the more sweeping reforms of 1833, when the last remnants of the Company's trade-rights were swept away; and of 1853, when the first appointments to the

* The real author of the Perpetual Settlement in Bengal.

Indian Civil service were thrown open to public competition.

Hastings' evidence may have pleased his friends and encouraged the witnesses who came after him. But all the arguments and the eloquence of the Company's champions failed to avert the blow which a Ministry, strong in the support o an approving nation, was prepared to deal at their commercial privileges. Under the Charter Act of 1813, little was left of those privileges save the China trade; Europeans became free to settle under certain conditions in the Company's territories; and in 1814, an Anglican bishop landed in Calcutta as the head of a Church establishment to be maintained at the Company's cost.

Soon after his return to Daylesford, Hastings learned that Oxford was about to confer upon him the tardy compliment of a degree. At his appearance in the noble theatre where he was to be installed a Doctor of Civil Law, the undergraduates rose to a man and greeted him with rounds of enthusiastic cheering. Dr. Phillimore presented him to the Vice-Chancellor in one of those elegant Latin speeches in which the University Orator is always supposed to excel.

The applause of a body of young men assembled at a time of yearly festival, to let off their surplus spirits in cheers, groans, or jokes, may not in itself be worth much. But it served as a test of the new comer's popularity, and at this time Hastings was certainly popular. The warmth of his reception inspired his friend, Elijah Impey, the student of Christchurch, to write a poetical address to Dr. Phillimore. Three copies of the poem were sent to Hastings, who declared himself unable to select passages from an effusion so admirable throughout. "How much I was pleased with the poem," he wrote, "I cannot tell you; but I have a greater pleasure in conveying to you the sentiments and words of my dear Mrs. Hastings. 'Tell him,' she said, 'that I am delighted with it. It is excellent, charming, and has nothing of sickness in the composition of it; nor is it possible to be better.'"

At the moment when Hastings took his place among the Dons of Oxford, he saw himself standing on the brink of pauperism. The term for which his pension had been granted him had well-nigh run out; and unless the Court of Directors came to his succour, beggary stared him in the face. The Court, however, were not unmindful of their debt to the great man who asked them as a favour for that which his past services demanded as a right. They renewed the pension for the term of his natural life. But to all suggestions that the name of Mrs. Hastings might be included in the grant to her husband, they turned a deaf ear. Hastings bore the disappointment with his wonted calmness, thankful at any rate for the boon secured to himself.

Fresh honours awaited him in the following year. In the May of that year the Prince Regent made him a member of his Privy Council. Hastings went through the ceremony of taking his seat, and returned home highly gratified with the long audience granted him by the most affable of princes. By that time all England was rejoicing over the downfal of the great Napoleon, whose defeat at Leipsic in the previous October had opened the way for the advance of the allied armies on the French capital. In April 1814 the spoilt child of Victory abdicated his throne and set out for the island of Elba. Early in June the allied sovereigns entered London as guests of the Prince

Regent. Their visit to Oxford in the same month added a rare lustre to the gay doings of that year's Commemoration. Among those who figured in that courtly gathering was Warren Hastings; and once more the Sheldonian Theatre rang with the noisy honours paid by young Oxford to the most illustrious of her guests.

On the 18th of June Hastings formed one of the splendid company that sat down to the great banquet given at Guildhall by the City of London to the Prince Regent and his august friends. On this occasion he was introduced by the Prince himself to the Emperor Alexander and the King of Prussia, as the most deserving and one of the worst-used men in England. "But I have made a beginning"—added the Prince—"and shall certainly not stop there. He has been created a Privy Councillor, which he is to regard as nothing more than an earnest of the esteem in which I hold him; he shall yet be honoured as he deserves."

In a letter to his friend Anderson, Hastings refers to this pretty speech as uttered "in a manner too flattering to be written, and more audible than was merely necessary for the great personages to whom it was addressed." * It was

* Gleig's "Warren Hastings," Vol. 3, Chap. xiv.

natural that he, like so many others, should be charmed by "the most gracious expressions of benevolence" on the part of one who had quite a princely knack of making pretty speeches. It was true enough, as Thackeray admits, that George IV. was "good-natured—not unkindly," ready sometimes to help a friend in need, or to save an old servant from disgrace. But selfishness, indolence and love of pleasure marked him for their own, and his best intentions fell like seed by the wayside. If Hastings, in spite of past experience, dreamed of any solid advantage from the good things so publicly said and promised by his royal patron, he was soon to find himself once more undeceived.

The excitement and the exertions he underwent at this time of general rejoicing told, at least for the moment, on his health. After the memorable Thanksgiving at St. Paul's, he had "a sharp but temporary fever." Rest and abstinence, however, and the pleasure of seeing his wife "improved to a state of unmixed health and exuberant spirits," soon brought him round; and on the 11th of July he was well enough to take the chair at a dinner given by "the Indian gentlemen" to the new-made Duke of Wellington, still fresh from his crowning victory over

Soult at Toulouse. His speech on this occasion contained some graceful references to the part which Wellington had once played in extending the British power in India, "thus uniting at the same time a brother's glory with his own," and to the train of events by which the victor of Assaye had become the instrument of retributive justice on the author of "the wanton and perfidious aggression at Bayonne." His voice was then so feeble, that only those who sat nearest him could hear him plainly; but his speech, according to the newspapers, was "received with much satisfaction." *

At a dinner given on the 16th July to the Duke of Wellington by the Court of Directors, the first health drunk was that of "Mr. Hastings and the Governments of India." Then followed "The Marquis Wellesley, with thanks to him for his distinguished services in India." On this occasion, Hastings himself does not seem to have been present; but his departure from London was delayed by an invitation to attend the fête given by the Prince Regent at Carlton House on

* Hastings, in a letter to Anderson, denied that his voice was weak, but I am inclined to think that in this instance the reporters were right.

the 21st July. Two days afterwards, Hastings returned with his wife to Daylesford, not sorry to exchange the stir and glitter of the scenes in which he had lately figured, for the quieter attractions of his country home.

Before his departure, some of his friends had been trying to obtain for him the honour of a statue in the India House. Nothing, however, came of this project. When Hastings heard of it through his friend, Sir George Dallas, he refused his assent to every attempt of the kind, "except what should arise from the Court of Directors themselves, and from their own mere motion." Sir George assured him that nothing should be done in the matter that could hurt his feelings; but Hastings insisted that the whole business should be "put an end to altogether."*

* Gleig's "Warren Hastings," Vol. 3, Chap. xiv.

CHAPTER V.

1814—1818.

Hastings returned to Daylesford in good spirits and fair health. But the shadow of coming fate was already falling on his path. In 1813, he had suffered from a numbness in his right side. During his stay in London in the following year, he found himself more than once deprived for a few minutes of the power of speech, by a seizure which affected the muscles of his mouth and of one hand. These atacks, however, soon passed by, leaving him apparently as well as ever. In September, 1815, he described himself to Anderson, with whom he regularly corresponded, as much better than he had been for months past, "happy in witnessing the good health, good spirits, and good looks of Mrs. Hastings, still unabated," and his own, "of each kind, perfect in all points, but memory of the past and present recollection."

He had now given up riding on horseback, but his strength was still equal to the old pursuits of farming and gardening, and he enjoyed as keenly as ever the society of his friends and his books. Nor did he relax from his old interest in the political movements of the day. In a letter to David Anderson, written soon after Bonaparte's triumphant return from Elba, Hastings looks upon the late events in France as falsifying Solomon's adage that there is nothing new under the sun, "for the imagination of man never conceived the invasion of a great empire by a mere adventurer at the head of six hundred men." Nor was he less amazed to contemplate the likelihood—*erelong to prove the fact*—of a foreign confederacy forcing "upon a whole people against their declared choice, a sovereign ruler, and that ruler the untainted blood of their own hereditary monarchs."* Like Fox, and a few other liberal-minded Englishmen of that day, he had always owned to a certain admiration of the great Corsican upstart, whose lurid genius and mad ambition were about to land him, a hopeless exile, on the lonely, well-guarded rock of St. Helena. He admired him much as one might

* Gleig's "Warren Hastings," Vol. 3, Chap. xiv.

admire a hurricane or a raging flood, or the fallen Archangel in *Paradise Lost.*

A few months later, we find his generous spirit vexed at "the miraculous transformation of the beautiful island of St. Helena into a state prison of a deposed emperor." He was "sorry for its degredation, and more so to contemplate the British nation in the character of the jailor of Europe." It was, no doubt, a disagreeable duty which fell to England, but in his sympathy with the famous prisoner Hastings seems to have overlooked the circumstances which justified the jailor's conduct. If Napoleon had been less closely guarded, would not the peace of Europe have soon been once more disturbed? The events that followed his return from Elba explain the sequel of his surrender to Captain Maitland.

Hastings watched the course of events in India with an interest heightened by his friendly relations with Lord Moira, the new Governor-General, and by the memory of his own experiences in the same post. With pardonable pride, the old man compares the success of his own plans in 1781 for defeating the Rajah of Banáras, with the blunders that marked the first year's campaign in Nepal. Our reverses in

1814 he ascribes, not to "the superior skill and courage of our enemies," but to our ignorance of the country invaded, our neglect of the discipline which makes up for inferior numbers, and to the folly of sending three columns "by three *undefined* lines, through an *unknown* labyrinth of thickets and rocks, with a plan for their converging in the same point of attack." His fears that the war might end in a peace that would lower the credit of our arms, and proclaim our "abandonment of the principle to which we owe all our present greatness in India," were happily falsified by the victories of Ochterlony and the treaty of 1816.

Falsified also, perhaps for the best, were his expectations regarding the latter years of Lord Hastings' rule.* Looking at Lord Hastings as "a man of superior talents, steady of purpose, and determined," who had no wish to make new conquests, he reckoned that the Marátha Princes would not care to provoke, at the hands of such a ruler, the punishment they would else receive. "These," he writes, in the winter of 1817, "are my reasons for believing that we shall have peace

* Lord Moira was made Marquis of Hastings at the end of the Gurkha war.

in his time." And yet at that very time Marátha intrigue had driven Lord Hastings to open the series of campaigns, which ended by annihilating the sovereignty of the Peshwas, and making the Company's power supreme in fact and form throughout India. Had Warren Hastings lived but a few months longer, he would have seen the glorious fulfilment of the dream he had begun to cherish sixty years before.

In July, 1816, we find him pleasantly engaged in restoring the ruinous old church at Daylesford, which stood upon his own land and was frequented chiefly by his own tenants and the members of his household "I feel," he wrote to Anderson in October, "a spice of vanity in relating that "I began the demolition of the old fabric on the 8th of July, and completed the whole of the renewed building on the 11th of September . . . . To this account must be added windows, pavements, and doors; against which I set the cove of a ceiling nearly finished, but not a part of the old church. This with the delay of a month for two coats of plaster already laid, and some ornamental additions, will about close the work, so as to admit of divine service in it on Sunday, the 6th of November, just four months from the dilapidation."*

About the same time he amused himself with reprinting a little tract he had once written "upon the means of guarding houses from fires." His letters of this period contain some touching references to that decay which was slowly creeping over his powers of mind and body. One night, "by way of experiment," as he tells Anderson, "I got by heart six lines of Walter Scott, on going to bed, and forgot them, without the power of recovering them, before I had composed myself." In another letter to the same friend, after telling of the "constant recreation, both of body and mind," which the rebuilding of the church had afforded him, he regrets his inability to walk so far as the village and give his orders to the workmen, as each occurs to him, on the spot. And to Elijah Impey, he writes in November, 1816, "You suffer only from the temporary depression of those energies which you inherently possess; and wait only the revolutionary change which every constitution, both of mind and body, possesses for their complete reproduction. That mine have passed that period,

* Gleig's "Warren Hastings," Vol. 3, Chap. xv.

this laboured and scarce intelligible, if intelligible, attempt to convey my meaning, too plainly demonstrates."

Still there was plenty of life in the old man, whose eighty-fourth birthday was close at hand when he thus wrote. If his handwriting was feeble, and his style prolix, his letters still showed a lively interest in the affairs of his friends and the world at large. Elijah Impey's last poem, a new pamphlet by Robert Owen, the Communist dreamer of New Lanark, the riots caused by the distresses consequent on war and bad harvests, the rumoured resignation of Lord Liverpool's Ministry, the fighting at Algiers and in Ceylon—these and suchlike topics are touched off by the same pen that discourses of the writer's home pursuits, of the health and virtues of Mrs. Hastings; that rejoices in the convalescence of Mrs. Anderson, and comments with kindly regret or pleasure on the news which the postman brings him from distant friends. Once in a way he is roused to momentary anger by some show of injustice to his official merits The reform of the salt department in Bengal was a measure which he had devised and carried out entirely by himself; and it hurt the old man's pride to see the credit of its conception claimed for some one who had acted under his orders. "I am angry," he writes to Thompson, "but I shall cool before I get to town."*

This was written in February, 1817. In the following month he went up to London for the last time; returning to Daylesford on the 8th of May. To pay his respects to the Prince Regent was for him a pleasant duty; and he also wrote his name at the Dukes of York and Clarence, besides making a round of other visits, formal or friendly. But that which gave him the most pleasure was the welcome offered him on the 13th of March, when he dined with thirty-nine old Indians at the Camden Hill Club. His health was "drunk with marks of the most expressive kindness." In such honours he read not only the testimony of those who had shared his friendship or served under him in former days, but "the corresponding sentiments of many besides to whom I am personally unknown."

The loss of blood from the extraction of a large tooth weakened him for a few days, and he returned home with a cold and cough which "troubled him all night." But a few days later

* Gleig's "Warren Hastings," Vol. I, Chap. xv.

he was well enough to make "two excursions" in his garden, and to feel "as stout at least as I was before my departure from home." Mrs. Hastings too had soon recovered from "a sudden and violent attack of the pleurisy." Her husband for his part still enjoyed, perhaps more than ever, the "long-seated visits"—as he called them—of his country neighbours; whom he loved too well, he says, to deem their coming an intrusion, whatever business he might have in hand.

It was in the last days of 1817 that he discoursed to Anderson on the chances against another Marátha war, in a letter which shows small trace of senile decay. Even as late as the following April, when his sight and "the memory of connected sentences" too often fáiled him, he could write to Elijah Impey about the inferior worth of contemporary history to that compiled by men "who have written so long after the events which they relate, as to have had no interest in them." He goes on to illustrate his theory by a reference to certain errors and omissions in Dr. Aikin's narrative of the events which led to his own impeachment. In this letter, which Mr. Gleig rightly deems "worthy of the best days of his manhood," there is only one line which betrays a consciousness of failing powers. After repeating the well-known story about the interview between Dundas and Pitt, which transformed the latter from an opponent into a supporter of Hastings' impeachment, he adds—"But I must stop, for my mind forsakes me."* But for that brief confession, the letter might have been written thirty years before.

The end indeed of a long, well-spent, and nearly blameless life, was drawing very near. In January, 1818, he had complained of "an inflamation in the roof of my mouth, and an inability to eat solids." A fresh train of unpleasant symptoms comes out in his diary for May. "Confused and indistinct sensations, as of the sounds of distant multitudes . . . . resembling slow music," began to visit him for several days running. On the last day of the same month he went to church, and his airings in the carriage seem to have been continued till the 13th July. On his return from that day's drive he was "seized with staggering," and had to be bled. From that time he grew daily weaker, but still managed to jot his feelings down in his diary. One day, the 15th, he passed "unexpectedly and

* Gleig's "Warren Hastings," Vol. 3, Chap. xv.

regretfully well." On the 20th he awoke with his throat "much swelled, and a difficulty of swallowing," which continued throughout the day.

From that date his diary remains a blank. The disease of his throat grew slowly worse, accompanied at times by fever. Loving friends, his wife, Sir Charles and Lady Imhoff, and his nephew and niece, Mr. and Mrs. Woodman, ministered to the wants and comforts of the dying statesman; and Sir Henry Halford gave him the poor benefit of first-rate medical skill. His sufferings, writes his beloved god-daughter, Mrs. Barton, were "very great indeed, borne with uncomplaining fortitude, the most touching meekness of temper, and pious resignation to the will of God." "Not one impatient expression," says Lady Imhoff, "ever escaped him," although he knew himself slowly starving to death. He was living, in fact, as Sir H. Halford said, "upon his own substance," for he had now lost all power of swallowing, and his only relief from suffering was to keep a little cold water in his fevered mouth.

Of death itself he had no fear. "At my age," he said, "it is time to go;" and his sufferings,

—"none of you know what I suffer," he replied to those around him—made him welcome the universal Peace-maker with a smile of contentment. But amidst his bodily ailments one anxiety still weighed upon his mind. What provision could he secure for the wife who would so soon be left a widow? He had lived up to his yearly income, and his pension would cease with his life. Mrs. Hastings' private fortune was very small; but the India House would surely take care of the widow for her husband's sake. On the 3rd August, Mrs. Hastings wrote from the dying man's dictation, to his old and faithful friend Toone, a letter which expressed in touching language his dread at leaving "the dearest object of all my mortal concerns, in a state of more than comparative indigence." Through her he had been enabled to maintain his masters' affairs for thirteen years "in vigour, strength, credit, and respect;" and in one case especially, when she was at Patna, and he "in a seat of greater danger, she proved the personal means of guarding one province of their Indian dominion from impending ruin by her own independent fortitude and presence of mind, varying with equal effect as every variation of event called upon her for fresh exertions of it." From his employers, towards whom he felt "the deepest gratitude," he asked only for "the continuance of that reward which they have thought proper equally to confer on my services and sufferings." To the hands of his friend Toone he would commit, "without further expression," the task of carrying his last appeal before the Court of Directors. "My latest prayers shall be offered for their service; for the welfare of my beloved country; and for that also of the land whose interests were so long committed to my partial guardianship."

When he had signed this letter, Hastings felt that he had done with worldly affairs. At that time and for some days later he could still swallow a little food; and he took the Sacrament in the midst of his sorrowing friends. But the inevitable hour was fast approaching; and on the evening of the 22nd August "his pure and gentle spirit" —in the words of Mrs. Barton—"quitted its earthly abode without a struggle or even a sigh." Not a trace of pain or suffering was left, according to Lady Imhoff, upon "his beloved, benign countenance;" nor did anyone know the exact moment of that peaceful ending. With characteristic delicacy he had drawn a handkerchief over his own face, and when, after a while, the watchers, alarmed by the stillness beneath it, removed the covering, he was dead.

A large number of the neighbouring gentry followed his body to its last resting-place behind the chancel of Daylesford Church.* It was not fated that the bones of one so great and so worthy of lasting honour should lie within St. Paul's or Westminster Abbey, "that temple of silence and reconciliation, where the enmities of twenty generations lie buried." But they rest fitly enough among the mouldering relics of those ancestral lords and squires of Daylesford, whose line never produced a more illustrious scion than Warren Hastings. Within the church itself a plain tablet of white marble, set up by Mrs. Hastings in memory or her noble husband, tells where he lies, and speaks of the rebuilding of the church where the last rites were so soon to be

* A new church was built in 1860 by the Lord of the Manor, Mr. Harman Grisewood, in the place of that rebuilt by Hastings in 1816. The new chancel partially covers the vault which holds his remains, so that his coffin which lay, when Mr. Gleig wrote, in the churchyard, now lies under the communion-table. Just outside the chancel is a railed enclosure containing a square stone pedestal surmounted by an urn, on one side of which is inscribed simply the great name of Warren Hastings.—See Mr. J. Tickford's letter in "Notes and Queries," 4th Series, Vol. 6, 1870, p. 192.

performed over him, as the last public effort of his "eminently virtuous and lengthened life."

In the same vault with the great proconsul lie the remains of his dearly-loved wife, who died in 1837 at the great age of ninety years. There too in 1853 was laid the body of her son, Sir Charles Imhoff, who died at the age of eighty-six. That the last years of Mrs. Hastings' life were not passed in "more than comparative indigence," was a mercy for which she had no cause to thank the Court of Directors. They gave no heed to the dying prayer of him whose genius had saved from ruin the empire founded by Clive, and whose achievements rendered possible the careers of Wellesley and Lord Hastings, the peaceful victories of Lord William Bentinck and the daring statesmanship of Dalhousie.

That Hastings was deficient in "the two great elements of all social virtue, in respect for the rights of others, and in sympathy for the sufferings of others;" that "his principles were somewhat lax," and "his heart was somewhat hard," are among the inferences which Macaulay drew from his reading of the great man's life-story. I venture to think that few readers of the foregoing pages will endorse on these points the verdict of the famous Essayist, whose party zeal sometimes overclouded his natural shrewdness and love of fairplay. Had Burke and Fox been Tories instead of Whigs, it is very probable that Macaulay would have done more justice to the moral worth of "the ablest of the able men who have given to Great Britain her Indian Empire."* Even he, however, calls upon us to admire "the amplitude and fertility" of Hastings' intellect, "his rare talents for command, for administration, and for controversy, his dauntless courage, his honourable poverty, his fervent zeal for the interests of the state, his noble equanimity, tried by both extremes of fortune, and never disturbed by either."

His public services may be summed up briefly in Macaulay's own words: "He had preserved and extended an empire. He had administered government and war with more than the capacity of Richelieu. He had patronised learning with the judicious liberality of Cosmo." His official industry has never, I think, been surpassed by the most painstaking of his successors; and in official courage and strength of will he may be said to stand alone, because none of his suc-

* Wilson's Note to Book V. Chap. 8 of Mill's "History."

cessors had to encounter all the trials, dangers, and disadvantages which fell to his lot. Few things in history are more admirable than the dauntless self-reliance, the patient energy, the unyielding grasp,—in a word, the marvellous pluck which enabled him, often single-handed, in spite of all hindrances, to carry out his plans for the public weal. A governor who held so high and arduous an office as Warren Hastings did for thirteen years, must in his time have made not a few mistakes. "Like other men"—says Horace Wilson—"he was occasionally ignorant or imperfectly informed; he doubted, he wavered, he changed his opinion, he was biassed by his feelings; he judged erroneously, he acted wrongly. He was not however judged like other men, by his acts, but every mistake or misconception, every hasty impression, every fluctuating purpose, every injudicious resolution, was hunted out, made public, and arrayed in evidence against him." Few statesmen indeed have paid so dearly for the faults of other men, have suffered such cruel injustice from the passions and the prejudices of their own age. But time and calmer inquiry have already raised him above the mists of contemporary slander;

and he begins to stand out clear in the light of honest criticism, as a Himalayan snow-peak stands out clear to the beholder from Masúri or Naini-Tal, at the close of the rainy season under the cool November sun.

NOTE.—Mrs. Hastings lived at Daylesford until her death in 1837, at the age of ninety. The estate then passed into the hands of her son, Sir Charles Imhoff, who died in 1853, aged 86. It was then bought by Mr. Harman Grisewood, who enlarged the house and rebuilt the church. His widow dying a few years ago, it has now become the seat of Mr. R. Nicholl Byass, J.P., the Lord of the Manor, under whose care the grounds and gardens retain all their former beauty. The house itself, as rebuilt by Hastings, stands on rising ground well-covered with trees and looking down upon a thickly-wooded glen. It is a handsome building, crowned by a light and airy dome. In the laying out of the gardens Mrs. Hastings' taste was called into profitable play. The little village of Daylesford has now grown into a thriving town, easily reached from the Adlestrop station of the Great Western Railway.—Neale's "Views of Seats," Vol. 5; and "Murray's "Handbook to Gloucestershire, Worcestershire and Herefordshire."

APPENDIX.

APPENDIX A.

In his "Early Records of British India," Mr. Talboys Wheeler gives the following picture of social life among the English in Bengal, at the time when Hastings first landed in Calcutta.

"Social life, whether at Calcutta or at the factories up country, was much the same in character. The Company's servants lived together in the factory; they boarded together like members of one family or firm. This practice was falling into disuse at Calcutta; marriages with English women had broken up the establishment into households. It was still kept up at the subordinate factories, where the English lived in greater isolation. The mornings were devoted to business. Then followed the mid-day dinner and the afternoon siesta. In the cool of the evening they took the air in palanquins or sailed on the river in budgerows. They angled for mango fish, or shot snipe and teal. The evening wound up with supper. There were quarrels, scandals and controversies. Possibly there were some excesses. There was always the show of religion and decorum which characterised the early half of the eighteenth century. The chaplain read prayers every morning, and preached on Sundays. There were intervals of excitement apart from the daily business. Ships broght news from Europe; from the outer Presidencies'; from the far-off settlements in China, Sumatra, Pegu, and other remote quarters. Above all, every ship that came from Madras brought tidings of the wars between the French and English in Southern India—the victories of Clive and gradual defeat of all the schemes of Dupleix."

APPENDIX B.

According to Grose (Voyage to the East Indies, Book 8, Chap. i.), Calcutta was a "very flourishing place" before its capture by Suraj-ad-daula in 1756. The town was "large, fair, and populous," being inhabited by "many private English merchants, and several rich Indian traders, who supplied the Company with the commodities of the country." The fort was strong, built of "brick and mortar called *puckah*, made of brickdust, lime, molasses, and hemp, which becomes as hard and durable as stone." The governor's house in the fort was "a handsome regular structure." There were also "convenient lodgings for the factors, storehouses for the Company's goods, and magazines for their ammunition. The Company had also good gardens and fish-ponds; with an hospital for the sick. On the other side of the river there were docks for repairing and careening the ships; near which the Armenians had a good garden . . . . About fifty yards from the fort was the English church, built by the contributions of the merchants and seamen who came to trade there." The trade of Bengal at that time "supplied rich cargoes for fifty or sixty ships yearly; besides what was carried in smaller vessels to the adjacent countries; and the article of saltpetre only was become of such great consequence to the European powers, that everything was attempted by the French and Dutch to deprive the English of that advantage."

The modern Calcutta may be said to date from 1757, when Fort William was begun by Clive, and the Maidan between it and Chowringhee was first cleared of jungle and native dwellings for the use of the European residents. New buildings for the merchants gradually arose on the site of the old fort; and the natives, who had fled at the approach of Suraj ad-daula, speedily flocked back to repair their ruined dwellings and grow rich under the shelter of English rule. During the famine of 1770, some 76,000 of them are said to have perished in the Black Town.

The city of Calcutta, as it was in 1780, is described by Sir James Mackintosh as "that scattered and confused chaos of houses, huts, sheds, streets, lanes, alleys, windings, gutters, sinks, and tanks, which jumbled into an undistinguished mass of filth and corruption, equally offensive to human sense and health, compose the capital of the English Company's Government in India." To jackals by night, and vultures, kites, and crows by day, it owed what little cleanliness it ever enjoyed. Ten years later, according to another witness, Grandpére, things were no better. The only drains were "open canals," where the filth and refuse of the town were left to putrefy; and jackals and birds of prey were the only scavengers. The plague of flies and mosquitoes was intolerable. As a defence against the latter, people used to wear pasteboard about their legs while they stayed indoors. Lord Valentia, in 1803, had little better to say of the Black Town, but he spoke of Chowringhee as "an entire village of palaces," and he admired the "magnificent buildings" of which the new Government House was then become the centre.—Newman's "Handbook to Calcutta."

APPENDIX C.

The following tribute to Hastings' memory appeared in the "Gentleman's Magazine," (Vol. 88, Part ii.), shortly after his death. It reads, if I may hazard a guess, like the work of Mr. Elijah Impey, who inherited his father's scholarly tastes, and had reason to appreciate the good qualities of his father's and his own good friend.

"In private life Mr. Hastings was one of the most amiable of human beings. He was the most tender and affectionate husband, he was the kindest master, he was the sincerest friend. He had "a tear for pity and a hand open as day for melting charity;" his generosity was unbounded in desire, and did not always calculate on his means of indulging it. He had that true magnanimity which elevated him above all selfish considerations, or personal resentments; his own private interest was always lost in his regard for the public welfare, and to those who had been his most implacable enemies he was ever ready to be reconciled, and to forgive. In his domestic intercourse, he was the most endearing partner, and in his social hours the most pleasing companion, instructive, affable, cheerful, and complaisant; his nature was full of "the milk of human kindness," without a tincture of gall in its composition. All who knew him loved him, and they who knew him most loved him best. This is a faint portrait of this great and good man; but as far as it goes, it is a faithful one; and it is drawn by one who knew him long and intimately, and who, if he had abilities equal to the design, would have given a more finished picture.

"Ossa quieta, precor, tutâ requiescite in urnâ;
Et sit humus cineri non onerosa tuo."

June, 1878.

BOOKS, &c.,

ISSUED BY

MESSRS. WM. H. ALLEN & Co.,

Publishers & Literary Agents to the India Office,

COMPRISING

MISCELLANEOUS PUBLICATIONS IN GENERAL LITERATURE. DICTIONARIES, GRAMMARS, AND TEXT BOOKS IN EASTERN LANGUAGES, MILITARY WORKS, INCLUDING THOSE ISSUED BY THE GOVERNMENT. INDIAN AND MILITARY LAW. MAPS OF INDIA, &c.

In January and July of each year is published in 8vo., price 10s. 6d.,

THE INDIA LIST, CIVIL & MILITARY.

BY PERMISSION OF THE SECRETARY OF STATE FOR INDIA IN COUNCIL.

CONTENTS.

CIVIL.—Gradation Lists of Civil Service, Bengal, Madras and Bombay. Civil Annuitants. Legislative Council, Ecclesiastical Establishments, Educational, Public Works, Judicial, Marine, Medical, Land Revenue, Political, Postal, Police, Customs and Salt, Forest, Registration and Railway and Telegraph Departments, Law Courts, Surveys, &c., &c.

MILITARY.—Gradation List of the General and Field Officers (British and Local) of the three Presidencies, Staff Corps, Adjutants-General's and Quartermasters-General's Offices, Army Commissariat Departments, British Troops Serving in India (including Royal Artillery, Royal Engineers, Cavalry, Infantry, and Medical Department), List of Native Regiments, Commander-in-Chief and Staff, Garrison Instruction Staff, Indian Medical Department, Ordnance Departments, Punjab Frontier Force, Military Departments of the three Presidencies, Veterinary Departments, Tables showing the Distribution of the Army in India, Lists of Retired Officers of the three Presidencies.

HOME.—Departments of the Office of the Secretary of State, Coopers Hill College, List of Selected Candidates for the Civil and Forest Services, Indian Troop Service.

MISCELLANEOUS.—Orders of the Bath, Star of India, and St. Michael and St. George. Order of Precedence in India. Regulations for Admission to Civil Service. Regulations for Admission of Chaplains. Civil Leave Code and Supplements. Civil Service Pension Code—relating to the Covenanted and Uncovenanted Services. Rules for the Indian Medical Service. Furlough and Retirement Regulations of the Indian Army. Family Pension Fund. Staff Corps Regulations. Salaries of Staff Officers. Regulations for Promotion. English Furlough Pay.

Adam W. (late of Calcutta) Theories of History.
8vo. 15s. (See page 27).

Advice to Officers in India.
By JOHN McCOSH, M.D. Post 8vo. 8s.

Allen's Series.
1.—World We Live In. (See page 30). 2s.
2.—Earth's History. (See page 6). 2s.
3.—Geography of India. (See page 8). 2s.
4.—2000 Examination Questions in Physical Geography. 2s.
5.—Hall's Trigonometry. (See page 9). 2s.
6.—Wollaston's Elementary Indian Reader. 1s. (See page 20.)
7.—Ansted's Elements of Physiography. 1s. 4d.

Analytical History of India.
From the earliest times to the Abolition of the East India Company in 1858. By ROBERT SEWELL, Madras Civil Service. Post 8vo. 8s.
*** The object of this work is to supply the want which has been felt by students for a condensed outline of Indian History which would serve at once to recall the memory and guide the eye, while at the same time it has been attempted to render it interesting to the general reader by preserving a medium between a bare analysis and a complete history.

Ancient and Mediæval India.
2 vols. 8vo. 30s. (See page 16).

Anderson's (P.) English in Western India.
8vo. 14s.

Andrew's (W. P.) India and Her Neighbours,
With Two Maps. 8vo. 15s.

Ansted's (D. T.) Water: Its Physical Properties, Source, Distribution over the Earth, and Uses for Engineering and Sanitary Purposes. (*In the Press.*)

Ansted's (D. T.) Elements of Physiography.
For the use of Science Schools. Fcap. 8vo. 1s. 4d.

Ansted's (D. T.) Physical Geography.
5th Edition. With Maps. Crown 8vo. 7s. (See page 22).

Ansted's (D. T.) World We Live In.
Fcap. 2s. 25th Thousand, with Illustrations. (See page 28).

Ansted's (D. T.) Earth's History.
Fcap. 2s. (See page 6).

Ansted's (D. T.)
Two Thousand Examination Questions in Physical Geography. pp. 180. Price 2s.

Ansted's (D. T.) Ionian Islands.
8vo. 8s. (See page 14.)

Ansted's (D. T.) and R. G. Latham's Channel Islands.
8vo. 16s. (See page 14).

Archer's (Capt. J. H. Laurence) Commentaries on the Punjaub Campaign—1848-49. Crown 8vo. 8s. (See page 6.)

Armies of the Powers of Europe, The.
Their Strength and Organisation, &c., with an Account of some of the Famous Regiments, their Composition, &c., &c.; also an Account of the Navies of the several Powers. By Captain H. B. STUART. (*In the press*).

At Home in Paris.
By BLANCHARD JERROLD. 2 Vols. Post 8vo. 16s.

Atterbury Memoirs, &c.
The Memoir and Correspondence of Francis Atterbury, Bishop of Rochester, with his distinguished contemporaries. Compiled chiefly from the Atterbury and Stuart Papers. By FOLKESTONE WILLIAMS, Author of "Lives of the English Cardinals," &c., 2 vols. 8vo. 14s.

Authors at Work.
By CHARLES PEBODY. Post 8vo. 10s. 6d.

Bengal Artillery.
A Memoir of the Services of the Bengal Artillery from the formation of the Corps. By the late CAPT. E. BUCKLE, Assist-Adjut. Gen. Ben. Art. Edit. by SIR J. W. KAYE. 8vo. Lond. 1852. 10s

Bernays, (Dr. A. J.) Students' Chemistry.
Crown 8vo. 5s. 6d. (See page 26).

Binning's (R. M.) Travels in Persia, &c.
2 vols. 8vo. 16s.

Birth of the War God.
A Poem. By KALIDASA. Translated from the Sanscrit into English Verse. By RALPH T. H. GRIFFITH. 5s.

Blanchard's (S.) Yesterday and To-day in India.
Post 8vo. 6s. (See page 30).

Blenkinsopp's (Rev. E. L.) Doctrine of Development
In the Bible and in the Church. 2nd edit. 12mo 6s. (See page 6).

Boileau (Major-General J. T.)
A New and Complete Set of Traverse Tables, showing the Differences of Latitude and the Departures to every Minute of the Quadrant and to Five Places of Decimals. Together with a Table of the lengths of each Degree of Latitude and corresponding Degree of Longitude from the Equator to the Poles; with other Tables useful to the Surveyor and Engineer. Fourth Edition, thoroughly revised and corrected by the Author. Royal 8vo. 12s. London, 1876.

Botany of the Himalaya Mountains.
And other Branches of Natural History of the Himalaya Mountains, and of the Flora of Cashmere. By J. FORBES ROYLE, M.D., V.P.R.S. 2 vols. folio London, 1839. £5 5s.

*** *This Book is now very scarce.*

Bowring's Flowery Scroll.
A Chinese Novel. Translated and Illustrated with Notes by SIR J. BOWRING, late H.B.M. Plenipo. China. Post 8vo. 10s. 6d.

Bradshaw (John) LL.D. The Poetical Works of John Milton, with Notes, explanatory and philological. 2 vols. post 8vo. 12s. 6d.

Brandis' Forest Flora of North-West and Central India.
Text and plates. £2 18s. (See page 7).

Briggs' (Gen. J.) India and Europe Compared.
Post 8vo. 7s.

Browne's (J. W.) Hardware; How to Buy it for Foreign Markets. 8vo. 10s. 6d. (See page 9).

Canal and Culvert Tables.
By LOWIS D'A. JACKSON. (*In the press*).

Catholic Doctrine of the Atonement.
An Historical Inquiry into its Development in the Church, with an Introduction on the Principle of Theological Development. By H. NUTCOMBE OXENHAM, M.A. 2nd Edit. 8vo. 10s. 6d.

"It is one of the ablest and probably one of the most charmingly written treatises on the subject which exists in our language."—*Times.*

Celebrated Naval and Military Trials.
By PETER BURKE, Serjeant-at-Law. Author of "Celebrated Trials connected with the Aristocracy." Post 8vo. 10s. 6d.

Central Asia (Sketches of).
By A. VAMBERY. 8vo. 16s. (See page 28).

Cochrane, (John) Hindu Law.
20s. (See page 13)

Commentaries on the Punjub Campaign 1848-49, including some additions to the History of the Second Sikh War, from original sources. By Captain J. H. LAWRENCE-ARCHER, late 60th Rifles. Crown 8vo. 8s.

Cruise of H.M.S. "Galatea,"
Captain H.R.H. the Duke of Edinburgh, K.G., in 1867—1868. By the REV. JOHN MILNER, B.A., Chaplain; and OSWALD W. BRIERLY. Illustrated by a Photograph of H.R.H. the Duke of Edinburgh; and by Chromo-Lithographs and Graphotypes from Sketches taken on the spot by O. W. BRIERLY. 8vo. 16s.

Danvers (Fred. Chas.) On Coal.
With Reference to Screening, Transport, &c 8vo. 10s. 6d.

Doctrine of Development in the Bible and in the Church.
By REV. E. L. BLENKINSOPP, M A., Rector of Springthorp. 2nd edition. 12mo. 6s.

Doran (Dr. J.) Annals of the English Stage.
Post 8vo. 6s (See p. 26.)

Drain of Silver to the East,
And the Currency of India. By W. NASSAU LEES. Post 8vo. 8s.

Drury.—The Useful Plants of India,
With Notices of their chief value in Commerce, Medicine, and the Arts. By COLONEL HEBER DRURY. Second Edition, with Additions and Corrections. Royal 8vo. 16s.

Earth's History,
Or, First Lessons in Geology. For the use of Schools and Students. By D. T. ANSTED. Third Thousand. Fcap. 8vo. 2s.

East India Calculator,
By T. THORNTON. 8vo. London, 1823. 10s.

Edgar's (J. G.) Modern History.
12mo. 6s. 6d.

Edinburgh (The Duke of) Cruise of the "Galatea."
With Illustrations. 8vo. 16s.

Edwards' (H. S.) Russians at Home.
With Illustrations. Post 8vo. 6s. (See page 25).

Edwards' (H. S.) History of the Opera.
2 Vols., 8vo. 10s. 6d. (See page 10).

Elementary Mathematics.

A Course of Elementary Mathematics for the use of candidate- for admission into either of the Military Colleges; of applis cants for appointments in the Home or Indian Civil Services; and of mathematical students generally. By Professor J. R. Young. In one closely-printed volume 8vo., pp. 648. 12s.

"In the work before us he has digested a complete Elementary Course, by aid of his long experience as a teacher and writer; and he has produced a very useful book. Mr. Young has not allowed his own taste to rule the distribution, but has adjusted his parts with the skill of a veteran."—*Athenæum.*

English Cardinals.

The Lives of the English Cardinals, from Nicholas Breakspeare (Pope Adrien IV.) to Thomas Wolsey, Cardinal Legate. With Historical Notices of the Papal Court. By Folkestone Williams. In 2 vols. 14s.

English Homes in India.

By Mrs. Keatinge. Part I.—The Three Loves. Part II.—The Wrong Turning. Two vols., Post 8vo 16s.

Final French Struggles in India and on the Indian Seas.

Including an Account of the Capture of the Isles of France and Bourbon, and Sketches of the most eminent Foreign Adventurers in India up to the period of that Capture. With an Appendix containing an Account of the Expedition from India to Egypt in 1801. By Colonel G. B. Malleson, C.S.I. Crown 8vo. 10s. 6d.

First Age of Christianity and the Church (The)

By John Ignatius Döllinger, D.D., Professor of Ecclesiastical History in the University of Munich, &c., &c. Translated from the German by Henry Nutcombe Oxenham, M.A., late Scholar of Baliol College, Oxford. Third Edition. 2 vols. Crown 8vo. 18s.

Forbes (Dr. Duncan) History of Chess.

8vo. 7s, 6d. (See page 10).

Forest Flora of North-Western and Central India.

By Dr. Brandis, Inspector General of Forests to the Government of India. Text and Plates. £2 18s.

Franz Schubert.

A Musical Biography, from the German of Dr. Heinrich Kreisle von Hellborn. By Edward Wilberforce, Esq., Author of "Social Life in Munich." Post 8vo. 6s.

Gazetteers of India.
Thornton, 4 vols., 8vo. £2 16s.
" 8vo. 21s.
" (N.W.P., &c.) 2 vols., 8vo. 25s.

Gazetteer of Southern India.
With the Tenasserim Provinces and Singapore. Compiled from original and authentic sources. Accompanied by an Atlas, including plans of all the principal towns and cantonments. Royal 8vo. with 4to. Atlas. £3 3s.

Gazetteer of the Punjaub, Affghanistan, &c.
Gazetteer of the Countries adjacent to India, on the north-west, including Scinde, Affghanistan, Beloochistan, the Punjaub, and the neighbouring States. By EDWARD THORNTON, Esq 2 vols. 8vo. £1 5s.

Geography of India.
Comprising an account of British India, and the various states enclosed and adjoining. Fcap. pp. 250. 2s.

Geological Papers on Western India.
Including Cutch, Scinde, and the south-east coast of Arabia. To which is added a Summary of the Geology of India generally. Edited for the Government by HENRY J. CARTER, Assistant Surgeon, Bombay Army. Royal 8vo. with folio Atlas of maps and plates; half-bound. £2 2s.

German Life and Manners
As seen in Saxony. With an account of Town Life—Village Life—Fashionable Life—Married Life—School and University Life, &c. Illustrated with Songs and Pictures of the Student Customs at the University of Jena. By HENRY MAYHEW, 2 vols. 8vo., with numerous illustrations. 18s.

A Popular Edition of the above. With illustrations. Cr. 8vo. 7s.
"Full of original thought and observation, and may be studied with profit by both German and English—especially by the German." *Athenæum.*

Glyn's (A. C.) Civilization in the 5th Century.
2 vols. post 8vo. £1 1s.

Goldstucker (Dr.) The Miscellaneous Essays of.
With a Memoir (*In the press*).

Grady's (S. G.) Mohamedan Law of Inheritance & Contract.
8vo. 14s. (See page 13).

Grady's (S. G.) Institutes of Menu.
8vo. 12s. (See page 13).

Griffith's Ralph (T. H.) Birth of the War God.

8vo. 5s. (See page 4).

Hall's Trigonometry.

The Elements of Plane and Spherical Trigonometry. With an Appendix, containing the solution of the Problems in Nautical Astronomy. For the use of Schools. By the REV. T. G. HALL, M.A., Professor of Mathematics in King's College, London. 12mo. 2s.

Hamilton's Hedaya.

A new edition, with the obsolete passages omitted, and a copious Index added by S. G. Grady. 8vo. £1 15s.

Handbook of Reference to the Maps of India.

Giving the Lat. and Long. of places of note. 18mo. 3s. 6d

**** This will be found a valuable Companion to Messrs. Allen & Co.'s Maps of India.*

Handbooks for India.

Bradshaw's Through Routes, Overland Guide, and Handbook to India, Egypt, Turkey, Persia, China, &c., &c. New Edition, 1875-76. With Maps, &c. 5s.; by post, 5s. 4d.

The "Times of India" Handbook of Hindustan; being a Short Account of the Geography, History, Present Administration, Native States, Sports and Places of Interest in India. Compiled by G. R. ABERIGH-MACKAY. With Maps. 8vo. 10s.

Maclean's Guide to Bombay; containing an Account of the Geography and History of the Island, Population, Trade and Industry, Government and Revenue, Descriptive Accounts of the Town and Neighbourhood, Native Festivals, Official and Mercantile Directories, &c., &c. With Map and Plans. 10s.

Hardware; How to Buy it for Foreign Markets.

By. J. WILSON BROWNE. (See page 5).

This is the most complete Guide to the Hardware Trade yet brought out; comprising all the principal Gross Lists in general use, with Illustrations and Descriptions. 8vo. 10s. 6d.

Hedaya.

Translated from the Arabic by WALTER HAMILTON. *A New Edition*, with Index by S. G. GRADY 8vo. £1. 15s.

Henry VIII.

An Historical Sketch as affecting the Reformation in England. By CHARLES HASTINGS COLLETTE. Post 8vo. 6s.

Hindu Law.

By Sir Thomas Strange. 2 vols. Royal 8vo., 1830. 24s. (See page 13).

Historical Results

Deducible from Recent Discoveries in Affghanistan. By H. T. PRINSEP. 8vo. Lond. 1844. 15s.

Histories of India.
Mill, 9 vols., cr. 8vo. £2 10s. (See page 22).
Thornton, 6 vols., 8vo. £2 8s. (See page 27).
Thornton, 1 vol., 8vo. 12s. (See page 27).
Trotter, 2 vols., 8vo. 32s. (See page 28).
Sewell (Analytical). Crown 8vo. 8s. (See page 3).
Owen, India on the Eve of the British Conquest. 8s. (See page 22).

History of the Indian Mutiny, 1857-1858.
Commencing from the close of the Second Volume of Sir John Kaye's History of the Sepoy War. By COLONEL G. B. MALLESON, C.S.I. 8vo. With Map. £1.

History of Civilization in the Fifth Century.
Translated by permission from the French of A. Frederic Ozanam, late Professor of Foreign Literature to the Faculty of Letters at Paris. By ASHBY C. GLYN, B.A., of the Inner Temple, Barrister-at-Law. 2 vols., post 8vo. £1 1s.

History of Chess,
From the time of the Early Invention of the Game in India, till the period of its establishment in Western and Central Europe. By DUNCAN FORBES, LL.D. 8vo. 7s. 6d.

History of China,
From the Earliest Records to A.D. 420. By THOMAS THORNTON, Member of the Royal Asiatic Society. 8vo., cloth. 8s.

History of the Opera,
From Monteverde to Donizetti. By H. SUTHERLAND EDWARDS Second edition. 2 vols., Post 8vo. 10s. 6d.

History of the Punjaub,
And of the Rise, Progress, and Present Condition of the Sikhs. By T. THORNTON. 2 Vols. Post 8vo. 8s.

Horses of the Sahara, and the Manners of the Desert.
By E. DAUMAS, General of the Division Commanding at Bordeaux, Senator, &c., &c. With Commentaries by the Emir Abd-el-Kadir (Authorized Edition). 8vo. 6s.

"We have rarely read a work giving a more picturesque and, at the same time, practical account of the manners and customs of a people, than this book on the Arabs and their horses."—*Edinburgh Courant.*

Hough (Lieut.-Col. W.) Precedents in Military Law.
8vo. cloth. 25s.

Hughes's (Rev. T. P.) Notes on Muhammadanism.
Second Edition, Revised and Enlarged. Fcap 8vo. 6s.

Hydraulic Manual and Working Tables, Hydraulic and Indian Meteorological Statistics. Published under the patronage of the Right Honourable the Secretary of State for India. By LOWIS D'A JACKSON. 8vo. 28s.

Illustrated Horse Doctor.

Being an Accurate and Detailed Account, accompanied by more than 400 Pictorial Representations, characteristic of the various Diseases to which the Equine Race are subjected; together with the latest Mode of Treatment, and all the requisite Prescriptions written in Plain English. By EDWARD MAYHEW, M.R.C.V.S. 8vo. 18s. 6d.

CONTENTS.—The Brain and Nervous System.—The Eyes.—The Mouth.—The Nostrils.—The Throat.—The Chest and its contents.—The Stomach, Liver, &c.—The Abdomen.—The Urinary Organs.—The Skin.—Specific Diseases.—Limbs.—The Feet.—Injuries.—Operations.

"The book contains nearly 600 pages of valuable matter, which reflects great credit on its author, and, owing to its practical details, the result of deep scientific research, deserves a place in the library of medical, veterinary, and non-professional readers."—*Field.*

"The book furnishes at once the bane and the antidote, as the drawings show the horse not only suffering from every kind of disease, but in the different stages of it, while the alphabetical summary at the end gives the cause, symptoms and treatment of each."—*Illustrated London News.*

Illustrated Horse Management.

Containing descriptive remarks upon Anatomy, Medicine, Shoeing, Teeth, Food, Vices, Stables; likewise a plain account of the situation, nature, and value of the various points; together with comments on grooms, dealers, breeders, breakers, and trainers; Embellished with more than 400 engravings from original designs made expressly for this work. By E. MAYHEW. A new Edition, revised and improved by J. I. LUPTON. M.R.C.V.S. 8vo. 12s.

CONTENTS.—The body of the horse anatomically considered PHYSIC.—The mode of administering it, and minor operations. SHOEING.—Its origin, its uses, and its varieties. THE TEETH.—Their natural growth, and the abuses to which they are liable.

FOOD.—The fittest time for feeding, and the kind of food which the horse naturally consumes. The evils which are occasioned by modern stables. The faults inseparable from stables. The so-called "incapacitating vices," which are the results of injury or of disease. Stables as they should be. GROOMS.—Their prejudices, their injuries, and their duties. POINTS.—Their relative importance and where to look for their development. BREEDING.—Its inconsistencies and its disappointments. BREAKING AND TRAINING.—Their errors and their results.

India Directory (The).

For the Guidance of Commanders of Steamers and Sailing Vessels. Founded upon the Work of the late CAPTAIN JAMES HORSBURGH, F.R.S.

PART I.—The East Indies, and Interjacent Ports of Africa and South America. Revised, Extended, and Illustrated with Charts of Winds, Currents, Passages, Variation, and Tides. By COMMANDER ALFRED DUNDAS TAYLOR, F.R.G.S., Superintendent of Marine Surveys to the Government of India. £1 18s.

PART II.—The China Sea, with the Ports of Java, Australia and Japan and the Indian Archipelago Harbours, as well as those of New Zealand. Illustrated with Charts of the Winds, Currents, Passages, &c. By the same. (*In the Press*).

India and Her Neighbours.

By W. P. ANDREW. 8vo. With 2 Maps. 15s.

Indian Administration.

By H. G. KEENE. Post 8vo. 5s.

The India List, Civil and Military,

Containing Names of all Officers employed by the Indian Government, including those of the Public Works, Educational, Political, Postal, Police, Customs, Forests, Railway and Telegraphs Departments, with Rules for Admission to these Services, Furlough Rules, Retiring Pensions, Staff Corps Regulations and Salaries, &c., with an Index. Issued in January and July of each year, by permission of the Secretary of State for India in Council. 8vo. 10s. 6d.

Indian Code of Civil Procedure.

In the Form of Questions and Answers. With Explanatory and Illustrative Notes. By ANGELO J. LEWIS. 12s. 6d.

Indian Criminal Law and Procedure,

Including the Procedure in the High Courts, as well as that in the Courts not established by Royal Charter; with Forms of Charges and Notes on Evidence, illustrated by a large number of English Cases, and Cases decided in the High Courts of India; and an APPENDIX of selected Acts passed by the Legislative Council relating to Criminal matters. By M. H. STARLING, ESQ., LL.B. & F. B. CONSTABLE, M.A. Third edition. 8vo. £2 2s.

Indian Penal Code.

In the Form of Questions and Answers. With Explanatory and Illustrative Notes. By ANGELO J. LEWIS. 7s. 6d.

Indian and Military Law.

Mahommedan Law of Inheritance, &c. A Manual of the Mahommedan Law of Inheritance and Contract; comprising the Doctrine of the Soonee and Sheea Schools, and based upon the text of Sir H. W. MACNAGHTEN'S Principles and Precedents, together with the Decisions of the Privy Council and High Courts of the Presidencies in India. For the use of Schools and Students. By STANDISH GROVE GRADY, Barrister-at-Law, Reader of Hindoo, Mahommedan, and Indian Law to the Inns of Court. 8vo. 14s.

Hedaya, or Guide, a Commentary on the Mussulman Laws, translated by order of the Governor-General and Council of Bengal. By CHARLES HAMILTON. Second Edition, with Preface and Index by STANDISH GROVE GRADY. 8vo. £1 15s.

Institutes of Menu in English. The Institutes of Hindu Law or the Ordinances of Menu, according to Gloss of Collucca. Comprising the Indian System of Duties, Religious and Civil, verbally translated from the Original, with a Preface by SIR WILLIAM JONES, and collated with the Sanscrit Text by GRAVES CHAMNEY HAUGHTON, M.A., F.R.S., Professor of Hindu Literature in the East India College. New edition, with Preface and Index by STANDISH G. GRADY, Barrister-at-Law, and Reader of Hindu, Mahommedan, and Indian Law to the Inns of Court. 8vo., cloth. 12s.

Indian Code of Criminal Procedure. Being Act X of 1872, Passed by the Governor-General of India in Council on the 25th of April, 1872. 8vo. 12s.

Indian Code of Civil Procedure. In the form of Questions and Answers, with Explanatory and Illustrative Notes. By ANGELO J. LEWIS, Barrister-at-law. 12mo. 12s. 6d.

Indian Penal Code. In the Form of Questions and Answers. With Explanatory and Illustrative Notes. BY ANGELO J. LEWIS, Barrister-at-Law. Post 8vo. 7s. 6d.

Hindu Law. Principally with reference to such portions of it as concern the Administration of Justice in the Courts in India. By SIR THOMAS STRANGE, late Chief Justice of Madras. 2 vols. Royal 8vo., 1830. 24s.

Hindu Law. Defence of the Daya Bhaga. Notice of the Case on Prosoono Coomar Tajore's Will. Judgment of the Judicial Committee of the Privy Council. Examination of such Judgment. By JOHN COCHRANE, Barrister-at-Law. Royal 8vo. 20s.

Law and Customs of Hindu Castes, within the Dekhan Provinces subject to the Presidency of Bombay, chiefly affecting Civil Suits. By ARTHUR STEELE. Royal 8vo. £1 1s.

Chart of Hindu Inheritance. With an Explanatory Treatise, By ALMARIC RUMSEY. 8vo. 6s. 6d.

Manual of Military Law. For all ranks of the Army, Militia and Volunteer Services. By Colonel J. K. PIPON, Assist. Adjutant General at Head Quarters, & J. F. COLLIER, Esq., of the Inner Temple, Barrister-at-Law. Third and Revised Edition. Pocket size. 5s.

Precedents in Military Law; including the Practice of Courts-Martial; the Mode of Conducting Trials; the Duties of Officers at Military Courts of Inquests, Courts of Inquiry, Courts of Requests, &c., &c. The following are a portion of the Contents:—

1. Military Law. 2. Martial Law. 3. Courts-Martial. 4. Courts of Inquiry. 5. Courts of Inquest. 6. Courts of Request. 7. Forms of Courts-Martial. 8. Precedents of Military Law. 9. Trials of Arson to Rape (Alphabetically arranged.) 10. Rebellions. 11. Riots. 12. Miscellaneous. By Lieut.-Col. W. HOUGH, late Deputy Judge-Advocate-General, Bengal Army, and Author of several Works on Courts-Martial. One thick 8vo. vol. 25s.

The Practice of Courts Martial. By HOUGH & LONG. Thick 8vo. London, 1825. 26s.

Indian Infanticide.

Its Origin, Progress, and Suppression. By JOHN CAVE-BROWN, M.A. 8vo. 5s.

Indian Wisdom,

Or Examples of the Religious, Philosophical and Ethical Doctrines of the Hindus. With a brief History of the Chief Departments of Sanscrit Literature, and some account of the Past and Present Condition of India, Moral and Intellectual. By MONIER WILLIAMS, M.A., Boden Professor of Sanscrit in in the University of Oxford. Third Edition. 8vo. 15s.

Ionian Islands in 1863.

By PROFESSOR D. T. ANSTED, M.A., F.R.S., &c. 8vo., with Maps and Cuts. 8s.

Jackson's (Lowis D'A.) Hydraulic Manual and Working Tables Hydraulic and Indian Meteorological Statistics.

8vo. 28s. (See page 10.)

Jackson (Lowis D'A.) Canal and Culvert Tables.

(*In the press*).

Japan, the Amoor and the Pacific.

With notices of other Places, comprised in a Voyage of Circumnavigation in the Imperial Russian Corvette *Rynda*, in 1858—1860. By HENRY A. TILLEY. Eight Illustrations. 8vo. 16s.

Jersey, Guernsey, Alderney, Sark, &c.

THE CHANNEL ISLANDS. Containing: PART I.—Physical Geography. PART II.—Natural History. PART III.—Civil History. PART IV.—Economics and Trade. By DAVID THOMAS

Ansted, M.A., F.R.S., and Robert Gordon Latham, M.A., M.D., F.R.S. New and Cheaper Edition in one handsome 8vo. Volume, with 72 Illustrations on Wood by Vizetelly, Loudon, Nicholls, and Hart; with Map. 16s.

"This is a really valuable work. A book which will long remain the standard authority on the subject. No one who has been to the Channel Islands, or who purposes going there will be insensible of its value."—*Saturday Review.*

"It is the produce of many hands and every hand a good one."

Jerrold's (Blanchard) at Home in Paris.
2 Vols. Post 8vo. 16s.

Kaye (Sir J. W.) The Sepoy War in India. (See page 25).
Vol. 1. 18s.
Vol. 2, £1.
Vol. 3. £1.

Kaye (Sir J. W.) History of the War in Affghanistan.
New edition 3 Vols. Crown 8vo. £1. 6s.

Kaye (Sir J. W.) H. St. G. Tucker's Life and Correspondence.
8vo. 10s.

Kaye's (Sir J. W.) Memorials of Indian Governments.
By H. St. George Tucker. 8vo. 10s.

Keene's (H. G.) Mogul Empire.
8vo. 10s. 6d. (See page 22.)

Keene's (H. G.) Administration in India.
Post 8vo. 9s.

Lady Morgan's Memoirs.
Autobiography, Diaries and Correspondence. 2 Vols. 8vo, with Portraits. 18s.

Latham's (Dr. R. G.) Nationalities of Europe.
2 Vols. 8vo. 12s. (See page 22).

Law and Customs of Hindu Castes,
By Arthur Steele. Royal 8vo. £1. 1s. (See page 13.)

Lee's (Dr. W. N.) Drain of Silver to the East.
Post 8vo. 8s.

Lewin's Wild Races of the South Eastern Frontier of India. Including an Account of the Loshai Country. Post 8vo. 10s. 6d

Lewis's (A. J.) Indian Penal Code. Post 8vo. 7s. 6d. (See page 12).

Lewis's Indian Code of Civil Procedure. Post 8vo. 12s 6d. (See page 12).

Leyden and Erskine's Baber. Memoirs of Zehir-ed-Din Muhammed Baber, Emperor of Hindustan, written by himself in the Jaghatai Turki, and translated partly by the late John Leyden, Esq., M.D., and partly by William Erskine, Esq., with Notes and a Geographical and Historical Introduction, together with a Map of the Countries between the Oxus and Jaxartes, and a Memoir regarding its construction. By Charles Waddington, of the East India Company's Engineers. 4to. Lond. 1826. £1 5s.

Liancourt's and Pincott's Primitive and Universal Laws of the Formation and development of language; a Rational and Inductive System founded on the Natural Basis of Onomatops. 8vo. 12*s*. 6*d*.

Lockwood's (Ed.) Natural History, Sport and Travel. Crown 8vo. With numerous Illustrations. 10s. 6d.

McBean's (S.) England, Egypt, Palestine & India by Railway. Popularly Explained. Crown 8vo., with a coloured Map. 4s.

Mahommedan Law of Inheritance and Contract. By Standish Grove Grady, Barrister-at-Law. 8vo. 14s. (See page 13).

Malleson's (Col. G. B.) Final French Struggle's in India. Crown 8vo. 10s. 6d. (See page 7).

Malleson's (Col. G. B.) History of the Indian Mutiny, 1857–1858, commencing from the close of the Second Volume of Sir John Kaye's History of the Sepoy War. Vol. I. 8vo. With Map. £1.

Manning (Mrs.) Ancient and Mediæval India. Being the History, Religion, Laws, Caste, Manners and Customs, Language, Literature, Poetry, Philosophy, Astronomy, Algebra, Medicine, Architecture, Manufactures, Commerce, &c., of the Hindus, taken from their writings. Amongst the works consulted and gleaned from may be named the Rig Veda,

Sama Veda, Vajur Veda, Sathapatha Brahmana, Baghavat Gita, The Puranas, Code of Menu, Code of Yajna-valkya, Mitakshara, Daya Bagha, Mahabharata, Atriya, Charaka, Susruta, Ramayana, Raghu Vansa, Bhattikavia, Sakuntala Vikramorvasi, Malali and Madhava, Mudra Rakshasa, Retnavali, Kumara Sambhava, Prabodah, Chandrodaya, Megha Duta, Gita Govinda, Panchatantra, Hitopadesa, Katha Sarit, Sagara, Ketala, Panchavinsati, Dasa Kumara Charita, &c. By Mrs. MANNING, with Illustrations. 2 vols., 8vo. 30s.

Manual of Military Law.
By Colonel J. K. PIPON, and J. F. COLLIER, Esq., of the Inner Temple, Barrister-at-Law. 5s.

Mayhew's (Edward) Illustrated Horse Doctor.
8vo. 18s. 6d. (See page 11).

Mayhew's (Edward) Illustrated Horse Management.
New edit. By J. I. LUPTON. 8vo. 12s. (See page 11)

Mayhew's (Henry) German Life and Manners.
2 vols., 8vo. 18s.

Also a cheaper edition, Post 8vo. 7s. (See page 8).

Max Muller's Rig-Veda-Sanhita.
The Sacred Hymns of the Brahmins; together with the Commentary of Sayanacharya. Published under the Patronage of the Right Honourable the Secretary of State for India in Council. 6 vols., 4to. £2 10s. per volume.

Meadow's (T.) Notes on China.
8vo. 9s.

Memorable Events of Modern History.
By J. G. EDGAR, Author of the Boyhood of Great Men, &c. Post 8vo. With Illustrations. 6s. 6d.

Military Works—chiefly issued by the Government.

Field Exercises and Evolutions of Infantry. Pocket edition, 1s.

Queen's Regulations and Orders for the Army. Corrected to 1874. 8vo. 3s. 6d. Interleaved, 5s. 6d. Pocket Edition, 1s.

Rifle Exercise and Musketry Instruction. 1878 (*in preparation*)

Musketry Regulations, as used at Hythe. 1s.

Dress Regulations for the Army. 1875. 1s. 6*d*.

Infantry Sword Exercise. 1875. 6d.

Infantry Bugle Sounds. 6d.

Handbook of Battalion Drill. By Lieut. H. C. SLACK. 2s; or with Company Drill, 2s. 6d.

Handbook of Brigade Drill. By Lieut. H. C. SLACK. 3s.

Red Book for Sergeants. By WILLIAM BRIGHT, Colour-Sergeant, 37th Middlesex R.V. 1s.

Handbook of Company Drill; also of Skirmishing, Battalion, and Shelter Trench Drill. By Lieut. CHARLES SLACK. 1s.

Elementary and Battalion Drill. Condensed and Illustrated, together with duties of Company Officers, Markers, &c., in Battalion. By Captain MALTON. 2s. 6d.

Cavalry Regulations. For the Instruction, Formations, and Movements of Cavalry. Royal 8vo. 4s. 6d.

Cavalry Sword, Carbine, Pistol and Lance Exercises, together with Field Gun Drill. Pocket Edition. 1s.

Trumpet and Bugle Sounds for Mounted Service and Artillery. 1s. 6d.

The Training of Cavalry Remount Horses. By the late Capt. L. E. NOLAN, of the 15th Hussars. 8vo. 10s.

Manual of Artillery Exercises, 1873. 8vo. 5s.

Manual of Field Artillery Exercises. 1877. 3s.

Standing Orders for Royal Artillery. 8vo, 3s.

Principles and Practice of Modern Artillery. By Lt.-Col. C. H. OWEN, R.A. 8vo. Illustrated. 15s.

Artillerist's Manual and British Soldiers' Compendium. By Major F. A. GRIFFITHS. 11th Edition. 5s.

Compendium of Artillery Exercises—Smooth Bore, Field, and Garrison Artillery for Reserve Forces. By Captain J. M. McKenzie. 3s. 6d.

Principles of Gunnery. By JOHN T. HYDE, M.A., late Professor of Fortification and Artillery, Royal Indian Military College, Addiscombe. Second edition, revised and enlarged. With many Plates and Cuts, and Photograph of Armstrong Gun. Royal 8vo. 14s.

Notes on Gunnery. By Captain Goodeve. Revised Edition. 1s.

Text Book of the Construction and Manufacture of Rifled Ordnance in the British Service. By STONEY & JONES. Second Edition. Paper, 3s. 6d., Cloth, 4s. 6d.

Handbooks of the 9, 16, and 64-Pounder R. M. L. Converted Guns. 6d. each.

Handbook of the 9 and 10-inch R. M. L. Guns. 6d. each.

Handbook of 40-Pounder B. L. Gun. 6*d*.

Handbooks of 9-inch Rifle Muzzle Loading Guns of 12 tons, and the 10-inch gun of 18 tons. 6d. each.

Treatise on Fortification and Artillery. By Major HECTOR STRAITH. Revised and re-arranged by THOMAS COOK, R.N., by JOHN T. HYDE, M.A. 7th Edition. Royal 8vo. Illustrated and Four Hundred Plans, Cuts, &c. £2 2s.

Military Surveying and Field Sketching. The Various Methods of Contouring, Levelling, Sketching without Instruments, Scale of Shade, Examples in Military Drawing, &c., &c., &c. As at present taught in the Military Colleges. By Major W. H. RICHARDS, 55th Regiment, Chief Garrison Instructor in India, Late Instructor in Military Surveying, Royal Military College, Sandhurst. Second Edition, Revised and Corrected. 12s.

Treatise on Military Surveying; including Sketching in the Field, Plan-Drawing, Levelling, Military Reconnaissance, &c. By Lieut.-Col. BASIL JACKSON, late of the Royal Staff Corps. The Fifth Edition. 8vo. Illustrated by Plans, &c. 14s.

Instruction in Military Engineering. Vol. 1., Part III. 4s.

Elementary Principles of Fortification. A Text-Book for Military Examinations. By J. T. HYDE, M.A. Royal 8vo. With numerous Plans and Illustrations. 10s. 6d.

Military Train Manual. 1s.

The Sappers' Manual. Compiled for the use of Engineer Volunteer Corps. By Col. W. A. FRANKLAND, R.E. With numerous Illustrations. 2s.

Ammunition. A descriptive treatise on the different Projectiles Charges, Fuzes, Rockets, &c., at present in use for Land and Sea Service, and on other war stores manufactured in the Royal Laboratory. 6*s*.

Hand-book on the Manufacture and Proof of Gunpowder, as carried on at the Royal Gunpowder Factory, Waltham Abbey. 5s.

Regulations for the Training of Troops for service in the Field and for the conduct of Peace Manœuvres. 2s.

Hand-book Dictionary for the Militia and Volunteer Services, Containing a variety of useful information, Alphabetically arranged. Pocket size, 3s. 6d.; by post, 3s. 8d.

Gymnastic Exercises, System of Fencing, and Exercises for the Regulation Clubs. In one volume. Crown 8vo. 1877. 2s.

Army Equipment. Prepared at the Topographical and Statistical Department, War Office. By Col. Sir HENRY JAMES, R.E., F.R.S., &c., Director.

PART. 1.—*Cavalry*. Compiled by Lieut. H. M. HOZIER, 2nd Life Guards. Royal 8vo. 4s.

PART 4.—*Military Train*. Compiled by Lieut. H. M. HOZIER, 2nd Life Guards. Royal 8vo. 2s. 6d.

PART 5.—*Infantry*. Compiled by Capt. F. MARTIN PETRIE. Royal 8vo. With Plates. 5s.

PART 6.—*Commissariat*. Compiled by Lieut. H. M. HOZIER, 2nd Life Guards. Royal 8vo. 1s. 6d.

PART 7.—*Hospital Service*. Compiled by Capt. MARTIN PETRIE. Royal 8vo. With Plates. 5s.

Text-Book on the Theory and Motion of Projectiles; the History, Manufacture, and Explosive Force of Gunpowder; the History of Small Arms. For Officers sent to School of Musketry. 1s. 6d.

Notes on Ammunition. 4th Edition. 1877. 2s. 6d.

Regulations and Instructions for Encampments. 6d

Rules for the Conduct of the War Game. 2s.

Medical Regulations for the Army, Instructions for the Army, Comprising duties of Officers, Attendants, and Nurses, &c. 1s. 6d.

Purveyors' Regulations and Instructions, for Guidance of Officers of Purveyors' Department of the Army. 3s.

Priced Vocabulary of Stores used in Her Majesty's Service. 4s.

Transport of Sick and Wounded Troops. By DR. LONGMORE. 5s.

Precedents in Military Law. By LT-COL. W. HOUGH. 8vo. 25s.

The Practice of Courts-Martial, by HOUGH & LONG. 8vo. 26s.

Manual of Military Law. For all ranks of the Army, Militia, and Volunteer Services. By Colonel J. K. PIPON, and J. F. COLLIER, Esq. Third and Revised Edition. Pocket size. 5s.

Regulations applicable to the European Officer in India. Containing Staff Corps Rules, Staff Salaries, Commands, Furlough and Retirement Regulations, &c. By GEORGE E. COCHRANE, late Assistant Military Secretary, India Office. 1 vol., post 8vo. 7s. 6d.

Reserve Force; Guide to Examinations, for the use of Captains and Subalterns of Infantry, Militia, and Rifle Volunteers, and for Serjeants of Volunteers. By Capt. G. H. GREAVES. 2nd edit. 2s.

The Military Encyclopædia; referring exclusively to the Military Sciences, Memoirs of distinguished Soldiers, and the Narratives of Remarkable Battles. By J. H. STOCQUELER. 8vo. 12s.

The Operations of War Explained and Illustrated. By Col. HAMLEY. New Edition Revised, with Plates. Royal 8vo. 30s.

Lessons of War. As taught by the Great Masters and Others; Selected and Arranged from the various operations in War. By FRANCE JAMES SOADY, Lieut.-Col., R A. Royal 8vo. 21s.

The Soldiers' Pocket Book for Field Service. By Col. SIR GARNET J. WOLSELEY. 2nd Edition. Revised and Enlarged. 4s. 6d.

The Surgeon's Pocket Book, an Essay on the best Treatment of Wounded in War. By Surgeon Major J. H. PORTER. 7s. 6d.

A Prec of Modern Tactics. By COLONEL HOME. 8vo. 8s. 6d.

Armed Strength of Austria. By Capt. COOKE. 2 pts. £1 2s.

Armed Strength of Denmark. 3s.

Armed Strength of Russia. Translated from the German. 7s.

Armed Strength of Sweden and Norway. 3s. 6d.

Armed Strength of Italy. 5s. 6d.

Armed Strength of Germany. Part I. 8s. 6d.

The Franco-German War of 1870—71. By CAPT. C. H. CLARKE. Vol. I. £1 6s. Sixth Section. 5s. Seventh Section 6s. Eighth Section. 3s. Ninth Section. 4s. 6d. Tenth Section. 6s.

The Campaign of 1866 in Germany. Royal 8vo. With Atlas, 21s

Celebrated Naval and Military Trials. By PETER BURKE. Post 8vo., cloth. 10s. 6d.

Military Sketches. By SIR LASCELLES WRAXALL. Post 8vo. 6s.

Military Life of the Duke of Wellington. By JACKSON and SCOTT. 2 Vols. 8vo. Maps, Plans, &c. 12s.

Single Stick Exercise of the Aldershot Gymnasium. 6*d*.

Treatise on Military Carriages, and other Manufactures of the Royal Carriage Department. 5s.

Steppe Campaign Lectures. 2s.

Manual of Instructions for Army Surgeons. 1s.

Regulations for Army Hospital Corps. 9d.

Manual of Instructions for Non-Commissioned Officers, Army Hospital Corps. 2s.

Handbook or Military Artificers. 3s.

Instructions for the use of Auxiliary Cavalry. 2s. 6d.

Equipment Regulations for the Army. 5s. 6d.

Statute Law relating to the Army. 1s. 3d.

Regulations for Commissariat and Ordnance Department 2s.

Regulations for the Commissariat Department. 1s. 6d.

Regulations for the Ordnance Department. 1s. 6d.

Artillerist's Handbook of Reference for the use of the Royal and Reserve Artillery, by WILL and DALTON. 5s.

An Essay on the Principles and Construction of Military Bridges, by SIR HOWARD DOUGLAS. 1853. 15s.

Mill's History of British India,
With Notes and Continuation. By H. H. WILSON. 9 vols. cr. 8vo. £2 10s.

Milton's Poetical Works, with Notes.
By JOHN BRADSHAW, LL.D., Inspector of Schools, Madras. 2 vols. post 8vo. 10s. 6d.

Mogul Empire.
From the death of Aurungzeb to the overthrow of the Mahratta Power, by HENRY GEORGE KEENE, B.C.S. 8vo. Second edition. With Map. 10s. 6d.
This Work fills up a blank between the ending of Elphinstone's and the commencement of Thornton's Histories.

Mysteries of the Vatican;
Or Crimes of the Papacy. From the German of DR. THEODORE GREISENGER. 2 Vols. post 8vo 21s.

Nationalities of Europe.
By ROBERT GORDON LATHAM, M.D. 2 Vols. 8vo. 12s.

Natural History, Sport and Travel.
By EDWARD LOCKWOOD, Bengal Civil Service, late Magistrate of Monghyr Crown 8vo. 10s. 6d. (*In the press.*)

Nirgis and Bismillah.
NIRGIS; a Tale of the Indian Mutiny, from the Diary of a Slave Girl: and BISMILLAH; or, Happy Days in Cashmere. By HAFIZ ALLARD. Post 8vo. 10s. 6d.

Notes on China.
Desultory Notes on the Government and People of China and on the Chinese Language. By T. T. MEADOWS, 8vo. 9s.

Notes on the North Western Provinces of India.
By a District Officer. 2nd Edition. Post 8vo., cloth. 5s.
CONTENTS.—Area and Population.—Soils.—Crops.—Irrigation.—Rent.—Rates.—Land Tenures.

Owen (Sidney) India on the Eve of the British Conquest.
A Historical Sketch. By SIDNEY OWEN, M.A. Reader in Indian Law and History in the University of Oxford. Formerly Professor of History in the Elphinstone College, Bombay. Post 8vo. 8s.

Oxenham's (Rev. H. N.) Catholic Doctrine of the Atonement.
8vo. 10s 6d. (See page 5).

Ozanam's (A. F.) Civilisation in the Fifth Century.
From the French. By The Hon. A. C. GLYN. 2 Vols. post 8vo. 21s.

Pathologia Indica,
Based upon Morbid Specimens from all parts of the Indian Empire. By ALLAN WEBB, B.M.S. Second Edit. 8vo. 14s.

Pharmacopœia of India.
By EDWARD JOHN WARING, M.D , &c. 8vo. 6s. (See page 2).

Physical Geography.
By PROFESSOR D. T. ANSTED, M.A., F.R.S., &c. Fifth Edition. Post 8vo., with Illustrative Maps. 7s
CONTENTS:—PART I.—INTRODUCTION.—The Earth as a Planet. —Physical Forces.—The Succession of Rocks. PART II.—EARTH —Land.—Mountains.—Hills and Valleys.—Plateaux and Low Plains. PART III.—WATER.—The Ocean.—Rivers. —Lakes and Waterfalls.—The Phenomena of Ice.—Springs. PART IV.—AIR.—The Atmosphere. Winds and Storms.—Dew, Clouds, and Rain.—Climate and Weather. PART V.—FIRE.—Volcanoes and Volcanic Phenomena.—Earthquakes. PART VI.—LIFE —The Distribution of Plants in the different Countries of the Earth.—The Distribution of Animals on the Earth.—The Distribution of Plants and Animals in Time.—Effects of Human Agency on Inanimate Nature.

"The Book is both valuable and comprehensive, and deserves a wide circulation."—*Observer*.

Pilgrimage to Mecca (A.)
By the Nawab Sikandar Begum of Bhopal. Translated from the Original Urdu. By MRS. WILLOUGHBY OSBORNE. Followed by a Sketch of the History of Bhopal. By COL. WILLOUGHBY-OSBORNE, C.B. With Photographs, and dedicated, by permission, to HER MAJESTY, QUEEN VICTORIA. Post 8vo. £1. 1s.

This is a highly important book, not only for its literary merit, and the information it contains, but also from the fact of its being the first work written by an Indian lady, and that lady a Queen.

Pebody (Charles) Authors at Work.
Francis Jeffrey—Sir Walter Scott—Robert Burns—Charles Lamb—R. B. Sheridan—Sydney Smith—Macaulay—Byron Wordsworth—Tom Moore—Sir James Mackintosh. Post 8vo. 10s 6d

Pollock (Field Marshal Sir George) Life & Correspondence.
By C. R. LOW. 8vo. With portrait. 18s.

Primitive and Universal Laws of the Formation and Development of Language. 8vo. 12s. 6d. (See page 16)

Prinsep's Political and Military Transactions in India.
2 Vols. 8vo. London, 1825. 18s.

Practice of Courts Martial.
By HOUGH & LONG. 8vo. London. 1825. 26s.

Precedents in Military Law;
By LIEUT.-COL. W. HOUGH. One thick 8vo. Vol. 25s.

Prichard's Chronicles of Budgepore, &c.
Or Sketches of Life in Upper India. 2 Vols., Foolscap 8vo. 12s.

Prinsep's (H. T.) Historical Results.
8vo. 15s.

Prinsep's (H. T.) Thibet.
Post 8vo. 5s.

Races and Tribes of Hindostan.
The People of India. A series of Photographic Illustrations of the Races and Tribes of Hindustan. Prepared under the Authority of the Government of India, by J. FORBES WATSON, and JOHN WILLIAM KAYE. The Work contains about 450 Photographs on mounts, in Eight Volumes, super royal 4to. £2. 5s. per volume.

Red Book for Sergeants.
By W. BRIGHT, Colour-Sergeant, 37th Middlesex R.V. Fcap. interleaved 1s.

Regiments of the Army (The)
Chronologically arranged. Showing their History, Services, Uniform, &c By Captain TRIMEN, late 35th Regiment.

Republic of Fools (The).
Being the History of the People of Abdera in Thrace, from the German of C. M. Von Wieland. By Rev. HENRY CHRISTMAS, M.A. 2 Vols, crown 8vo. 12s.

Richards (Major W H.) Military Surveying, &c.
12s. (See page 19).

Royle's (Dr. J. F.) Botany of the Himalaya Mountains.
2 Vols. royal 4to. £5 5s. (See page 5).

Russians at Home.
Unpolitical Sketches, showing what Newspapers they read, what Theatres they frequent; and how they eat, drink and enjoy themselves; with other matter relating chiefly to Literature, Music, and Places of Historical and Religious Interest in and about Moscow. By H. Sutherland Edwards. Second Edition, post 8vo., with Illustrations. 6s.

Sanderson's (G. P.) Thirteen Years among the Wild Beasts of India. Small 4to. 25s. (See page 27).

Sepoy War in India.
A History of the Sepoy War in India, 1857—1858. By Sir John William Kaye, Author of "The History of the War in Affghanistan." Vol. I, 8vo. 18s. Vol. II. £1. Vol. III. £1

Contents of Vol. I:—Book I.—Introductory.—The Conquest of the Punjab and Pegu.—The "Right of Lapse."—The Annexation of Oude.—Progress of Englishism. Book II.—The Sepoy Army: its Rise, Progress, and Decline—Early History of the Native Army.—Deteriorating Influences—The Sindh Mutinies.—The Punjaub Mutinies. Discipline of the Bengal Army. Book III.—The Outbreak of the Mutiny.—Lord Canning and his Council.—The Oude Administration and the Persian War.—The Rising of the Storm.—The First Mutiny.—Progress of Mutiny.—Excitement in Upper India—Bursting of the Storm.—Appendix.

Contents of Vol. II.:—Book IV.—The Rising in the North-west.—The Delhi History.—The Outbreak at Meerut.—The Seizure of Delhi.—Calcutta in May.—Last Days of General Anson.—The March upon Delhi Book V.—Progress of Rebellion in Upper India—Benares and Allahabad.—Cawnpore.—The March to Cawnpore.—Re-occupation of Cawnpore. Book VI.—The Punjab and Delhi.—First Conflicts in the Punjab.—Peshawur and Rawul Pinder.—Progress of Events in the Punjab.—Delhi.—First Weeks of the Siege.—Progress of the Siege.—The Last Succours from the Punjab.

CONTENTS OF VOL. III.:—BOOK VII.—BENGAL, BEHAR, AND THE NORTH-WEST PROVINCES.—At the Seat of Government.—The Insurrection in Behar.—The Siege of Arrah.—Behar and Bengal. BOOK VIII.—MUTINY AND REBELLION IN THE NORTH-WEST PROVINCES.—Agra in May.—Insurrection in the Districts.—Bearing of the Native Chiefs.—Agra in June, July, August and September. BOOK IX.—LUCKNOW AND DELHI.—Rebellion in Oude.—Revolt in the Districts.—Lucknow in June and July.—The siege and Capture of Delhi.

Sewell's (Robert) Analytical History of India.
Crown 8vo. 8s. (See page 3).

Social Life in Munich.
By EDWARD WILBERFORCE, Second Edition. Post 8vo. 6s.

"A very able volume. Mr. Wilberforce is a very pleasant and agreeable writer whose opinion is worth hearing on the subject of modern art which enters largely into the matter of his discourse."—*Saturday Review.*

Student's Chemistry.
Being the Seventh Edition of Household Chemistry, or the Science of Home Life. By ALBERT J. BERNAYS, PH. DR. F.C.S., Prof. of Chemistry and Practical Chemistry at St. Thomas' Hospital, Medical, and Surgical College. Post 8vo. 5s. 6d.

Sin: Its Causes and Consequences.
An attempt to Investigate the Origin, Nature, Extent and Results of Moral Evil. A Series of Lent Lectures. By the REV. HENRY CHRISTMAS, M.A., F.R.S. Post 8vo. 5s.

Starling (M. H.) Indian Criminal Law and Procedure.
Third edition. 8vo. £2 2s.

Strange's (Sir T.) Hindu Law.
2 Vols. Royal 8vo. 1830. 24s. (See page 13).

Stuart's (Capt. H, B.) Armies of the Powers of Europe.
(*In the press.*)

"Their Majesties Servants":
Annals of the English Stage. Actors, Authors, and Audiences. From Thomas Betterton to Edmund Kean. By Dr. DORAN, F.S.A., Author of "Table Traits," "Lives of the Queens of England of the House of Hanover." &c. Post 8vo. 6s.

"Every page of the work is barbed with wit, and will make its way point foremost. . . . . . provides entertainment for the most diverse tastes."—*Daily News.*

Textile Manufactures and Costumes of the People of India,

As originally prepared under the Authority of the Secretary of State for India in Council. By J. FORBES WATSON, M.A., M.D., F.R.A.S., Reporter on the Products of India. Folio, half-morocco. With numerous Coloured Photographs. £3. 5s.

This work—by affording a key to the Fashions of the People, and to the Cotton, Silk, and Wool Textiles in actual use in India—is of special interest to Manufacturers, Merchants, and Agents; as also to the Student and lover of ornamental art.

Theories of History.

An Inquiry into the Theories of History,—Chance,—Law,—Will With Special Reference to the Principle of Positive Philosophy. By WILLIAM ADAM 8vo. 15s.

Thirteen Years among the Wild Beasts of India: their

Haunts and Habits, from Personal Observation; with an account of the Modes of Capturing and Taming Wild Elephants. By G. P. SANDERSON, Officer in Charge of the Government Elephant Keddahs at Mysore With 21 full page Illustrations and three Maps. Fcp. 4 to. £1 5s

Thomson's Lunar and Horary Tables.

For New and Concise Methods of Performing the Calculations necessary for ascertaining the Longitude by Lunar Observations, or Chronometers; with directions for acquiring a knowledge of the Principal Fixed Stars and finding the Latitude of them. By DAVID THOMSON. Sixty-fifth edit. Royal 8vo. 10s.

Thornton's History of India.

The History of the British Empire in India, by Edward Thornton, Esq. Containing a Copious Glossary of Indian Terms, and a Complete Chronological Index of Events, to aid the Aspirant for Public Examinations. Third edition. 1 vol. 8vo. With Map 12s

**** The Library Edition of the above in 6 volumes, 8vo., may be had, price £2. 8s.*

Thornton's Gazetteer of India.

Compiled chiefly from the records at the India Office. By EDWARD THORNTON. 1 vol., 8vo., pp. 1015. With Map. 21s.

**** The chief objects in view in compiling this Gazetteer are:—*

1st. To fix the relative position of the various cities, towns, and villages, with as much precision as possible, and to exhibit with the greatest practicable brevity all that is known respecting them; and

2ndly. To note the various countries, provinces, or territorial divisions, and to describe the physical characteristics of each, together with their statistical, social, and political circumstances.

To these are added minute descriptions of the principal rivers and chains of mountains; thus presenting to the reader, within a brief compass, a mass of information which cannot otherwise be obtained, except from a multiplicity of volumes and manuscript records.

The Library Edition.
4 vols., 8vo. Notes, Marginal References, and Map. £2 16s.

Thugs and Dacoits of India.
A Popular Account of the Thugs and Dacoits, the Hereditary Garotters and Gang Robbers of India. By JAMES HUTTON. Post 8vo. 5s.

Tibet, Tartary, and Mongolia.
By HENRY T. PRINSEP, Esq. Second edition. Post 8vo. 5s

Tilley's (H. A.) Japan, &c.
8vo. 16s (See page 14).

Tod's (Col. Jas.) Travels in Western India.
Embracing a visit to the Sacred Mounts of the Jains, and the most Celebrated Shrines of Hindu Faith between Rajpootana and the Indus, with an account of the Ancient City of Nehrwalla. By the late Lieut.-Col. JAMES TOD, Illustrations. Royal 4to. £3 3s.

*** *This is a companion volume to Colonel Tod's Rajasthan.*

Trimen's (Capt. R., late 35th Regiment) Regiments of the British Army chronologically arranged. 8vo. 10s. 6d.

Trotter's History of India.
The History of the British Empire in India, from the Appointment of Lord Hardinge to the Death of Lord Canning (1844 to 1862). By LIONEL JAMES TROTTER, late Bengal Fusiliers. 2 vols. 8vo. 16s. each.

Turkish Cookery Book (The).
A Collection of Receipts from the best Turkish Authorities. Done into English by FARABI EFENDI. 12mo. Cloth. 3s. 6d.

Vambery's Sketches of Central Asia.
Additional Chapters on My Travels and Adventures, and of the Ethnology of Central Asia. By Armenius Vambery. 8vo. 16s.

" A valuable guide on almost untrodden ground."—*Athenæum.*

View of China,
For Philological Purposes. Containing a Sketch of Chinese Chronology, Geography, Government, Religion, and Customs. Designed for the use of Persons who study the Chinese Language. By Rev. R. MORRISON. 4to. Macao, 1817. 6s.

Waring's Pharmacopœia of India.
8vo. 6s. (See page 2).

Watson's (Dr. J. Forbes) Textile Manufactures of India.
Folio. £3. 5s. (See page 27).

Watson's (Dr. J. F.) and J. W. Kaye, The People of India.
A Series of Photographs. Vols. 1 to 8, £18.

Webb's (Dr. A.) Pathologia Indica.
8vo 14s (See page 23).

Wellesley's Despatches.
The Despatches, Minutes, and Correspondence of the Marquis Wellesley, K.G., during his Administration in India. 5 vols. 8vo. With Portrait, Map, &c. £6. 10s.

This work should be perused by all who proceed to India in the Civil Services.

Wellington in India.
Military History of the Duke of Wellington in India. 1s

Wilberforce's (Edward) Social Life in Munich.
Post 8vo. 6s. (See page 26)

Wilberforce's (E.) Life of Schubert.
Post 8vo. 6s.

Wilk's South of India.
3 vols. 4to £5. 5s.

Williams' (F.) Lives of the English Cardinals.
2 vols., 8vo. 14s. (See page 7).

Williams' (F.) Life, &c., of Bishop Atterbury.
2 vols., 8vo. 14s. (See page 4).

Williams' Indian Wisdom.
8vo. 15s. (See page 14).

Wollaston's (Arthur N.) Anwari Suhaili, or Lights of Canopus
Commonly known as Kalilah and Damnah, being an adaptation of the Fables of Bidpai. Translated from the Persian. Royal 4to., with illuminated borders, designed specially for the work, cloth, extra gilt. £3 13s. 6d.

Wollaston's (Arthur N.) Elementary Indian Reader.
Designed for the use of Students in the Anglo-Vernacular Schools in India. Fcap. 1s.

Woolrych's (Serjeant W. H.)
Lives of Eminent Serjeants at-Law of the English Bar. By HUMPHRY W. WOOLRYCH, Serjeant-at-Law. 2 vols. 8vo. 30s.

World we Live In.
Or First Lessons in Physical Geography. For the use of Schools and Students. By D. T. ANSTED, M.A., F.R.S, &c. 25th Thousand. Fcap. 8vo. 2s.

Wraxall's Caroline Matilda.
Queen of Denmark, Sister of George 3rd. From Family and State Papers. By Sir Lascelles Wraxall, Bart. 3 vols., 8vo. 18s.

Wraxall's Military Sketches.
By SIR LASCELLES WRAXALL, Bart. Post 8vo. 6s.

"The book is clever and entertaining from first to last."—*Athenæum.*

Wraxall's Scraps and Sketches, Gathered Together.
By SIR LASCELLES WRAXALL, Bart. 2 vols., Post 8vo. 12s

Yesterday and To-Day in India.
By SIDNEY LAMAN BLANCHARD. Post 8vo. 6s.

CONTENTS.—Outward Bound.—The Old Times and the New.—Domestic Life.—Houses and Bungalows.—Indian Servants—The Great Shoe Question.—The Garrison Hack—The Long Bow in India.—Mrs. Dulcimer's Shipwreck.—A Traveller's Tale, told in a Dark Bungalow.—Punch in India.—Anglo-Indian Literature.—Christmas in India.—The Seasons in Calcutta.—Farmers in Muslin.—Homeward Bound.—India as it Is.

Young's (J. R.) Course of Mathematics.
8vo. 12s. (See page 7).

A SELECTION FROM

MESSRS. ALLEN'S CATALOGUE

OF BOOKS IN THE EASTERN LANGUAGES, &c.

HINDUSTANI, HINDI, &c.

[*Dr. Forbes's Works are used as Class Books in the Colleges and Schools in India.*]

Forbes's Hindustani-English Dictionary in the Persian Character, with the Hindi words in Nagari also; and an English Hindustani Dictionary in the English Character; both in one volume. By DUNCAN FORBES, LL.D. Royal 8vo. 42s.

Forbes's Hindustani Grammar, with Specimens of Writing in the Persian and Nagari Characters, Reading Lessons, and Vocabulary. 8vo. 10s. 6d.

Forbes's Hindustani Manual, containing a Compendious Grammar, Exercises for Translation, Dialogues, and Vocabulary, in the Roman Character. New Edition, entirely revised. By J. T. PLATTS. 18mo. 3s. 6d.

Forbes's Bagh o Bahar, in the Persian Character, with a complete Vocabulary. Royal 8vo. 12s. 6d.

Forbes's Bagh o Bahar in English, with Explanatory Notes, illustrative of Eastern Character. 8vo. 8s.

Eastwick (Edward B.) The Bagh-o-Bahar—literally translated into English, with copious explanatory notes. 8vo. 10s. 6d.

Forbes's Tota Kahani; or, "Tales of a Parrot," in the Persian Character, with a complete Vocabulary. Royal 8vo. 8s.

Small's (Rev. G.) Tota Kahani; or, "Tales of a Parrot." Translated into English. 8vo. 8s.

Forbes's Baital Pachisi; or, "Twenty-five Tales of a Demon," in the Nagari Character, with a complete Vocabulary. Royal 8vo. 9s.

Platts' J. T., Baital Pachisi; translated into English. 8vo. 8s.

Forbes's Ikhwanu s Safa; or, "Brothers of Purity," in the Persian Character. Royal 8vo. 12s. 6d.

[*For the higher standard for military officers' examinations.*]

Platts' Ikhwanu S Safa; translated into English. 8vo. 10s. 6d.

Platts' Grammar of the Urdu or Hindustani-Language. 8vo. 12s.

Forbes's Oriental Penmanship; a Guide to Writing Hindustani in the Persian Character. 4to. 8s.

Forbes's Hindustani-English and English Hindustani Dictionary, in the English Character. Royal 8vo. 36s.

Forbes's Smaller Dictionary, Hindustani and English, in the English Character. 12s.

Forbes's Bagh o Bahar, with Vocaby., English Character. 5s.

Singhasan Battisi. Translated into Hindi from the Sanscrit. A New Edition. Revised, Corrected, and Accompanied with Copious Notes. By SYED ABDOOLAH. Royal 8vo. 12s. 6d.

Robertson's Hindustani Vocabulary. 3s. 6d.

Eastwick's Prem Sagur. 4to. 30s.

Akhlaki Hindi, translated into Urdu, with an Introduction and Notes. By SYED ABDOOLAH. Royal 8vo. 12s. 6d.

Sakuntala. Translated into Hindi from the Sanskrit, by FREDERIC PINCOTT. 4to. 12s. 6d.

SANSCRIT.

Haughton's Sanscrit and Bengali Dictionary, in the Bengali Character, with Index, serving as a reversed dictionary. 4to. 30s.

Williams's English-Sanscrit Dictionary. 4to., cloth. £3. 3s.

Williams's Sanskrit-English Dictionary. 4to. £4 14s. 6d.

Wilkin's (Sir Charles) Sanscrit Grammar. 4to. 15s.

Williams's (Monier) Sanscrit Grammar. 8vo. 15s.

Williams's (Monier) Sanscrit Manual: to which is added, a Vocabulary, by A. E. GOUGH. 18mo. 7s. 6d.

Gough's (A. E.) Key to the Exercises in Williams's Sanscrit Manual. 18mo. 4s.

Williams's (Monier) Sakuntala, with Literal English Translation of all the Metrical Passages, Schemes of the Metres, and copious Critical and Explanatory Notes. Royal 8vo. 21s.

Williams's (Monier) Sakuntala. Translated into English Prose and Verse. Fourth Edition. 8s.

Williams's (Monier) Vikramorvasi. The Text. 8vo. 5s.

Cowell's (E B.) Translation of the Vikramorvasi. 8vo. 3s. 6d.

Thompson's (J. C.) *Bhagavat Gita*. Sanscrit Text. 5s.

Haughton's Menu, with English Translation. 2 vols. 4to. 24s.

Johnson's Hitopadesa, with Vocabulary. 15s.

Hitopadesa, Sanscrit, with Bengali and English Trans. 10s. 6d.

Johnson's Hitopadesa, English Translation of the. 4to. 5s.

Wilson's *Megha Duta*, with Translation into English Verse, Notes, Illustrations, and a Vocabulary. Royal 8vo. 6s.

PERSIAN.

Richardson's Persian, Arabic, and English Dictionary. Edition of 1852. By F. JOHNSON. 4to. £4.

Forbes's Persian Grammar, Reading Lessons, and Vocabulary. Royal 8vo. 12s. 6d.

Ibraheem's Persian Grammar, Dialogues, &c. Royal 8vo. 12s. 6d.

Gulistan. Carefully collated with the original MS., with a full Vocabulary. By JOHN PLATTS, late Inspector of Schools, Central Provinces, India. Royal 8vo. 12s. 6d.

Gulistan. Translated from a revised Text, with Copious Notes. By JOHN PLATTS. 8vo. 12s. 6d.

Ouseley's Anwari Soheili. 4to. 42s.

Wollaston's (Arthur N.) Translation of the Anvari Soheili. Royal 8vo. £2 2s.

Keene's (Rev. H. G.) First Book of The Anwari Soheili. Persian Text. 8vo. 5s.

Ouseley's (Col.) Akhlaki Mushini. Persian Text. 8vo. 5s.

Keene's (Rev. H. G.) Akhlaki Mushini. Translated into English. 8vo. 3s. 6d.

Clarke's (Captain H. Wilberforce, R E) The Persian Manual. A Pocket Companion.

PART I.—A CONCISE GRAMMAR OF THE LANGUAGE, with Exercises on its more Prominent Peculiarities, together with a Selection of Useful Phrases, Dialogues, and Subjects for Translation into Persian.

PART II.—A VOCABULARY OF USEFUL WORDS, ENGLISH AND PERSIAN, showing at the same time the difference of idiom between the two Languages. 18mo. 7s. 6d.

A Translation of Robinson Crusoe into the Persiân Language. Roman Character. Edited by T. W. H. TOLBORT, Bengal Civil Service. (*In the press*).

BENGALI.

Haughton's Bengali, Sanscrit, and English Dictionary, adapted for Students in either language; to which is added an Index, serving as a reversed dictionary. 4to. 30s.

Forbes's Bengali Grammar, with Phrasesand dialogues. Royal 8vo. 12s. 6d.

Forbes's Bengali Reader, with a Translation and Vocabulary Royal 8vo. 12s. 6d.

Nabo Nari. 12mo. 7s.

ARABIC.

Richardson's Arabic, Persian and English Dictionary. Edition of 1852. By F. JOHNSON. 4to., cloth. £4.

Forbes's Arabic Grammar, intended more especially for the use of young men preparing for the East India Civil Service, and also for the use of self instructing students in general. Royal 8vo., cloth. 18s.

Palmer's Arabic Grammer. 8vo. 18s.

Forbes's Arabic Reading Lessons, consisting of Easy Extracts from the best Authors, with Vocabulary. Royal 8vo., cloth. 15s.

Beresford Arabic Syntax. Royal 8vo 6s.

Matthew's Translation of the Mishkāt-ul-Masābih. 2 vols in 1. By the REV. T. P. HUGHES, Missionary to the Afghans at Peshawur. (In the Press).

TELOOGOO.

Brown's Dictionary, reversed: with a Dictionary of the Mixed Dialects used in Teloogoo. 3 vols. in 2, royal 8vo. £5.

Campbell's Dictionary. Royal 8vo. 30s.

Bromn's Reader. 8vo. 2 vols. 14s.

Brown's Dialogues, Teloogoo and English. 8vo. 5s. 0d.

Pancha Tantra. 8s.

Percival's English-Teloogoo Dictionary. 10s. 6d.

TAMIL.

Rottler's Dictionary, Tamil and English. 4to. 42s.

Babington's Grammar (High Dialect). 4to. 12s.

Percival's Tamil Dictionary. 2 vols. 10s. 6d.

GUZRATTEE.

Mavor's Spelling, Guzrattee and English. 7s, 6d.

Shapuaji Edalji's Dictionary, Guzrattee and English. 21s.

MAHRATTA.

Molesworth's Dictionary, Mahratta and English. 4to. 42s.

Molesworth's Dictionary, English and Mahratta. 4to. 42s.

Stevenson's Grammar. 8vo., cloth. 17s. 6d.

Esop's Fables. 12mo. 2s. 6d.

Fifth Reading Book. 7s.

MALAY.

Marsden's Dictionary. 4to. £3. 3s.

Marsden's Grammar. 4to. £1 1s.

CHINESE.

Morrison's Dictionary. 6 vols. 4to. £10.

Marshman's—Clavis Sinica, a Chinese Grammar. 4to. £2 2s.

Morrison's View of China, for Philological purposes; containing a Sketch of Chinese Chronology, Geography, Government, Religion and Customs, designed for those who study the Chinese language. 4to. 6s.

MISCELLANEOUS.

Reeve's English-Carnatica and Carnatica-English Dictionary. 2 vols. (Very slightly damaged). £8.

Collett's Malayalam Reader. 8vo. 12s. 6d.

Esop's Fables in Carnatica. 8vo. bound. 12s. 6d.

David's Turkish Grammar. 15s.

Wilson's Glossary of Judicial and Revenue Terms, and of useful Words occurring in Official Documents relating to the Administration of the Government of British India. From the Arabic, Persian, Hindustani, Sanskrit, Hindi, Bengali, Uriya, Marathi, Guzarathi, Telugu, Karnata, Tamil, Malayalam, and other Languages. Compiled and published under the authority of the Hon. the Court of Directors of the E. I. Company. 4to., cloth. £1 10s.

Messrs. Wm. H. Allen & Co.'s Catalogues of Printed and Lithographed Books in the Eastern Languages, to which is added a list of Oriental Manuscripts, may be had gratis on application.

A CHRONOLOGICAL AND HISTORICAL

CHART OF INDIA,

Price, fully tinted, mounted on roller or in case, 20s. size, about 40 in. by 50 in.

Showing, at one view, all the principal nations, governments, and empires which have existed in that country from the earliest times to the suppression of the Great Mutiny, A.D. 1858, with the date of each historical event according to the *various eras used in India.*

BY

ARTHUR ALLEN DURTNALL,

Of the High Court of Justice in England.

By this Chart, any person, however ignorant of the subject, may, by an hour's attention, obtain a clear view of the broad lines of Indian History, and of the evolutions which have resulted in the dominion of Her Majesty as EMPRESS OF INDIA. It will be found invaluable for EDUCATIONAL PURPOSES, especially in Colleges and Schools, where an Indian career is in contemplation. It will also be found of PERMANENT UTILITY in all Libraries and Offices as a work of ready reference for the connection of events and dates. Besides the History of India, it includes the contemporaneous histories of AFGHANISTAN, CENTRAL ASIA, and EUROPE.

A RELIEVO MAP OF INDIA.

BY

HENRY F. BRION.

In Frame, 21s.

A map of this kind brings before us such a picture of the surface of a given country as no ordinary map could ever do. To the mind's eye of the average Englishman, India consists of 'the plains' and 'the hills,' chiefly of the former, the hills being limited to the Himalayas and the Nilgiris. The new map will at least enable him to correct his notions of Indian geography. It combines the usual features of a good plain map of the country on a scale of 150 miles to the inch, with a faithful representation of all the uneven surfaces, modelled on a scale thirty-two times the horizontal one; thus bringing out into clear relief the comparative heights and outlines of all the hill-ranges, and showing broad tracts of uneven ground, of intermingled hill and valley, which a common map of the same size would hardly indicate, except to a very practised eye. The plains of Upper India are reduced to their true proportions; the Central Provinces, Malwa, and Western Bengal reveal their actual ruggedness at a glance; and Southern India, from the Vindhyas to Cape Comorin, proclaims its real height above the sea-level. To the historical as well as the geographical student such a map is an obvious and important aid in tracing the course of past campaigns, in realising the conditions under which successive races carried their arms or settlements through the Peninsula, and in comprehending the difference of race, climate, and physical surroundings which make up our Indian Empire. Set in a neat frame of maplewood, the map seems to attract the eye like a prettily-coloured picture, and its price, a guinea, should place it within the reach of all who care to combine the useful with the ornament[al]."—*Ho[me] N[ews].*

MAPS OF INDIA, etc.

Messrs. Allen & Co.'s Maps of India were revised and much improved during 1874, with especial reference to the existing Administrative Divisions, Railways, &c.

District Map of India; corrected to 1874;
Divided into Collectorates with the Telegraphs and Railways from Government surveys. On six sheets—size, 5ft. 6in. high; 5ft. 8in. wide, £2; in a case, £2 12s. 6d.; or, rollers, varn., £3 3s.

A General Map of India; corrected to 1874;
Compiled chiefly from surveys executed by order of the Government of India. On six sheets—size, 5 ft. 3 in. wide; 5 ft. 4 in. high, £2; or, on cloth, in case, £2 12s. 6d.; or, rollers, varn., £3 3s.

Map of India; corrected to 1874;
From the most recent Authorities. On two sheets—size, 2 ft. 10in. wide; 3 ft. 3 in. high, 16s.; or, on cloth, in a case, £1 1s.

Map of the Routes in India; corrected to 1874;
With Tables of Distances between the principal Towns and Military Stations On one sheet—size, 2 ft. 3 in. wide; 2 ft. 9 in. high, 9s.; or, on cloth, in a case, 12s.

Map of the Western Provinces of Hindoostan,
The Punjab, Cabool, Scinde, Bhawulpore, &c., including all the States between Candahar and Allahabad. On four sheets—size, 4 ft. 4in. wide; 4 ft. 2 in. high, 30s.; or, in case, £2; rollers, varnished, £2 10s.

Map of India and China, Burmah, Siam, the Malay Peninsula, and the Empire of Anam. On two sheets—size, 4 ft. 3 in. wide; 3 ft. 4 in. high, 16s.; or, on cloth, in a case, £1 5s.

Map of the Steam Communication and Overland Routes between England, India, China, and Australia. In a case, 14s.; on rollers, and varnished, 18s.

Map of Affghanistan and the adjacent Countries.
On one sheet—size, 2 ft. 3 in. wide; 2 ft. 9 in. high, 9s.; in case, 12s.

Map of China,
From the most Authentic Sources of Information. One large sheet—size, 2 ft. 7 in. wide; 2 ft. 2 in. high, 6s.; or, on cloth, in case, 8s.

Map of the World;
On Mercator's Projection, showing the Tracts of the Early Navigators, the Currents of the Ocean, the Principal Lines of great Circle Sailing, and the most recent discoveries. On four sheets—size, 6ft. 2 in. wide; 4 ft. 3 in. high, £2; on cloth, in a case, £2 10s.; or, with rollers, and varnished, £3.

Handbook of Reference to the Maps of India.
Giving the Latitude and Longitude of places of note. 18mo. 3s. 6d.

THE

ROYAL KALENDAR,

AND

COURT & CITY REGISTER

FOR

England, Ireland, Scotland, and the Colonies

FOR THE YEAR

1878.

CONTAINING A CORRECT LIST OF THE TWENTY FIRST IMPERIAL PARLIAMENT, SUMMONED TO MEET FOR THEIR SESSION— MARCH 5TH, 1874.

House of Peers—House of Commons—Sovereigns and Rulers of States of Europe—Orders of Knighthood—Science and Art Department—Queen's Household—Government Offices—Mint —Customs—Inland Revenue—Post Office—Foreign Ministers and Consuls—Queen's Consuls Abroad—Naval Department—Navy List—Army Department—Army List—Law Courts—Police—Ecclesiastical Department—Clergy List—Foundation Schools—Literary Institutions—City of London—Banks—Railway Companies—Hospital and Institutions—Charities—Miscellaneous Institutions—Scotland, Ireland, India, and the Colonies; and other useful information.

Price with Index, 7s.; without Index, 5s.